David Joris

and Dutch Anabaptism
1524-1543

Gary K. Waite

Wilfrid Laurier University Press

Canadian Cataloguing in Publication Data

Waite, Gary K., 1955-
    David Joris and Dutch Anabaptism, 1524-1543

Includes bibliographical references.
ISBN 0-88920-992-8

1. Joris, David, b. 1501 or 2.   2. Anabaptists –
Netherlands – History.   3. Anabaptists – Netherlands –
Biography.   4. Davidists – Biography.   I. Title.

BX4946.J8W35 1990   284'.3'092   C90-095288-1

BX
5946
.J8
W35
1990

∞

Copyright © 1990
Wilfrid Laurier University Press
Waterloo, Ontario, Canada
N2L 3C5

Cover design by Rick McLaughlin

Printed in Canada

David Joris and Dutch Anabaptism, 1524-1543 has been produced from a manuscript supplied in electronic form by the author.

To the memory of my parents

Audrey and Robert Waite

Contents

List of Illustrations vii
List of Tables and Maps viii
Acknowledgements ix
Abbreviations xi
Introduction 1

Part I. The Reformation in the Netherlands, 1519-35
Chapter
One   The Early Reform Movement in the Netherlands 7
Two   The Anabaptist Movement in Holland, 1531-35 23

Part II. David Joris: Life, Thought and Following, 1501-43
Three From Sacramentarian Lay Reformer to Melchiorite
       Sympathiser, 1501-33 49
Four   From Anabaptist to Nicodemite, 1534-39 65
Five   Joris' Early Theology, 1534-36 89
Six   Joris and the Post-Münster Radicals, 1536-39 113
Seven Confrontation with the Elders of Israel:
       The Strasbourg Debate 129
Eight Joris' Followers and Supporters: A Social Analysis 145
Nine   Joris' Asylum in Antwerp, 1539-44 163
Ten   Joris in Basel, 1544-56 177

Appendix
I   Anabaptist Leaders Active after 1535 195
II   Jorien Ketel's Confession 197
III   Ketel's Letter to His Wife 201
IV   Leonard van Dam's Vision of the Heavenly Man 203
V   Public Confession of Sins 207
VI   The Internal Restitution 211

Bibliography 213
Index 229

List of Illustrations

Portrait of David Joris; Frisian School, *c.* 1550-55 xii

Glass round portraying allegorical virtues: Charity/Love;
c. 1544-56. Ascribed to David Joris 6

Glass round portraying allegorical virtue: Righteousness;
c. 1544-56. Ascribed to David Joris 22

Title page: David Joris, *A Very Lovely Tract on the*
Beauty of the Beloved (Deventer: Albert Pafraet, 1539) 48

David Joris, "The Fountain of Life" from *Wonder*
Book (Deventer: Dirk van Borne, *c.* 1543) 64

David Joris, "The New Man" from *Wonder Book,*
Part II 88

Engraving by Hieronymus Wiericx, after David Joris, "The True
Restoration or Restitution, the Image of the Bride of Christ"
from *Wonder Book*, 1551 edition (n.p., [1584]), Part III 95

David Joris, "The Lamb of God and the Lion of Judah" from
Wonder Book, Part I 112

Engraving by Hieronymus Wiericx, after David Joris, "The
Steps to the Way, the Truth and the Life" from *Wonder*
Book, 1551 edition, Part IV 128

Title page: *Wonder Book* (Deventer: Dirk van Borne,
c. 1543) 162

Joris' château in Binningen, near Basel 176

List of Tables and Maps

Table

I	Occupations of Anabaptists in Amsterdam, 1531-35	29
II	Amsterdam and Frisian Leaders	30
III	Occupations of Reformers, 1525-28	31
IV	Prosecutions of Reform Activity, 1514-28	33
V	Amsterdam Anabaptist Migrants	36
VI	Anabaptist Leaders	114
VII	Localities of Davidites	147
VIII	Occupations of Davidite Leaders	150
IX	Anabaptist Progression	169

Map

1	Location of Anabaptist Leaders	115
2	Davidite Groups and Davidites in Delft	146

Acknowledgements

Like most major projects, this book was not completed in solitude. While responsibility for any errors belongs entirely to the author, he acknowledges an immense debt of gratitude for the helpful criticism and suggestions of numerous people which aided the transformation of a mass of research notes into a coherent whole.

In an earlier form the project existed as my doctoral dissertation. Inestimable thanks, therefore, are due to my mentor, Professor Werner O. Packull, whose constant support, encouragement and criticism helped form the backbone of this study. I would also like to thank my former colleagues at the University of Waterloo, Professors John English, Stanley Johannesen, Walter Klaassen, David John, John New, and Arnold Snyder; and Professor James M. Stayer of Queen's University and Dr. Samme Zijlstra of Groningen, for reading all or portions of the dissertation and offering many illuminating and helpful suggestions. Throughout the process of revision Colleen Johnston of Waterloo successfully trod the fine line between patient literary critic and close friend.

The transition from dissertation to book was aided inestimably by the two anonymous readers appointed by the Canadian Federation for the Humanities whose remarks were both objective and insightful. In the later stages, Professor Peter Erb of Wilfrid Laurier University graciously took the time to go through the manuscript, helping to reshape it into its final form. I am also thankful for the many friendly and useful comments from members of the Anabaptist Colloquium, to whom I read portions of chapters in various times and places. I have furthermore profited from the scholarly dialogue experienced at other conferences, in particular the Sixteenth Century Studies Conference (1984 and 1986), the Canadian Society for Renaissance Studies (1985 and 1987), and the Waterloo Consortium for Reformation Studies (1987).

I would like to thank the staffs of the Gemeente Archief Amsterdam, Stad Antwerpen Stadsarchief, and of the Archives and Libraries of the Universities of Amsterdam, Basel, Waterloo and New Brunswick for their courteous and efficient service. Having to put up most with my research needs were Sam Steiner and the staff of the Library of Conrad Grebel College, who handled my frequent queries with both professionalism and personal concern. The director of Wilfrid Laurier University Press, Sandra Woolfrey, and her staff are to be commended for making the process of publication as painless as possible.

Friends and relatives have provided emotional support. My brother, Brian Waite, has provided continuous and unwavering encouragement, as well as a home for my frequent research trips to Toronto. Rick and Anita Pybus also furnished emotional support during some of the roughest periods of my tenure as a doctoral candidate. Vic Neglia and Desh Sharma of the University of Waterloo Arts Computing Office and the staff of the Computer Services Department at the University of New Brunswick provided much assistance in working out many computer-related problems. Other friends and colleagues, too numerous to mention, have provided suggestions and support at various times. Thank you all.

This book has been published with the help of a grant from the Canadian Federation for the Humanities, using funds provided by the Social Sciences and Humanities Research Council of Canada.

Abbreviations

ARG   *Archiv für Reformationsgeschichte*

BRN   Cramer, S. and F. Pijper (eds.). *Bibliotheca Reformatoria Neerlandica.* 10 vols. The Hague: Martinus Nijhoff, 1903

CDI   Fredericq, Paul (ed.). *Corpus documentorum Inquisitionis Haereticae Pravitatis Neerlandicae.* 5 vols. Ghent and The Hague: Martinus Nijhoff, 1889-1900

DAN   Mellink, A.F. (ed.). *Documenta Anabaptistica Neerlandica.* Vol. 1: *Friesland en Groningen (1530-1550).* Vol. 2: *Amsterdam, 1536-1578.* Vol. 5: *Amsterdam, 1531-1536.* Leiden: E.J. Brill, 1975-

ME   *Mennonite Encyclopedia*

MQR   *Mennonite Quarterly Review*

SCJ   *The Sixteenth Century Journal*

Portrait of David Joris; Frisian School, *c.* 1550-55. Courtesy Öffentliche
Kunstsammlung, Basel, Kunstmuseum.

Introduction

The central figure of this study is the Dutch Radical Reformer, David Joris (1501-56). Joris, a glasspainter from the city of Delft, Holland, became an important figure in both the early Reform (1524-34) and Anabaptist (1534-44) movements in the Netherlands. In his time he was one of the most infamous men in the Low Countries, hounded by the imperial authorities and adored by perhaps thousands of supporters who willingly risked their lives and shared their resources to keep their beloved leader alive. For a number of years he was one of the most influential Dutch Anabaptist leaders and competed successfully for adherents with other prominent figures in the movement, Menno Simons in particular. But in 1544 he escaped the relentless persecution in his home country and lived in voluntary exile, under the pseudonym Johann van Brugge, in the Swiss city of Basel. Here he died of natural causes in 1556 and was buried as a honoured gentleman of the community.

Posterity has not been kind to Joris. Until recently, the more charitable image of him, when there was one at all, conjured up thoughts of a slightly deranged narcissist whose enigmatic writings deluded a generation of otherwise sincere Anabaptists.[1] In some respects, Joris himself is to blame for the condition of his reputation. He tended to obscure his teachings, partly in an attempt to win support from both radical and pacifist Anabaptist camps, and partly through his murky writing style. Unfortunately, much of the hostility towards Joris which was expressed by his contemporary opponents was carried over into the modern scholarly debate about this controversial figure.

Since the initiation of the modern study of the Radical Reformation, much attention has been devoted to those figures of the various radical movements who could be most simply claimed by their religious descendants.[2] Mennonite scholars from the 1930s on saw their religious ancestors in the early Swiss Anabaptists, and came to regard the Schleitheim Confession of 1527 as providing the theological definition of "Evangelical Anabaptism." In this schema, all Radical Reformers not measuring up to the Schleitheim standard were not worthy of serious study. Applied to the Low Countries, the yardstick of Evangelical Anabaptism meant that Dutch Anabaptists such as Menno Simons (after whom Mennonites are named) have been the subject of much research on the part of Mennonite scholars, while others who deviated from the norm, such as Obbe Philips, David Joris and

---

Notes to the Introduction are found on page 3.

Adam Pastor, have been neglected.[3] The 1960s and 1970s witnessed a growth in the interest in the more mystical wings of the Radical Reformation and attention turned to South German Anabaptists such as Hans Denck and Pilgram Marpeck.[4] Study of the prominent Spiritualist, Caspar Schwenckfeld, has been promoted by his descendants in North America, the Schwenckfeldians. Even radicals such as Thomas Müntzer and the violent Anabaptist kingdom of Münster (1534-35) have been extensively analysed by Marxist scholars.[5] Unfortunately, these trends have meant that equally significant figures whose descendants, by quirk of history, have not survived, have been relegated to the scholarly sidelines. One of these is David Joris. The study that follows is therefore intended to demonstrate the important role played by Joris in the Radical Reformation and to delineate the relationship between Joris and Anabaptism in the Low Countries.

In the first section of my monograph, I review the history of the early reform and Anabaptist movements in the Netherlands which form the backdrop to Joris' career. Emphasis here is placed on the reform movements which most directly influenced laymen such as Joris. While important in their own right, Dutch humanists, whose primary audience consisted of a small group of classically trained scholars, receive therefore only cursory attention. In the second and major part of the book I deal with the life and thought of Joris. Chapters three and four examine in detail his life and career from his adoption of reform ideas *circa* 1524 to his move to Basel in the summer of 1544. The following four chapters discuss questions relating to the relative importance of Joris to Dutch Anabaptism, including his early theology, his relationship to other Anabaptist groups (both peaceful and violent), his debate with the important Dutch Anabaptist refugees in Strasbourg in 1538, and the nature and import of his following. The penultimate chapter then describes Joris' gradual transition from Anabaptism to Spiritualism. In the final chapter the last years of Joris' life in Basel are briefly surveyed.

The reasons for curtailing my detailed investigation at the year Joris emigrated to Basel are several. First, this transition in the Anabaptist leader's life was more than a geographical one. By his exile Joris had removed himself from direct leadership over the Anabaptist movement in the Low Countries. Other Dutch Anabaptist leaders, such as Menno, were able therefore to more effectively counteract Joris' influence and to bring more of the Dutch Anabaptists into the Mennonite fold. Second, the geographical move corresponded to a significant shift in Joris' ideas. Theologically Joris became much more of a Spiritualist than an Anabaptist while in Basel. Third, Joris' literary production increased dramatically once he had found refuge in the Protestant Swiss Cantons.[6] An analysis of this voluminous corpus and of Joris' ideological changes would require a monograph of its own. Fourth, Joris' Basel period has been more extensively studied than his Anabaptist period. The now classic investigation of Joris' contribution to religious toleration written by Roland Bainton over fifty years ago gave much more attention to Joris' life as a leisured gentleman in the Swiss city than to his existence as a religious refugee in the Netherlands.[7] Therefore, while a brief synopsis of Joris' last years provides the conclusion to our study, the central theme remains the relationship between David Joris and Dutch Anabaptism.

Notes

1. See, for example, the comments of Karel Vos, in "Revolutionary Reformation," in James M. Stayer and Werner O. Packull (eds.), *The Anabaptists and Thomas Müntzer* (Dubuque, Iowa: Kendall/Hunt Publ. Co., 1980), p. 91. Anabaptists were so called because they not only rejected the validity of their baptism as infants, but also practised believer's baptism, a consideration which led their opponents to call them ana- or re-baptisers.
2. The distinction between the Radical Reformation and the Magisterial Reformation of Luther and Calvin is described by George H. Williams, *The Radical Reformation* (Philadelphia: The Westminster Press, 1962).
3. For the archetypal description of the position of this school, see Harold S. Bender, "The Significance of Sixteenth-Century Anabaptism," in Stayer and Packull, *Anabaptists and Thomas Müntzer*, pp. 13-22. The most recent advocate of the "Evangelical Anabaptism" standard has been the Baptist scholar, Kenneth R. Davis, in *Anabaptism and Asceticism* (Scottdale: Herald Press, 1974). Adam Pastor was in 1547 expelled from the Mennonite fold for his anti-trinitarian views.
4. See Packull, *Mysticism and the Early South German-Austrian Anabaptist Movement* (Scottdale: Herald Press, 1977); Walter Klaassen, "Spiritualization in the Reformation," *Mennonite Quarterly Review*, Vol. XXXVII, 1963, pp. 67-77; and William Klassen, *Covenant and Community* (Grand Rapids: Wm. Eerdmans Publishing, 1968).
5. For the prototype Marxist statement on revolutionary Anabaptism see Gerhard Zschäbitz, "The Position of Anabaptism on the Continuum of the Early Bourgeois Revolution in Germany," in Stayer and Packull, *Anabaptists and Thomas Müntzer*, pp. 28-32. For recent Marxist research on Münster, see Günter Vogler, "The Anabaptist Kingdom of Münster in the Tension Between Anabaptism and Imperial Policy," in Hans J. Hillerbrand (ed.), *Radical Tendencies in the Reformation: Divergent Perspectives* (Kirksville, MO: Sixteenth Century Journal Publishers, 1988), pp. 99-116.
6. His works, according to the most complete bibliography, number over 230, only 62 of which appear from the earlier period. The major bibliography is A. van der Linde, *David Joris. Bibliografie* (The Hague, 1867; available in the Radical Reformation Microfiche Project, Section I, Mennonite and Related Sources up to 1600 [Inter Documentation Company, AG, Zug, Switzerland], No. 400). Van der Linde did not include the *Jorislade*, a fifteen-volume collection of manuscripts in the Universität Basel. Several other works were discovered by Roland Bainton (*David Joris. Wiedertäufer und Kämpfer für Toleranz im 16. Jahrhundert* [Leipzig, 1937], pp. 108-11). See also Hillerbrand (ed.), *A Bibliography of Anabaptism, 1520-1630* (Elkhart: Institute of Mennonite Studies, 1962). For a summary of Joris' early works, see Gary K. Waite, "Spiritualizing the Crusade: David Joris in the Context of the Early Reform and Anabaptist Movements in the Netherlands, 1524-1543," Ph.D. diss., University of Waterloo, 1986, pp. 46-62. There is need for a more complete and up-to-date critical bibliography.
7. Joris' place in the Anabaptist movement was therefore never clearly delineated. This is the problem also with Paul Burckhart's "David Joris und seine Gemeinde in Basel," *Basler Zeitschrift für Geschichte und Altertumskunde*, Vol. XLVIII, 1949, pp. 5-106.

PART I

THE REFORMATION IN THE NETHERLANDS, 1519-35

Glass round portraying allegorical virtues: Charity/Love; c. 1544-56. Ascribed to David Joris. From Historical Museum, Basel.

CHAPTER ONE

The Early Reform Movement in the Netherlands

The Reformation initiated by the Augustinian monk and Wittenberg professor Martin Luther and symbolised by the posting of his 95 Theses on the subject of Indulgences on October 31, 1517, quickly extended beyond the boundaries of Electoral Saxony. Luther's reform message and example left the realm of university debate and were propagated throughout the empire by clerical and lay preachers and popularised by pamphleteers, artists and printers. If a complaint made by Dominican friars can be believed, the new teaching was well known in the Low Countries as early as 1519.[1] Understandably, the greatest initial response to the Reformation message in the Netherlands is discovered within Luther's own Augustinian Order. The Priors of several Augustinian Houses, particularly those of Dordrecht, Ghent and Antwerp, were accused by their inquisitors of promoting Luther's teaching among their inmates.[2] Naturally authorities attempted to suppress the spread of the new ideas. As a result the first martyrs of the Dutch Reformation were "Lutheran" Augustinians. Two members of the Augustinian Order in Antwerp were executed at Brussels in 1523.[3] Another from Dordrecht was drowned in 1525.[4] The Antwerp House was razed to the ground in 1523 in an attempt to stem the heresy.[5] These measures, although harsh, were effective — after 1525 the Augustinians were no longer leaders in the reform movement.[6]

Sacramentarians

In spite of this repression the reform movement spread among spiritual and secular clergy, humanists and educated artisans. Sometime around 1520 a Dominican, Wouter of Utrecht, was publicly decrying abuses in the church; he established several conventicles (groups of lay people and clerics gathered to read and discuss the Scriptures), the most important of which was located at Delft.[7] Whether such conventicles preceded the Reformation is as yet unclear. Wouter, it seems, preached a more popular form of Luther's reform message, which included attacking Indulgences. He allegedly advocated that one should not seek remission of sins with money, "otherwise God ... would not have sent his only begotten Son in the flesh to atone by his blood and death for sins."[8] Among those possibly influenced by Wouter were a Georgius Sylvanus; Johannes Sartorius (a teacher in Amsterdam);

Notes to Chapter One are found on pages 16-20.

Cornelis Hoen (a lawyer at the Court of Holland at The Hague); Jan Pistorius (a priest); Willem Gnapheus (rector of the school at The Hague); Canirivus (rector of the Latin school at Delft); and David Joris (a glasspainter), all of whom were to play important roles in the reform movement.[9] Hoen's symbolical interpretation of the eucharist was to influence both Andreas Bodenstein von Karlstadt and Ulrich Zwingli.[10] It is therefore clear that the reform program of Martin Luther was not normative in every respect for those in the Netherlands who took up his call for reform. In particular, a symbolic interpretation of the eucharist appears to have been widespread among the early supporters of the Dutch Reformation. Adherents of this position, generally referred to as Sacramentarians, held that what was important in the celebration of the eucharist was its inner spiritual meaning, not participation in the external act. Sacramentarians, chief among whom was Hoen, were deeply influenced by the monastic reform movement, the Brethren of the Common Life (more commonly known as the *Devotio Moderna*), although none of the important spokesmen of the Brethren, such as their fourteenth-century founder Gerard Groote or Thomas à Kempis, presumed author of *The Imitation of Christ*, ever denied the validity of the external observance of the sacraments.[11] The prominent Dutch theologian of the fifteenth century, Wesel Gansfort, however, appears to have brought together the devotionalists' emphasis on the inner meaning of the sacraments with a careful indifference to the external rites.[12] With Hoen's symbolic interpretation, the doctrine of transubstantiation — that with the words of consecration the bread and wine are actually transformed into the body and blood of Christ — had been repudiated. With this denial of the most central tenet of the medieval sacramental system, Dutch Sacramentarians seemed poised to reject the Catholic church, priesthood, and sacramental system in their entirety.[13]

The Popular Phase

Governmental pressure was brought to bear on those who sided with the reform tradition and by 1524 many of the humanist or clerical leaders were forced to either recant or flee.[14] In 1525, one of the central figures in the early Dutch reform movement, Jan Pistorius (Jan van Woorden), was executed, although his martyrdom remained a rallying force for other reformers.[15] In spite of the subsequent decline in what may be considered educated leadership, membership in reform conventicles and anticlerical activity both continued to increase. As early as 1525, moreover, an increasing number of the laity, particularly artisans, were brought before the courts for heresy.[16] Sources indicate that the Sacramentarian emphasis on the symbolic meaning of the sacraments, when propagated in the context of popular anticlerical sentiment, frequently led to violent and law-breaking acts of iconoclasm.

Laymen, most significantly artisans, who joined the early reform movement did so with zeal. They were moved most strongly by the more blatant aspects of anticlericalism. This is clearly apparent on even the most superficial examination of court records.[17] Of those arraigned, most had been arrested for either acts of iconoclasm or for publicly blaspheming the church and its sacraments. In November 1526, for example, two weavers were arrested in Delft for destroying a monstrance.[18] In July 1528 a woman, Dieuwer Reyersdochter, was arrested because she had, in the presence of many people, asked the rhetorical question "Surely you do not believe that under the host in the Mass . . . is the body of Christ?" and had stated that she could perform the Mass as well as any priest. She had also ridiculed those who were going to church.[19] Dieuwer was charged with blasphemy against Mary, the saints, holy days and fasting. She was sentenced to have her tongue bored and to be exiled for three years.

The activities of persons like Reyersdochter demonstrate that the desacralization of sacred objects was perceived to be a crucial step in the gaining of freedom from clerical domination.[20] Indirect evidence of this can be seen in the widespread absenteeism from church functions in the Low Countries. This lack of enthusiasm for a clerically centred worship vividly contrasts with the religious fervour shown by those who distributed anticlerical broadsheets in the churches, confessionals, and during processionals, or who tacked such literature to church doors. One such pamphlet, summarised in the court records, appeared in Leiden in 1526. It suggested that as far as God was concerned, going to church was of little value, "since He is not there."[21] A verse, possibly part of the same pamphlet, was nailed to St. Peter's Church in Leiden earlier in that year and distributed in the confessionals. It included an evident disdain for the sacrament of confession and insisted as well that husbands needed to keep their wives away from all monks, "or [they] will regret it."[22]

Another key factor in the rise of the Dutch reform movement was the fervent and frequent appeal on the part of the laity to a vernacular form of the Scriptures (as opposed to the traditional Latin Vulgate) as the sole authority in religious matters. This position arose out of and supported rampant Dutch anticlericalism. There was a rapid growth of conventicles in which the Bible was read and discussed, a clear result of the rising literacy rate among urban artisans of the Netherlands.[23] In the early sixteenth century printed books were as yet a novelty and often regarded by the laity with awe. Printers could barely keep up with the demand for Bibles and "pocket-sized" New Testaments.[24] Church authorities, not without reason, often equated literacy with heresy. The increasing number of literate artisans in the urban centres of the Netherlands was particularly disturbing to those who preferred the *status quo*. Literate laymen were perceived by authorities to adhere to a self-reliant reading of the Scriptures. In this sense, the adoption of reformation ideas may have reflected an intellectual "coming of age" on the part of many laymen who joined reform conventicles. Iconoclasm in this regard reflected the aspirations of these literate townspeople to move religious instruction from the visual or aural media to more modern printed or literary ones. Certainly the positive image of the artisan or common man as presented in early Reformation literature helped to reinforce this factor.[25]

Such reform literature called for the reformation of both church and state in both theory and practice. The first step of this particular reformation involved an attack on the "supporting pillars of the Catholic Church." Because of the contemporary urban religio-political situation any attack on the existing church was "an attack on the whole *corpus christianum*," on the medieval concept of a united Christian commonwealth.[26] The central attitudes of this reform movement can be clearly illustrated with reference to the interrogation of Jan Pistorius in 1525.[27] Pistorius exhibited a defiant attitude throughout his interrogation, stating that he considered his inquisitors to be the "new scribes and Pharisees" who "roar like wolves in order to devour the sheep."[28] In addition he showed disdain for his own ordination, stating: "I regard the priesthood as chaff, for we were ordained to it with money . . . for this reason I regard my own status as priest of no worth."[29] Against the church with its special caste of priests, Pistorius went on to postulate the priesthood of all believers:

> the holy church is an invisible and spiritual gathering of all those who will be preserved through Christ and who make do only with the Word of God. Your church . . . is the *Ecclesia malignantium*, and the Pope sits there on the uppermost throne, which is the *Cathedra Pestilentie*. I will have nothing to do with this your church and I will be happy to be banned from it.[30]

Pistorius, moreover, affirmed congregational election of ministers as opposed to the ordination of priests by the bishop. There was also for him no true "holy doctor in the holy Church" except "the Holy Spirit, who teaches us all truth."[31] According to Pistorius, believers no longer needed a professional elite to explain the Word of God to them, for the Scriptures are "rich and full enough to explain themselves."

> The meaning of the holy Scriptures is not hidden under the glosses of the doctors or in the deliberations of the Councils, but their meaning is given to us through the clear and certain word of God.[32]

When Pistorius asked for a public disputation, one of the inquisitors asked, "Who would then be the judges, furriers and weavers?" Pistorius replied simply that "the whole community is able to judge the Scriptures."[33] In the place of priestly absolution, Pistorius affirmed the evangelical belief that Jesus Christ was the sole mediator.[34] He further undercut the sacerdotal system and advocated the emancipation of the laity who were to be fully responsible for their own salvation.[35]

As the case of Pistorius indicates, the early reform movement in the Lowlands was not merely negative. It insisted on a number of central theological tenets. These positive beliefs included the belief that Christ is the sole mediator between God and believers; that the spiritual meaning of the Lord's Supper is more important than its external act; and that such theological tenets are clearly enunciated in the vernacular version of the Scriptures. Nevertheless the reformers' status as a protesting opposition led to the overshadowing of these positive tenets by the negative. These latter elements were, in short, the denial of the role of Mary as co-redemptrix; the rejection of the doctrine of the invocation of the saints; the renunciation of the interpretation of the Mass as a sacrifice; and an insistence on the ability of laymen to gain knowledge of the Word of God without the assistance of priests. What the leaders of the movement repudiated was the exalted status of the clergy either as dispensers of grace or custodians of truth. This anticlericalism was expressed both by the former clerics and by the laity.

Anticlericalism manifested itself as well in the strong iconoclastic tradition of the Netherlands.[36] The reformers felt strongly that images detracted both from the spiritual significance of what the images portrayed and from what they regarded as the true source of spiritual help, the Scriptures. Such images, instead of providing important religious information, merely reinforced old superstitions and unenlightened practices. The anonymous author of *Concerning the Prophet Baruch* wrote:

> And is it not a great stupidity that someone says that the saints would be glad that people visit their images which are wood and stone, or their bones, which are earth . . . because they [the saints] themselves did not want to do such things. Even if they had preferred that we visited their images and bones, what does that accomplish?[37]

A social critic, the author of the treatise went on to insist that money spent on images would be better spent on the poor. It was foolish to dress idols with velvet, silver and gold while "living saints" went naked and suffered from hunger.[38]

The connection between anticlericalism and iconoclasm is reinforced in the writings of Willem Gnapheus. Gnapheus, arrested with Pistorius in 1523, was by happenstance released in 1525.[39] Four years later Gnapheus published his dialogue, "Comfort and Mirror for the Sick," a widely disseminated work that went through forty-seven editions.[40] The overall popularity of Gnapheus' piece indicates that this work is a particularly good source for our understanding of the early reform movement. Gnapheus' tract echoes the concerns of the author of "Concerning the Prophet Baruch," arguing that to seek help from saints "whom we mean to honour in their wooden images" was not only mere foolishness but a breaking of the first commandment.[41] Monies spent on such 'frills' as chapels, churches, cloisters, singers, caps, cups, clocks, images and altars should instead be "used by each city to take care of its own poor." Christian schools should be established, Gnapheus states, in order that society "prepare young Christians in all good arts."[42]

Gnapheus also expressed dismay at the poor example set by the clergy, "who flee at the sign of wolves and leave the lambs helpless."[43] He complained about priests who "preach the Gospel like . . . angels" but who in reality only aid the needy for a piece of gold. True Christian life for Gnapheus was not one of ceremonies, such as blindly attending church and taking the sacraments, but "it is a life of the Spirit of truth, of love and mercy, it is one of death to sensuality, of peace and rest in God alone."[44]

In Gnapheus' writings there is a parallel between anticlericalism and an emphasis on the spiritual significance of external religious acts. For him, true spiritual life was only hindered by the sacerdotal system. The most important act of a Christian was not attendance at Mass, but the mortification of sensual lusts — the old Adam — as a step toward the "rebirth of the inward man."[45] It was crucial for Gnapheus and his contemporaries that everyone be able to read and understand the Scriptures. This they believed was best accomplished through translations of the Bible into the vernacular.[46]

The Chambers of Rhetoric

One of the more vivid instruments of communication aiding the spread of the anticlerical and iconoclastic sentiment of the early reform movement were the Chambers of Rhetoric. The Chambers were acting societies, originating in the medieval French *Rhétoriqueurs*, that in the fifteenth century came to be centred in the court of the Dukes of Burgundy. It is natural, considering the culturally and politically dominant role played by the Burgundians in the Low Countries, that Rhetoricians should become a popular sight in first the French and then Dutch-speaking areas of the Netherlands. The extraordinary popularity of Rhetorician performances is indicated by the fact that by the end of the first half of the sixteenth century, at least 133 Chambers had been created in some 94 cities and towns of the Low Countries.[47] While the *Rhétoriqueurs'* activities had been closely associated with Church processions and festivities, the Burgundians and local authorities soon recognised the important role of Dutch Rhetoricians, or *rederijkers*, in the cultivation of civic pride by means of their pageants and dramatic performances.[48]

The Chambers were organised along the lines of craft guilds and ranged in size from a dozen to over a hundred associates. Members wrote and performed songs, poems, and farces, as well as the more serious allegorical plays (*Spelen van Zinne*) for which they became most famous. Rhetoricians were at the same time entertainers and teachers; the allegorical plays in particular were primarily didactic in function and exerted considerable influence on their audiences.[49] Inter-city *rederijker* festivities (*landjuweels*) often involved hundreds of lavishly costumed participants who entered the host city riding horseback or performing plays on wagons.[50] Aside from their noble figureheads and well-educated playwrights, most members were from the artisanal and merchant strata of society.[51] Clearly membership in the chambers provided ordinary citizens with a cultural outlet that had hitherto been the sole preserve of the first two social estates.[52] They also furnished artisans with a popular vernacular counterpoint to the humanists' elite Latin culture.[53]

These guilds acted as the sixteenth-century equivalent of modern mass media, both moulding and reflecting popular opinion by their plays. The scripts therefore provide remarkable insights into the popular mentality during the time of the Reformation. From those plays that remain, it is evident that well before the 1530s the Chambers of Rhetoric had become notorious for anticlerical sentiment. For example, in 1526, the Court of Holland sent a representative to Amsterdam to investigate

> certain plays which were performed by some *Retorijkers* in front of the *Stadhuys* and inside other buildings there, to the confusion, derision and ridiculing of the sacraments of the holy church and other good institutions.[54]

Further reports of subversive activity on the part of *rederijkers* date from 1524 in Amsterdam, 1526 in Hoorn, different places in Holland and Zealand in 1528, from 1533 in Louvain and Amsterdam again, and from 1535 in Zierikzee.[55]

One of the best examples of this expression of anticlericalism by *rederijkers* is the well executed anonymous play, "A Good Comedy with Three Characters: A Priest, Sexton and a Weaver." The Priest and Sexton represent the religious establishment, while the Weaver, as is so often the case, speaks for evangelical reform.

The play opens with the priest's lamentation that common people were now so bold as to read the Scriptures for themselves.[56] He admits that despite his clerical training he is barely able to understand his Breviary. How could "rude ignorant men" discover the wisdom of the Scriptures? Confronting the Weaver, the Priest then demands that the artisan leave the Scriptures to those called to interpret them and adhere instead to the faith of his forefathers.[57] The Weaver defends the right and ability of laymen to read the Scriptures and to decide their own religious fate. As the play progresses fifteen aspects of the new teachings and their implications for the audience are outlined. These include the accusations, enunciated by the Priest and Sexton, that the reformers (called Lutherans) refuse to attend either church or confession, but instead set themselves against the authorities; and that they do not trust in any good works, such as praying to saints or honouring their images, fasting, celebrating holy days, or paying taxes to support the papacy. Furthermore, the reformers reject priests as scribes and Pharisees, claim that priests could marry, and depreciate the value of the whole sacramental system, especially the Mass and Purgatory. What is worse in the view of the Priest is that these "Lutherans" desire to teach their opinions to everyone and appeared more than willing to suffer martyrdom.[58]

The Weaver is permitted throughout the play to defend these points and in due process the artisan gives the work its anticlerical thrust. There is no need for a confessor since confession is best made to God alone, the Weaver says. Indeed, "you priests ought to confess to us!"[59] The Weaver further states that the pope should not be honoured, because God was jealous of His glory.[60] Evangelicals refuse to attend the sacraments because the Weaver says they "find nothing but idolatry in the church." Externals are insignificant, he goes on to say, for the "true temple of Christ" is a "pure, believing heart."[61] Moreover, the clergy are responsible for the cult of the saints, which, to the artisan, is nothing short of idolatry.[62] The clergy are in fact scribes and Pharisees because they "sell their wares to the common people" and persecute true believers. Because the Weaver sees the pope as the head of the anti-Christian church, the figurehead of Catholicism comes in for special verbal abuse:

> How can you undertake to blaspheme the Spirit of God,
> and exalt the holiness of the pope?
> Was he not also born in sin,
> and conceived in sin, just like other men?
> Why are we concerned about his demands and wishes,
> About his benedictions or damnations?
> I regard them all as arts of sorcery,
> For he seeks nothing but money and worldly honour.
> He acts through the power of the great Antichrist,
> which he himself is and eternally remains.[63]

The papal hierarchy could hardly be treated any less severely. Christ said the "greatest will be the least among you," the Weaver continued:

> Where abides now your pope with all his splendour,
> With all his bishops and cardinals?
> They are Balaam's servants, full of idolatry . . .
> who prophesy against God.[64]

Later the question of the prohibition of working on holy days becomes a particular vexation to the Weaver, as indeed it must have been for many artisans attempting to make a living in the economically depressed Netherlands of the 1520s and early 1530s to whom this play was addressed.[65] He asks why it is that pastry cooks are allowed to work on holy days. The Priest in response argues that they perform necessary work. To this the Weaver responds sarcastically:

> Yes, it is in order to fill your mouths with sweets,
> Therefore you say it is necessary, you canons,
> For it is truly a food for priests and monks,
> And not for weavers, furriers or smiths,
> Who are happy merely with a piece of cheese,
> and coarse bread and water, as is the rooster.[66]

Since Christ had come to fulfill the Sabbath, the Weaver argues that all craftsmen ought to have the freedom to work on holy days. Feast days, the Weaver laments, were instituted only for the material benefit of the clergy, who

> . . . run always with both hands open,
> It is only money that you seek, more than the spirit,
> And on the feast days you earn the most.[67]

When the Sexton then attempts to support the value of images in the churches as the books of the unlearned, the Weaver responds that all this is merely idolatry and an excuse for the clergy to avoid their responsibility to teach the laity according to the Word of God.[68] To the Priest's assertion that "a weaver should weave, a mender should mend but leave us to watch over the Scriptures," the Weaver replies that all believers have been called to proclaim the gospel, and this in spite of persecution.[69]

The Mass is likewise regarded as idolatry by the Weaver, especially when the "simple man" by way of attending is led to conclude "I have now heard a Mass, therefore no harm will come to me this day."[70] Besides, the Weaver argues, only the work of the Spirit and not external things can make one holy:

> It [the Mass] benefits indeed you alone!
> It is not a communion, which leads to Christ,
> For you take your cup and wipe and empty it,
> Just like the drunkards, who drink themselves into a stupor.[71]

The Weaver also has harsh words concerning celibacy. Priests, he proclaims to the cleric, were forbidden to marry so that "you can live your fleshly lives. A fresh whore every day pleases you well!"[72] Finally, with the Weaver quoting from Scripture his interpretation of the non-existence and injustice of purgatory, the play moves to its climax. The Sexton, convinced by the Weaver, asks "what must I do to be saved?" The Weaver replies,

> In the sweat of your brow must you eat your bread.
> This is the first requirement, you should know,
> For whoever will not work, should not eat.[73]

To this the Sexton replies despondently, "Yes, but poor me, I do not know how to work." The Weaver then offers to teach the Sexton the craft of weaving and the former Sexton accepts.

This final action in the play sums up well the position of the early reform movement in the Netherlands. Anticlerical, protesting and negative in emphasis, its ultimate end was the reform of society. There was an expressed desire to improve systems of poor relief and education, and to focus more specifically on preaching and teaching in the churches. The Scriptures were to be both expounded in detail by educated preachers and read by the laity itself. Reformers hoped for a more egalitarian church in which lay people, freed from clerical tutelage, would be more intellectually and actively engaged in religious life. Their ultimate goal was a deeper religious commitment on the part of all Christians, not merely a priestly elite.

Notes

1. See J.G. de Hoop Scheffer, *Geschiedenis der Kerkhervorming in Nederland van haar ontstaan tot 1531* (Amsterdam: 1873), pp. 82-3; and Helmut Isaak, "The Struggle for the Evangelical Town," in Irvin B. Horst (ed.), *Dutch Dissenters* (Leiden: E.J. Brill, 1986), pp. 68-74.
2. Alastair Duke, "Popular Religious Dissent in the Low Countries, 1520-1530," *Journal of Ecclesiastical History*, Vol. XXVI, 1975, p. 42.
3. *CDI*, Vol. IV, pp. 265 and 416-17. Brussels was the seat of the Imperial Court for the Southern Netherlands.
4. Ibid., pp. 92, 209, 420.
5. Ibid., pp. 209, 415.
6. After 1525 there are only scattered references to Augustinian Evangelicals: in 1526 an Augustinian preached evangelical sermons at Delft (ibid., Vol. V, pp. 133-35, 168). In 1527, another, Loderijk Roelants, was imprisoned in Louvain (ibid., pp. 243-45). Generally the authorities called all reformers "Lutherans." For an example, see ibid., Vol. IV, p. 349. See also Duke, "Popular Religious Dissent," p. 42.
7. There is a report that Wouter already in 1510 was preaching against abuses in the Church but recanted under pressure from the Bishop of Utrecht (*CDI*, Vol. I, p. 498).
8. Ibid., Vol. IV, pp. 18-19. I am indebted to James R. Coggins for help in translating this passage from the Latin. See Isaak, "The Struggle," pp. 68-74 and de Hoop Scheffer, *Geschiedenis*, pp. 62-63, 350-56, 533, 538. All translations, unless otherwise indicated, are mine.
9. *CDI*, Vol. IV, p. 19.
10. See Cornelius Krahn, *Dutch Anabaptism* (Scottdale: Herald Press, 1981), pp. 53-56, and Isaak, "The Struggle," pp. 68-69. Cornelius Hoen was apparently the first to enunciate the symbolic interpretation. It was transported in the form of a letter by Hinne Rode to Karlstadt and Zwingli. Luther opposed this teaching in "The Sacrament of the body and blood of Christ against the Fanatics," in Helmut T. Lehmann (ed.), *Luther's Works*, Vol. 36 (Philadelphia: Fortress Press, 1959), pp. 335-61.
11. For the *Devotio Moderna*, see Albert Hyma, *The Christian Renaissance* (New York: The Century Company, 1924); R.R. Post's rejoinder to Hyma's overly positive thesis in *The Modern Devotion* (Leiden: E.J. Brill, 1968); and the more recent discussion by Josef IJsewijn, "The Coming of Humanism to the Low Countries," in Thomas Brady and Heiko A. Oberman (eds.), *Itinerarium Italicum* (Leiden: E.J. Brill, 1975), esp. pp. 223-24. While the most prominent of Dutch humanists, Erasmus, in works such as *Praise of Folly* and *A Pilgrimage for Religion's Sake*, attacked popular superstitious attitudes toward the sacraments and relics, he never denied the importance of the rites themselves. See John P. Dolan (ed.), *The Essential Erasmus* (New York: New American Library, 1964) and Craig R. Thompson (ed.), *Erasmus, Ten Colloquies* (Indianapolis: The Bobbs-Merrill Co., 1957).
12. Post (*The Modern Devotion*, pp. 477-85) depreciates, but cannot deny completely, Gansfort's intellectual roots in the *Devotio Moderna*.
13. A certain Jan Vitrier, who was examined by the Inquisition in October of 1498, had apparently suggested to his fellows that, among other things, "when you observe the sacrament [of the Mass], do not listen; when it is raised, look at the floor, not at the

sacrament" (*CDI*, Vol. III, p. 490).

14. In line with the recent research of Cornelis Augustijn and others, this discussion will use the phrase "reform movements" to refer to the early Reformation in the Netherlands, instead of attempting to make rigid distinctions between Sacramentarians, Lutherans, and other reform groups in the Low Countries (Augustijn, "Anabaptism in the Netherlands: Another Look," *MQR*, Vol. LXII, pp. 197-210).

15. His trial record was published by Willem Gnapheus as *Een Suuerlicke ende seer schoone Disputacie, welcke gheschiet is in den Haghe in Hollant, tusschen die kettermeesters ende eenen christelijcken priester ghenaemt Jan van Woorden, aldaer gheuanghen ende oock verbrant* (n.p., n.d.), and his martyrdom immortalised in song. The trial record is contained in *CDI*, Vol. IV, pp. 452-96 and the song in ibid., p. 79. See also Isaak, "The Struggle," p. 74.

16. See below, chapter 2.

17. See Duke, "Popular Religious Dissent," p. 65.

18. *CDI*, Vol. V, p. 170. According to J. Huizinga (*The Waning of the Middle Ages* [Middlesex: Penguin Books, 1985], p. 193), the use of the monstrance was one of the many innovations introduced into Catholic worship in the late Middle Ages.

19. *CDI*, Vol. V, p. 347. Wolfert the keymaker was arrested in 1528 for having remarked to a priest, "It must be indeed a fool's God who would come between your priests' hands!" (ibid., p. 364).

20. Hans-Christoff Rublack, "Martin Luther and the Urban Social Experience," *SCJ*, Vol. XVI, 1985, esp. pp. 29-31.

21. The anonymous author continued, "Ghy en wilt den Euangelie nyet zwygen, daerom zullen u die monicken bedriegen" (*CDI*, Vol. V, p. 142).

22. Ibid., p. 106.

23. Duke, "Popular Religious Dissent," p. 45.

24. From 1522 to 1530 there were 25 editions of the New Testament printed in Dutch (ibid., p. 65).

25. See Werner O. Packull, "The Image of the 'Common Man' in the Early Pamphlets of the Reformation (1520-1525)," *Historical Reflections*, Vol. XII, 1985, p. 254. "However short lived, an upgraded literary image of the common man constituted the novel achievement of early Reformation propaganda."

26. Isaak, "The Struggle," pp. 74-75.

27. It took place between July 11 and September 15 at The Hague. For the full title of the published account, see above, footnote 15.

28. "Een Suuerlicke ende seer Schoone Disputacie," *CDI*, Vol. V, p. 455. Even if the account does not accurately record Pistorius' own words, it still reflects the attitudes of the members of his reform circle.

29. Ibid., p. 458.

30. Ibid., p. 477.

31. Ibid., p. 457.

32. Ibid., p. 473. An anonymous evangelical pamphlet which was published in Dutch and circulated widely was *Van olden en nieuwen God geloove ende leere*. In it the author remarked that it was a shameful lie "dat men seyt, dat Euangelium en can niemant verstaen sonder die Doctoren, want die heylige scrift is een alsulcker maten door den heylighen gheest wt ghesproken" (*BRN*, Vol. I, p. 96).

33. *CDI*, Vol. V, p. 467.

34. Ibid., p. 491. Pistorius also affirmed the right of priests to marry. His own marriage was a matter of considerable inquiry.

35. Two verses of Pistorius' martyr song in particular reflect the anticlerical sentiment, contrasting the man of God, Pistorius, with his inquisitors:

Een christen man heeft daer gheweest,
Van God begaeft met den heyligen Geest,
Van Woerden was he gheboren;
Seer heylich van leven en wel gheleert,
Een vat Gods, wtvercoren.

Daer waren vergaert met fellen moet
De meesters van Louvain, heel verwoet,
Met monicken en met papen;
Sy zijn vervolgers des godlicken woorts,
Sy en connens niet missaken. (ibid., p. 79)

36. Keith P.F. Moxey's study of iconoclastic sentiment in the early Reformation does not deal adequately with the issue of anticlericalism ("Image Criticism in the Netherlands Before the Iconoclasm of 1566," *Nederlands Archief voor Kerkgeschiedenis*, Vol. LVII, 1977, pp. 148-62).

37. "Vanden Propheet Baruch" (published around 1525), *BRN*, Vol. I, p. 261; translated in Moxey, "Image Criticism," p. 149.

38. *BRN*, p. 263.

39. Ibid., p. 137. Cornelis Hoen had also been arrested but died in prison. Gnapheus was arrested for a second time and released again in 1530, whereupon he fled. Eventually he became tutor of the sons of Countess Anna of East Frisia (Krahn, *Dutch Anabaptism*, p. 63).

40. It was likely written before 1529. *BRN*, Vol. I, pp. 139-40. Moxey says it was written in 1525, the year Gnapheus published his account of Pistorius' martyrdom ("Image Criticism," p. 150).

41. *BRN*, Vol. I, p. 188.

42. Ibid., p. 163.

43. "Het verdriet my so seer, dat wi arme luden, so cleyne exempelen der liefden sien, aen de ghenen die hem seluen wtgeuen voor onse Herders ende sielbewaerders" (ibid., p. 153).

44. Ibid., p. 162. The phrase "death to sensuality" illustrates the anti-materialistic thrust of Sacramentarian literature and could be interpreted to add fuel to the fire of iconoclasm.

45. Ibid., p. 220.

46. "*Timothy [Evangelical]*: Have you read your Pater Noster? *Lazarus*: Of course! Do you take me for a Turk? *Timothy*: In Latin or Dutch? *Lazarus*: I read it as my father taught me [i.e., in Latin]. *Timothy*: It is fitting that you read it in Dutch, then you can better understand it, for you are not able in Latin" (ibid., p. 169).

47. Taken from the list in A. van Elslander, "Lijst van Nederlandse rederijkerskamers uit de XVe en XVIe eeuw," *Koninklijke Soevereine Hoofdkamer van Retorica De Fonteine Jaarboeck*, Vol. XVIII, 1968, pp. 29-60 (hereafter *Jaarboeck De Fonteine*).

48. See Reinder P. Meijer, *Literature of the Low Countries* (Assen: Van Gorcum & Co., 1971), pp. 49-52.

49. Most scholars affirm the influence of the Chambers in the increase in anticlerical sentiment in the Netherlands. Furthermore, Leenert Meeuwis van Dis (*Reformatorische Rederijkersspelen uit de Eerst Helft van de Zestiende Eeuw* [Haarlem: Drukkerij Vijlbrief, 1937]), argues that the Chambers were important elements in the spread of the Reformation ideas. Some contemporary observers suggested that the Ghent *Landjuweel* of June 12-23, 1539, played a role in the major rebellion which occurred a scant three weeks later. The Englishman Richard Clough remarked that "those plays waas one of the prynsypall occasyons of the dystrouccyon of the towne of Gannt" (cited in M. Vandecasteele, "Letterkundig Leven te Gent van 1500 tot 1539," *Jaar-*

boeck De Fonteine, Vol. XVI, 1966, pp. 56-57).

50. On July 22, 1515, the Antwerp Chamber "De Violieren" participated in a competition in Mechelen. Leading the entourage were a number of the city's nobility and magistracy, along with six hundred men "zoo te peerd als opkonstrijke praelwagens en te voet; allen hadden eenderley kleedsel en hoeden." For their efforts the Chamber won the prize for the most "glorious entrance" (J.B. van der Straelen [ed.], *Geschiedenis der Antwerpsche Rederykkamers* [Antwerpen, 1863], p. 20; and Freddy Puts, "Geschiedenis van de Antwerpse rederijkerskamer De Goudbloem," *Jaarboeck De Fonteine*, Vol. XXIII-XXIV, 1973-4, pp. 9-10).

51. See E. van Autenboer, *Volksfeesten en Rederijkers te Mechelen (1400-1600)* (Gent: Secretariaat van de Koninklijke Vlaamse Academy voor Taal-en Letterkunde, 1962).

52. See Autenboer, "Organisaties en stedelijke cultuurvormen 15de en 16de eeuw," *Varia Historica Brabantica*, Vol. VI-VII, 1978, p. 148. In the newly formed religious confraternities the third estate had also begun to take over the functions of religious orders. See Lionel Rothkrug, "Holy Shrines, Religious Dissonance and Satan in the Origins of the German Reformation," *Historical Reflections*, Vol. XIV, 1987, pp. 191-2.

53. J.F.M. Sterck, "Onder Amsterdamsche Humanisten," *Het Boeck*, 2nd Reeks, Vol. VI, 1917, p. 296.

54. Those actors named were Pieter Jacobssen, Lou Jacobsz and Dalem Gerytssoen from Monnikendam (*CDI*, Vol. V, pp. 168, 172).

55. Dis, *Reformatorische Rederijkersspelen*, p. 30.

56. Ibid., p. 152:
    En is dit niet een plaghe, een pestilentie,
    Ergher dan pocken, Lelmten oft Enghels sweet,
    Dat tgemeyn volck nu maect sulcken mencie,
    Vander scriftueren, dwelc hem niet en versteet!

57. Ibid., p. 156.

58. Ibid., p. 162.

59. Ibid., p. 165. The abolition of clerical confession however would have removed from the church an important practice for the maintenance of social control. Thomas N. Tentler (*Sin and Confession on the Eve of the Reformation* [Princeton: Princeton University Press, 1977], p. 345) suggests that "In theory and practice, sacramental confession provided a comprehensive and organised system of social control. Its first principle was the sacramentally ordained priest's dominance which was expressed in a variety of ways."

60. Dis, *Reformatorische Rederijkersspelen*, p. 166.

61. Ibid., pp. 169-70.

62. Ibid., p. 176. "So seg ic datter geen meer duyvels en wesen Dan de Heyligen, sout so zijn also ghyse acht, Want Lucifer en hadde maer een hooveerdich gedacht, Men werp hem wten hemel naer tschrifts vertellen, Om dat he zijnen stoel als God wilde stellen."

63. Ibid., p. 181. If the pope turned from his errors,
    Maer sochte he de rechte Apostolische leere,
    Hoe de menschen moeten op Christum staen,
    So sout hem also Paus Adrianus gaen,
    Die van zijn valsche Apostles wert vergheven.
    Later the Weaver said "So zijt ghy den Antechrist oft Antechrists knecht" (p. 193).

64. Ibid., p. 183.

65. For a discussion of the economic conditions of the Low Countries in these decades,

see below, chapter 2.
66. Dis, *Reformatorische Rederijkersspelen*, p. 189.
67. Ibid., p. 190. This particular criticism may have reflected the concerns of the merchant class, which was strongly represented in the Chambers.
68. "*Coster*: Gregorius seyt: tzijn der ongeleerden boecken . . . *Weaver*: Ja, maer God spreect, ghy en sult geen gelyckenisse maken . . . Hoe God alle Godemakers sal verderven . . . Ghi sultse wel leeren, preect haer trechte Gods woort / En leert haer, als der heligen, Christi voetstappen gaen" (ibid., pp. 197-98). This suggests a parallel to what Packull has called the celebration of lay emancipation from the tutelage of clergy in the pamphlet literature in the German Reformation between 1520 and 1525 ("The Image of the Common Man," p. 260).
69. At this point the Sexton asked the Weaver, "Are you not an Anabaptist?" The Weaver replied, "Ich houdse even voor Monicken, als ghy zijt / Vaten superstitieus, kuerieus van wercken, / Sy bannen, sy schelden, sy blijven wter kercken . . ." (Dis, *Reformatorische Rederijkersspelen*, pp. 201-2).
70. Ibid., p. 208.
71. Ibid., p. 209.
72. Ibid., p. 211.
73. "Ist so, so moet de Paus wel een Tyrant zijn, / Heeft he sulcke macht en is hy so snoode, Dat hy de seelen daer laet siten in noode? So is hy erger dan Judas den verrader! Is hy niet bermhertich als zijn hemelsche vader?" (ibid., p. 218). Purgatory, like confession, may have served as a form of social control, particularly in its emphasis on rewards for good behaviour and punishment for undesirable conduct.

Glass round portraying allegorical virtue: Righteousness; *c.* 1544-56. Ascribed to
David Joris. From Historical Museum, Basel.

CHAPTER TWO

The Anabaptist Movement
in Holland, 1531-35

David Joris' work cannot be understood aside from the Netherlands reform movement. Nor can it be comprehended apart from the history of the various Anabaptist traditions that drank from the same stream as the Sacramentarians and Dutch reformers. In fact, the egalitarian thrust of the early reform movement in the Netherlands has interesting parallels in the rise of the Anabaptist movement.

The first sample we have of a movement that can be clearly defined as Anabaptist is in the Swiss city of Zurich in 1525. There, under the leadership of two young humanists, Conrad Grebel and Felix Mantz, a number of important issues were raised regarding the depth and pace of reform conducted by the prominent Reformer Ulrich Zwingli and the Zurich city council. Central to these was Grebel and Mantz's belief that the church of God consisted of those who chose to be members of a believer's conventicle set apart from the mass of nominal Christians.[1] Membership was symbolised by believer's baptism, hence those who joined one of these conventicles were known as ana-baptists (rebaptisers). The theological position held by the Grebel group was more fully expressed two years later in the famous Schleitheim Confession penned by the former Benedictine prior, Michael Sattler.[2] Schleitheim set out seven doctrinal points which became formative for Swiss Anabaptism. These tenets helped formulate the rationale for a separatist, voluntary church, the baptised members of which refused to carry a sword or swear an oath, chose and supported their own pastors, enforced church discipline, and regularly partook of the Lord's Supper as a sign of their membership in the body of Christ.[3]

Zurich and Schleitheim cannot be seen, however, as providing the genesis for the entire Anabaptist movement. There is evidence of groups who held similar positions arising on their own elsewhere in Europe.[4] The proliferation of Anabaptist ideals throughout Europe makes it difficult to speak of it as a single integrated tradition. The origins of South German Anabaptism, for example, were linked to the peasant uprising of 1525 and to the work of the Radical Reformer of Mühlhausen, Thomas Müntzer. Müntzer identified the confrontation between peasant and lord as the final conflict between the godly and ungodly before the return of Christ.[5] Instead of establishing a more egalitarian society, peasant resistance was crushed. South German

---

Notes to Chapter Two are found on pages 39-46.

Anabaptism was formed, in part, in this context of disillusionment.[6] Hans Hut, an admirer of Müntzer, managed to survive the battle of Frankenhausen, while Müntzer was captured and executed.[7] Hut became convinced that the peasants had been defeated because they had not been the "pure, unselfish champions of God's honour for which he had taken them."[8] When in the spring of 1526 he joined the Anabaptist group centred around Hans Denck, Hut naturally associated these people with the truly godly. The baptism he received at the hands of the mystically-inclined Denck, however, did not involve a break with his Müntzerian past.[9] Instead, Hut regarded his baptism as a sign of the sealed who would be spared in the coming judgement. He took on the burden of administering this mark on as many of the 144,000 elect of Revelation 7 in the short time remaining before the return of Christ.[10]

In spite of this wide divergence in practice, there is little doubt that some common principles held differing Anabaptist groups together. The idea of a people set apart by their baptism into a separatist elect was a commonplace. While the differences between Swiss and North German/ Dutch Anabaptism were considerable, Anabaptism in the Low Countries had much in common with the apocalyptical ideas of Hut and his circle. This is seen most clearly in the career of the visionary South German prophet Melchior Hoffman.

Hoffman came from the South German Imperial Free City of Schwäbisch Hall. By trade he was a furrier, but already in 1523 he was a lay missionary in Livonia on behalf of the Lutheran Reformation (as he understood it).[11] Hoffman's success as a lay reform preacher was indeed remarkable. The support he gained in Livonia (1523-26), Stockholm (1526-27), and Schleswig-Holstein (1527-29) on the part of both the populace and the authorities frustrated more orthodox Lutherans who were suspicious of some of his views. Disputed points included Hoffman's belief that the end of the world would occur in a mere seven years (in 1533) with the last three and a half years being filled with apocalyptical tribulation.[12] Furthermore, he claimed that he had a unique gift to understand the figurative meaning of the Scriptures, an ability which was superior to that of the formally educated theologians whom he called the servants of the letter. In 1529 Hoffman visited the religiously tolerant South Germany city of Strasbourg, where he came in contact with the Denck Anabaptists. He was also enamoured of the small group centred around the "Strasbourg Prophets" led by Leonard and Ursula Jost and Barbara Rebstock.[13] Both groups emphasised the superiority of the "inner Word" over the "outer Word." The truth of God was communicated by the Holy Spirit to the heart of the believer and not found in the text itself. Hence, for the Strasbourg radicals, visions and other forms of direct revelations were important means for the mediation of religious knowledge. Under the influence of the Strasbourg Anabaptists, Hoffman altered his reform program, rejecting Luther's doctrine of predestination and revising his apocalyptical expectations. He adopted the Josts' idea that the world required a great cleansing before the return of Christ. During this cleansing, the Imperial Free Cities such as Strasbourg would defend the truth of the gospel against the combined ungodly forces of the antichristian emperor, papacy and clergy. After a difficult siege, the attacking forces would be destroyed and the following period of peace would set the stage for the return of Christ. While Hoffman affirmed that Anabaptists would not themselves take up the sword, they were to assist the cities by non-violent means. Hoffman at this time also developed his new doctrine of the "heavenly flesh of Christ," which affirmed that Christ had not taken his flesh from Mary and hence had remained sinless.[14]

In April 1530 Hoffman demanded that the Strasbourg city council provide a church for the Anabaptist fellowship. The year before, however, an imperial mandate had made rebaptism a capital offence and a warrant was therefore issued for Hoffman's arrest. He fled to Emden in East Frisia, where persecuted dissenters from the Low Countries had also fled. Here Hoffman won a sizeable following with his message of eschatalogical hope. Upon their return to their home territories, these now Anabaptist refugees became the prime carriers of Hoffman's ideas throughout the Low Countries.[15] Hoffman stamped his personality, theology and apocalyptic mood so decisively upon the Dutch Anabaptist movement that its early adherents are also called Melchiorites. This lay missionary, however, did not stay long in East Frisia. On the strength of a vision on the part of one of his followers, Hoffman allowed himself to be arrested in Strasbourg in 1533. He still regarded Strasbourg as the location of the forthcoming kingdom of God and he therefore expected that within six months Christ himself would deliver him from jail. To his dismay, the day of deliverance did not appear and Hoffman most likely died in prison some time around 1543.[16]

Before Hoffman had left his successful campaign in Emden, he had appointed Jan Volkerts Trijpmaker, another artisan, as his primary apostle to Holland.[17] Trijpmaker began his baptising activity in Amsterdam some time around Christmas 1530.[18] He and nine others were, however, arrested and executed the following December at The Hague, and the leadership of Hoffman's movement fell into the hands of those who had been converted in Amsterdam. The death of Trijpmaker and his fellows also caused Hoffman to suspend the practice of believer's baptism for a two-year period in order to avoid further martyrdom.[19] In spite of this setback, the movement, directed by several artisans, such as the Frisian barber-surgeon Obbe Philips, gained a wide measure of support in Amsterdam, which then became one of two foci for the movement.[20] The other focus for Dutch Anabaptism was the Bishop-city of Münster in Westphalia.[21]

The Münsterite Revolution

As in most other German cities, advocacy of reform received widespread support in Münster. By 1531 the key Reformer of the city was the evangelical preacher, Bernhard Rothmann. His reform proposals were in line with the civic, communal Reformation common to the Swiss and South German cities in the 1520s, "at a time and in a region in which magisterial Reformation and conformity to Lutheran theology were politically inescapable."[22] Rothmann's Sacramentarian ideas and communal Reformation appealed to both the magistracy and the guild leaders of Münster. City fathers favoured his calls for political autonomy from the prince-bishop, while the city's guilds hoped to use the groundswell of reform sentiment to wrest control of the city council from the ruling elite. The bishop's efforts to remove Rothmann from his office therefore met with popular opposition. Moreover, attempts by Wittenberg's theologians to force Münster to conform to official Lutheranism merely made Rothmann and many residents of the city more receptive to the radical message of Heinrich Rol and his fellow refugees from Wassenberg in Jülich, who arrived in Münster in September 1532. These so-called Wassenberg preachers promoted the Anabaptist practice of baptism upon confession of faith. By the following summer Rothmann had been won over to the concept of believer's baptism and wrote an elegant defence of it in the *Confession of the Two Sacraments*.[23] Its practice was not reinstated until Jan Matthijs received a copy of Rothmann's tract. Matthijs, a Haarlem baker residing in Amsterdam, claimed to be the new prophet (presumably replacing the imprisoned Hoffman), terminated Hoffman's suspension of believer's baptism (*Stillstand*) and reinstituted the rite.[24] Messengers of Matthijs were the first to baptise adults in Münster in January 1534. The following month Rothmann and the Anabaptists, although comprising a minority faction in the city council and facing seemingly impossible odds, were granted control over the city council as a means to preserve the Münster Reformation against the bishop. Matthijs arrived shortly afterwards and took over leadership of the reform movement, affirming that Münster, not Strasbourg, was to be the site of the New Jerusalem, which would see the return of Christ in Easter (April 5) of 1534.[25] In the meantime, Rothmann was relegated to the post of propagandist for the Anabaptist community. While the prince-bishop (Franz von Waldeck) laid siege to his city, Matthijs gained absolute control over the city council. But when on the day appointed the divine deliverance failed to appear, Matthijs marched out of the city to be cut into pieces by the besiegers.[26] Jan van Leiden, a Dutch merchant and innkeeper, took Matthijs' place, reinforced his adoption of community of goods and the use of violence, and set up the more infamous characteristics which have become part of the legend of the Münster kingdom — an Old Testament style theocracy and enforced polygamy. Rothmann was called upon to write justifications for all of these radical ideas.[27] Münsterite emissaries attempted to raise support for the New

Jerusalem by distributing Rothmann's tracts throughout the Low Countries and North Germany.

Excited by the prophetic predictions of Hoffman and Matthijs and driven to desperation by the poor economic conditions and the pressure of persecution, thousands of Dutch believers had attempted in March 1534 to find refuge in Münster from the coming wrath of God, although only a few actually made it past the forewarned authorities.[28] A year later several hundred Anabaptists captured Oldeklooster, a Frisian monastery near Bolswart.[29] Inspired by the Münsterite apostles, small groups of Melchiorites attempted twice to take over the city of Amsterdam.[30] The second attempt was made on May 10, 1535. During this attack by fewer than forty Anabaptists led by Jan van Geelen, a survivor of Oldeklooster, the Amsterdam city hall was captured and held for one night, with the loss of one of the city's burgomasters and several of the watch. Decisive action was taken against the rebels and Amsterdam, which to this point had been one of the more religiously tolerant cities in Holland, undertook a serious campaign to rid the city of religious dissenters.[31] For their part, the Anabaptists, both peaceful and violent, underwent a terrible period of persecution, and many of their number subsequently died on the scaffold while countless others were forced to flee. Certainly van Geelen and his cohorts had expected that large numbers of their brethren in the city would join with them to create a second urban Anabaptist kingdom analogous to Münster. They were, as it turned out, mistaken.[32]

After a sixteen-month siege, Münster itself fell in June 1535 to the bishop's forces, initiating a period of severe disillusionment and reappraisal on the part of Melchiorites. Great hopes had been pinned on the success of that endeavour, and with its fall confusion, apathy and anger set in. It seems that many Anabaptists or sympathisers had second thoughts, recanted, returned to their homes and disappeared from the historian's field of view.[33] Most of those who remained gathered into six or more major camps under the leadership of several key leaders.[34] Guiding a portion of the peaceful element was Menno Simons, a priest from Witmarsum, Friesland. Even before the fall of Münster, Simons held views regarding the Lord's Supper and baptism which resembled those of the Anabaptists, but he did not officially join the movement until 1536. He, along with Obbe Philips' brother Dirk (a former monk), took their followers in the direction of a separated, pacifist fellowship, enforcing the purity of the church by the use of the ban and guarding the flock from the subversive ideas of the leaders of the other Anabaptists camps such as David Joris.[35] Joris' emphasis was to retain as much of the original ideology and zeal of the earlier Melchiorite movement without taking part in insane revolutionary attempts. He also allowed his supporters to participate in Catholic or Reformed services in order to avoid detection by the authorities, a practice known as Nicodemism and which Simons took great pains to counteract.[36]

Four other camps competed less successfully for the devotion of Dutch Anabaptists. These included a remnant of Münsterites who, under the direction of the former chancellor of Münster, Heinrich Krechting, found a place of refuge in Oldenburg in northern Westphalia and continued to plan for the restoration of the New Jerusalem. Another group of radicals formed around the Dutch nobleman Jan van Batenburg who continued the campaign of vengeance against the godless as well as the traditions of polygamy and community of goods, albeit on a much smaller scale.[37] A small group of Melchiorites remained devoted to the imprisoned Hoffman in Strasbourg, although by 1539 several of them were active in restoring Anabaptists in the region of Strasbourg to the Reformed Church.[38] Finally, a significant number of Melchiorites followed the path taken by Obbe Philips, who spiritualised all Anabaptist tenets. Influenced by more famous Spiritualists such as Sebastian Franck and the Silesian nobleman Caspar Schwenckfeld, Philips eventually denied that any group, including the Anabaptists, had the monopoly on religious truth and that all external rites and organisations were insignificant.[39] What truly mattered in the minds of Spiritualists was the spiritual devotion of the individual. David Joris himself was eventually to take up this position.

The Socio-Economic Context

The Anabaptist tradition in the Netherlands cannot be understood simply within the framework of the apocalypticism and theology of the Radical Reformation. Although many studies have dealt with the theological issues at stake in the various Dutch Anabaptist disputes, little attention has been directed to the socio-economic framework within which that Anabaptism arose. Even Claus-Peter Clasen's groundbreaking study of the social history of Anabaptism neglected the movement in the Low Countries, which, according to Klaus Deppermann, took on the characteristics of a mass movement.[40]

There is a good deal of material relating to Anabaptism in the Netherlands and the social framework out of which David Joris arose. Although most sources relating to the early reform and Anabaptist movements in Joris' home city of Delft were destroyed in a fire in 1536, a considerable body of information is available for Amsterdam, the pivotal centre for Anabaptism in Holland.[41] A study of the movement in Amsterdam illuminates not only the nature of developments in Holland generally, but also developments in other urban centres of the Netherlands. The following study emphasises the Anabaptist movement in Amsterdam between 1531 and 1535, but Amsterdam records are supported by almost half as many from urban centres outside that city.[42] These Anabaptists are here analysed in terms of their social background, leadership positions and migratory patterns. The resulting picture is then compared with a similar survey of non-Anabaptist reformers brought before the courts between 1525 and 1528,[43] as well as with conclusions reached by Clasen in his study. The early Anabaptist movement in Holland, and particularly in Amsterdam, was in part an attempt by a segment of the artisanal estate to cope with the social, economic, political and religious problems of the third and fourth decades of the sixteenth century, which affected them far more severely than it did any other social group. The large numbers of artisans who joined the Anabaptist movement, their enthusiastic adoption of apocalypticism, their almost complete lack of an educated leadership, and the desperate nature of their hope and migrations, all attest to the fact that most of those who joined the Anabaptist movement in the Netherlands did so out of a profound sense of crisis.

As noted, Holland Melchiorites were overwhelmingly from the artisanal stratum of society. Given that Hoffman himself was an artisan, it comes as no surprise that his preaching was well received by that same social stratum. Of the 192 Anabaptists brought before or identified in the Court of Amsterdam between 1534 and 1535, and the fifty brought before The Hague between 1531 and 1535, 140, or 58%, were identified by gender and occupation. Of these, 38 (37%) were women, mostly wives of Anabaptist artisans. Aside from one surgeon, Gerrit van Campen, (beheaded in May of 1534 for planning the overthrow of the city), and one priest (sentenced at The Hague in 1533), the rest were artisans or craftsmen (see Table I).[44]

Table I. Occupations of Anabaptists in Amsterdam, 1531-35

Intellectuals 2	**Metals 21**	**Agriculture 2**
surgeon 1	swordmakers 6	
priest 1	armour makers 4	**Construction 5**
	kettlemakers 3	ditchdiggers 3
Textiles 18	goldsmiths 2	blockmakers 2
tailors 6	needlemakers 2	
fullers 4	pumpmakers 2	**Others Identified 13**
sailmakers 3	smiths 1	glassmakers 4
weavers 3	lanternmakers 1	bargemen 3
furrier 1		merchants 2
cloakmaker 1	**Leather 10**	barber 1
	shoemakers 10	soapmaker 1
Wood 10		sexton 1
cabinetmakers 3	**Foods 6**	cardmaker 1
basketweavers 2	bakers 4	
coopers 2	milkers 2	
carpenters 2		
woodpiler 1		

What is most remarkable in this survey is the nearly complete lack of any theologically trained leaders within the movement. A similar state of affairs with respect to leadership existed in Friesland, where only one of 85

Anabaptists named in the sources could be considered formally educated.[45] Although Dirk Philips, a former Franciscan monk, had been baptised by 1534, in leadership before 1535 he was dramatically overshadowed by his barber brother, Obbe.[46] In Amsterdam artisans dominated both the leadership and membership of the Melchiorites. The movement which had been instituted by an artisan was, in fact, carried on and nurtured by lay leaders within the same social stratum and found its greatest response among their confreres or social inferiors.[47]

Table II. Amsterdam and Frisian Leaders

Amsterdam:		
Jan Pouwels	carpenter	(d.1534)
Gerrit van Campen	surgeon	(d.1534)
Dominicus Abelsz	goldsmith	baptiser (d.1534)
Jacob Symons	layman	baptiser (d.1534)
Jan Paeuw	master blockmaker	deacon
Hans van Leeuwarden	ditchdigger	baptiser
Steven	shoemaker	deacon
Jan Matthijs van Middelburg	goldsmith	baptiser
Gherrijt van Wou	layman	baptiser
Adriaen van Benscop	merchant	prophet
Jacob van Campen	barber	bishop (d.1535)
Cornelius uit Briell	shoemaker	baptiser
Peter Claeszn	sexton	baptiser
Barent Bacher	baker	baptiser
Frisian:		
Bartholomeus Boeckbinder	bookbinder	elder and apostle
Melchior Hoffman	furrier	chief evangelist
Peter Houtsager	layman	baptiser and elder
Jacob Tyetteye van Goegna		
Peter Simonszoen van Tyrnes		apostle from Münster
Obbe Scherrier (Philips)	barber	baptiser or elder

Melchiorites naturally looked for leadership from within their own ranks. Most of their leaders, however, came from the higher-ranked crafts or had achieved a measure of success in their field. A surgeon, two goldsmiths, two barbers, a baker, a master blockmaker (with at least one apprentice) and a bookbinder were all included in their number (see Table II).[48] More famous leaders, such as Jan Matthijs (baker), Jan van Leiden (Rhetorician and merchant) and David Joris (glasspainter) also fit this description.[49]

The exclusively lay leadership of the Dutch Anabaptists can also be contrasted with the wider reform movement in the Low Countries which preceded it. Of the 115 non-Anabaptist reformers brought before the Court at The Hague between 1525 and 1528 whose occupations are known, 46, or a full 40%, were priests or monks and nine more were intellectuals (see Table III).[50]

Table III. Occupations of Reformers, 1525-28

	1525	1526	1527	1528	Total
Clerics	26	8	12	7	53
(Religious:	21	8	10	7)	
Bookworkers	4	6	0	0	10
Metalworkers	2	1	3	2	8
Clothworkers	1	4	8	4	17
Others*					26+

*Painters (6), Glassworkers (4), Barbers (3), Merchants (3), Free Thinkers (2), Others (8+).

The remainder of those identified (approximately half), were again artisans. An interesting factor is that the number of clerics examined by the courts declined over the period, with 26 in 1525 and only seven in 1528. It would appear, then, that the early reformers in the Netherlands were directed by a clerical leadership, but with increasing lay involvement as the educated leaders were martyred or forced to flee.

The Reform and Anabaptist Movements

These statistics put the question of the interrelationship between the non-Anabaptist Dutch Reformers and Anabaptists into a rather new light. Several Anabaptist leaders — notably Jan Pouwels of Amsterdam,[51] David Joris of Delft and Jan Matthijs of Haarlem — had in fact been tried earlier for their reform activities. Also, at least sixteen Anabaptists confessed before the Court of Amsterdam that they had been religious dissenters for up to fifteen years.[52] This relationship can be seen quite clearly in the case of David Joris. Joris had settled in the city of Delft in 1524 to practise his craft of glasspainting. He came under the influence of the former Dominican Wouter (also referred to as the ''Lutheran monk'') mentioned in the preceding chapter, who had established a reform conventicle in that city.[53] Joris became an enthusiastic supporter of the Reformation and on Ascension Day, 1528, he interrupted and publicly denounced the Procession of the Host while standing before the door of the New Church. The authorities feared an uprising of the common people and Joris was arrested.[54] Nevertheless, Joris was just one member (albeit a radical one) of the Delft conventicle, which was led by clerics such as Wouter.[55]

While the clerics restricted their reforming activities to teaching and preaching (which offices they already held), it appears that many lay members were so moved that they publicly denounced the priesthood and interrupted church services.

It is evident then that many of the Anabaptist leaders had received their initial training from educated reform leaders. By 1531, however, most of these leaders had disappeared, and leadership of the newly forming Anabaptist conventicles fell to reform lay members such as Joris.[56] As a result, the anticlericalism (and according to Irvin Horst, the Nicodemism)[57] of the earlier protests seems to have moved unaltered into the ideology of the Dutch Anabaptists.

There is a tendency today to assume that because of the divergent developments of the Dutch Calvinist and Mennonite traditions, the early reform and Anabaptist movements were from the beginning two distinct phenomena. While there were differences, more prominent were the very close ties between the two. In its initial stages Anabaptism grew out of and followed the lines of the earlier reform legacy. This development accounts for the relative ease of transition of members from one movement to another. The close association between non-Anabaptist and Anabaptist reform movements also helps explain the apparent discrepancy between the respective developments regarding Anabaptist leadership in the North and South. The leadership of the popular reform movement in the Netherlands shifted from clerics to artisans between 1525 and 1535, just as it had in the South. The ideological differences between the earlier reform and the Anabaptist manifestations, particularly the apocalypticism of the latter, were not important enough to hinder many devoted followers of reformers such as Wouter from moving into Anabaptism. Anticlericalism was, in fact, the ideological thread which tied the two reform streams together.[58]

The example of Wouter Deelen indicates the close ties between the early reform movement and Anabaptism. Deelen, a teacher of biblical languages in Amsterdam, is reported to have done the radical Anabaptist Frans Frederycxz (later involved in the May 10, 1535 uprising) a daring favour.[59] Wouter was asked by Frederycxz for the key to the *Rederijkerscamer* (the Rhetoricians' meeting hall) and Wouter gave it to him. Interestingly, Frederycxz also claimed that one of the more important Anabaptist leaders, Jan Matthijs van Middelburg, had stayed with Wouter Deelen in an Amsterdam inn known as the "Spain" (*Spaengnen*).[60] Wouter may have been unaware of the Anabaptist plot to capture Amsterdam, but he clearly was on close terms with several of the Anabaptists and, if the later governmental report can be believed, it was his reform proposals that spurred his disciples into even worse blasphemies.[61] It is not at all clear whether or not Wouter would have cooperated with Frederycxz's request for the Chamber key had he been fully cognizant of the radicals' desire to use the banners and drums of the *rederijkers* in an attempted revolt.

There were definite centres of radical or iconoclastic dissent for both the early non-Anabaptist and Anabaptist phases of popular reform. There is also a very clear correlation between the localities of the earlier reform and Anabaptist activities; generally those cities which were noted for anticlerical and iconoclastic activities before 1528 were also the major centres of Anabaptism in the Netherlands. Amsterdam, Delft, Haarlem, Monnikendam and Leiden had all experienced significant iconoclastic outbursts or the activities of reform conventicles before they became the centres of Anabaptism. There was, however, a shift in the geographic centre of this activity. Between 1514 and 1524, Antwerp, in the southern Netherlands, had investigated at least 69 cases of heresy. This figure far surpassed that of the next city, Amsterdam, with only fifteen. Between 1525 and 1528, Antwerp investigated a further 26, indicating a levelling off or even a drop in activity. Amsterdam, however, more than doubled its investigations to 31, and the other cities of Holland, such as Haarlem, Delft, Monnikendam, and Leiden practically exploded from only a few cases between 1514 and 1524 to 91, 26, 23, and nineteen respectively between 1525 and 1528. The southern cities, however, continued to prosecute reformers, and one purge in Brussels in 1527 netted more than 60 names (see Table IV).[62] The centre of the reform movement therefore had moved north, particularly to Amsterdam, Haarlem and Delft.[63]

Table IV. Prosecutions of Reform Activity,
1514-28

Amsterdam	1514-20	0	Delft	1514-24	4
	1521-24	15		1525	12
	1525-28	31		1526-28	14
Antwerp	1514-20	5	Haarlem	1514-24	0
	1521-23	26		1525-27	1
	1524	38		1528	90
	1525-26	19			
	1527-28	3	Leiden	1514-20	2
				1521-24	4
Brussels	1514-20	1		1525-28	18
	1521-24	4			
	1525-26	0	Monnikendam	1514-24	0
	1527-28	60		1514-25	2
				1526-28	21
Hoorn	1514-24	1			
	1525-28	11			

This shift was due in part to the persecution undertaken against the radicals in the southern Netherlands, particularly in Antwerp and Brussels, where the first Dutch martyrs of the Reformation were executed in 1523. The southern cities were far easier for the emperor to control than were the northern territories. The cities of Holland to the north found the attempts of the inquisitors (representatives of the emperor and pope) to prosecute heretics within their jurisdiction especially heinous as well as unlawful. They argued that such interference went against the privileges of the cities and they desired to deal with the heretics in their own fashion.[64] This usually meant that the heretics were dealt with more humanely than if tried by the

Inquisition. David Joris is again a case in point. The court of Delft had initially sentenced him to only a token punishment. The representative of the Inquisitor found this exceedingly lenient, and won a new trial before the Court of Holland (the Imperial Court) at The Hague. His previous sentence was overturned, and instead he was to be

> bound upon the scaffold built upon the marketplace in the city of Delft and there to be severely lashed and then an iron is to be bored through his tongue and left there for half an hour. He is then to be banned from the city for the next three years. He is not to return inside this time except at the loss of his right hand. And then not to return until he has paid Jan de Heuter [the sheriff at Delft] the sum of 40 Karolus guilders and the cost of these proceedings.[65]

In spite of what may seem to modern readers to have been harsh treatment, the cities of Holland tended to be more tolerant of the Reformation than the southern territories and hence many of the radicals fled to the north.

Amsterdam as the New Jerusalem

There is another factor in this geographic shift. In the early sixteenth century, Amsterdam was just beginning its rise to prominence among the cities of Europe.[66] In fact, Amsterdam was the only city in the province of Holland to experience numerical and economic growth in the first half of the sixteenth century.[67] Many religiously radical artisans in particular may simply have moved to Amsterdam to find employment. This is particularly evident when one examines Anabaptist migrations. Of the 192 Amsterdam Anabaptists examined between 1534 and 1535, at least 96, or 50%, had migrated to that city within the last few years. Amsterdam was regarded by these immigrants as the "Holy City" or the "New Jerusalem."[68] As was the case with Hoffman's choice of Strasbourg and Matthijs' choice of Münster, these Anabaptists chose Amsterdam in part because of its relatively tolerant stance towards heretics, especially before the attempted revolt. Yet this explanation does not suffice on its own, for the persecution of Anabaptists in the northern provinces did not become extensive until after the winter of 1534, when the Bishop of Münster began to besiege his city. It appears that Anabaptists fleeing to Amsterdam because of persecution were also part of a larger wave of unemployed artisans who were migrating to better areas of employment.[69] Jacob van Campen reported that at the beginning of his office he had baptised sixty to seventy strangers whom he did not know.[70] An example of this economically motivated migration is provided by Annetgen Baelhuys from Brussels. She had migrated from Brussels with her husband Gelis, a fuller, the previous Easter in order to "win their bread by fulling." Gelis had become an Anabaptist, but his wife had not accepted his argument that she too ought to be baptised. She therefore reported their motives for the move without the religious terminology found in most other reports.[71]

In the light of economic considerations, the Anabaptists' choice of Amsterdam as the New Jerusalem becomes quite sensible. Any decision to migrate to this locale was, moreover, "supported and given wings by the apocalyptic expectation of the 'godly city.'"[72] While Münster was the ultimate "example for the whole world"[73] of the Lord giving a city over to his people with no innocent blood shed, Amsterdam was to follow suit. Jan van Reenen was reported to have said that

> the Lord has given us two cities of faith and that the prophet of the pure people had said such. Münster was one city and Amsterdam the other . . . the Anabaptists would not have to fight the people of Amsterdam

for only those who opposed the Lord would be slain.[74] Once the city belonged to "the people of God," then "all the people who are hurt or cast away should come here, for there was a merciful people here and everyone would be received."[75] One of the Amsterdam radicals, Gerrit van Campen, wrote a letter to other Anabaptists outside of Amsterdam confirming that the godless would be forced out of the city. After this cleansing, he continued, the Melchiorites would then "hold all the goods of the city for each other and the servants [i.e., leaders] of the fellowship would have the most beautiful houses."[76] The city was to be a refuge for the oppressed.

These considerations would seem to imply that those choosing to be Anabaptists were impoverished and desperate to improve their lot. Published archival sources, however, give little concrete evidence regarding the wealth of the captured Anabaptists. It is clear that many of the resident Anabaptists owned homes or other considerable property, and the city council decreed that, in line with traditional privileges, Anabaptist citizens could have their property seized only to a value of one hundred pounds.[77] This indicates that there must have been some resident Anabaptists who were worth more than that amount. That there were many poor, however, is also evident. The city council felt that Jacob van Campen and Jan Matthijs van Middelburg were both principal in deceiving "the poor, simple people."[78] Jan Paeuw made reference to the distribution of ten to eleven pounds in poor relief and expressed surprise at its quick dispersal, although this is the only reference to mutual aid among the Amsterdam Anabaptists.[79] What is probably the case is that the resident Anabaptists were better off than their immigrant brothers and sisters. The degree of distress on the part of the latter is hard to measure at this point.[80] One must avoid the simplistic assumption that all artisans were poor, for social upheaval can equally affect both the well-off and the destitute.

For any city in the Netherlands to experience growth, immigration from other regions was required in order to offset the high urban mortality rate of this period.[81] That Holland's industrial cities, especially Leiden, Gouda and Haarlem, were stagnating in terms of population growth indicates a lack of significant migration into these cities after 1496.[82] It seems that Amsterdam, on the other hand, became the new centre for migration, for its population, which had been less than that of Haarlem as late as 1514, experienced a rapid growth shortly thereafter.[83] This "pattern of migration, in turn, suggests that vigorous economic development acted as the stimulant to this mobility."[84] What is striking about the Anabaptist migration is the sheer number of workers from the stagnating cities who made their way to Amsterdam. Of the 96 Anabaptists whose migrations are known, 22 (23%) came from the cities of Delft, Haarlem and Leiden, and another twelve from other nearby cities. A further ten came from the town of Monnikendam to the north and sixteen from the city of Groningen. In all, 74, or 77% came from other cities in the Netherlands (see Table V).[85]

Table V. Amsterdam Anabaptist Migrants

South Holland	34	(35%)
Delft, Haarlem, Leiden: 22 (23%)		
North Holland	10	(10%)
Monnikendam: 9 (9%)		
North Netherland cities	20	(21%)
Groningen City: 16 (17%)		
East Netherland cities	9	(9%)
Southern Netherlands	1	(1%)
Netherlands villages	13	(14%)
Other localities	9	(9%)
Total of known immigrants	96	(100%)

Amsterdam, because of its singular economic growth, became the centre not only for "religious salvation," but for economic salvation as well.

These conditions were exacerbated by the economic crises of the 1520s and 1530s.[86] The first two decades of the sixteenth century had been characterised by devastation: flood, harsh winters and great mortality. Recovery began around 1520, when the population and economy showed signs of rallying. New crises in the late 1520s and early 1530s were particularly damaging therefore to a population which was only beginning to recover. The great war between Emperor Charles V and Duke Karel van Gelder culminated in the plundering of The Hague in 1528 and the war between Lübeck and Holland saw the blockading of the Baltic trade route in 1533.[87] Food prices, especially for grain, jumped dramatically.[88] In 1531 the increase in the number and desperation of the poor in their city forced the Amsterdam magistrates to institute new regulations regarding the distribution of bread.[89] The continuing population growth at the same time produced an overabundance of labour, most especially in Holland where at least half the population was even at this early stage urbanised.[90] Wages lagged seriously behind the rise in prices, and remained inadequate throughout the remainder of the 1530s.[91] Urban artisans in particular suffered from the loss of markets when prospective buyers were forced to spend most of their wages on foodstuffs.[92] Many urban craftsmen were forced to join the ranks of the impoverished, despite their skills and social standing. Migration to Amsterdam, a city which had achieved a virtual stranglehold on the commerce of Holland in 1533,[93] appeared to offer a singular opportunity for economic prosperity. Amsterdam, therefore, acted as an oasis in the economically depressed region of the Northern Netherlands.

Thus, the message that the Lord would deliver Amsterdam into the hands of the ''Christian brothers'' and that well over ''five thousand of the brothers were there,'' which had been promulgated by Anabaptist prophets such as Adriaen van Benscop in the spring of 1535, came as good news to many Anabaptist artisans.[94] Whether the figure of five thousand ''brothers'' in this city is accurate is difficult to ascertain from the available data, especially since these possibly inflated figures came from an advocate of revolution and were clearly useful for propaganda purposes. Earlier in January of that year, Meynart van Emden estimated their number at thirty-five hundred.[95] Another Anabaptist placed their numbers inside the city at ''over a thousand strong.''[96] In any case it would appear that there were enough Anabaptists or sympathisers to take over the city, so that the city council's fears of an impending insurrection were well grounded. The difficulty in ascertaining an exact figure is exacerbated by the fact that most of the Amsterdam Melchiorites were successful in hiding themselves from the authorities, perhaps continuing Melchior Hoffman's earlier two-year suspension of adult baptism in order to avoid further martyrdoms. This would have allowed his followers to conform outwardly to Amsterdam society (Nicodemism) and thus avoid detection. Those who were brought before the court were generally the more radical of the Anabaptists. For example, the forty who were apprehended after the 1535 attempt to capture Amsterdam by and large divulged names of only those from their own groups, implicating but a handful of members from other factions.

Other factors, aside from the partisan estimates given above, suggest that the numbers of Anabaptists in the city were substantial. First, the great influx of strangers into the city became a source of increasing alarm on the part of the magistrates. Many of these immigrants were in fact Anabaptists who had been arrested and then released during the ''Great Trek'' in March of 1534. They sought shelter in attics and other concealed places in the residences of Amsterdam, and the acts issued against them by the City Council indicate that their numbers were perceived as considerable.[97] The difficulties which the magistrates experienced in attempting to root out these dissidents indicate the degree of support which the Anabaptists had in the city. Second, the Anabaptist leaders obviously hoped that once the small band of radicals began the rebellion, the mass of their fellows would support them, although the radicals may not have differentiated clearly enough between Anabaptist radicals and Anabaptist sympathisers or non-Anabaptist reformers, thus swelling the estimates. The differentiation between Anabaptism and other manifestations of reform was neither clear-cut nor easily discernible, especially if Amsterdam Anabaptists still practised Hoffman's *Stillstand*. While the numbers of rebaptised in Amsterdam were most likely exaggerated, their impact and threat to the city and its magistrates can be judged, for the above reasons, as considerable.

The obvious question then arises – if there were so many Anabaptists and sympathisers in the city, why did the attempted revolution of May 1535 fail? Reasons for this may be found in the division of Anabaptists into two or three groups, whose cooperation was hindered both by a need for concealment from authorities and by the disagreements among their leaders. The radical Münsterites, led by Jan Pouwels and Gerrit van Campen in 1534 and Jan van Geelen and Peter Gael in 1535 were followers of Jan Matthijs' and Jan van Leiden's programs. The more moderate Melchiorite faction, under the leadership of Jan Paeuw and Jacob van Campen, seems to have had an ambivalent relationship with Münster and with the radicals in Amsterdam. That van Campen kept himself somewhat aloof from the radical Münsterites is borne out not only by his own testimony, but also by the witness of Peter Gael, who remarked that "Jacob van Campen had not been in their company."[98]

On the question of the use of the sword, van Campen agreed with Jan van Geelen that it was permissible for "each one of the fellowship to buy arms to defend their lives against those who would capture them." Van Campen further stipulated that "they should only defend themselves, and not further offend anyone." He also was waiting, like Hoffman, for a definite sign from the Lord before taking any further steps. As a result van Campen refused to have anything to do with the planned revolt, despite the pleading of the radicals.[99]

Van Campen's relationship to Obbe Philips and his supporters in Amsterdam was also one of both agreement and discord. Obviously these two leaders were closer to each other when it came to the use of the sword in fulfilling the plan of God than to the radicals, and hence they also stood closer to Hoffman himself in this respect. The major area of disagreement came in the question of the interpretation of the Scriptures. Van Campen held to a Hoffmanite interpretation which allowed for a literal fulfilment of the Kingdom of God, organised according to Old Testament precepts, such as in Münster (or Strasbourg for Hoffman), while Philips expressed reservations about this during a brief debate between the two men in the fall of 1534.[100] Van Campen and his supporters, therefore, attempted to provide a middle ground between the Münsterite radicals and the Obbenites. The hope of a temporal salvation among the membership seems to have transcended the differences between the leaders regarding how that salvation was to come about. Most Melchiorites, however, were reluctant to participate in an armed revolt, regardless of the fact that they were allowed by their leaders to carry weapons. As artisans, they were not acquainted with fighting against trained soldiers and were no doubt terrified at the thought. The ease with which the authorities captured thousands of armed Melchiorites on their way to Münster in March of 1534 suggests a natural reluctance on the part of the common folk to fight the authorities. Seeing that a good number of the immigrant Anabaptists in Amsterdam were drawn from these same "trekkers," it is no wonder that they refused to join the revolt.[101] Anabaptists in belief may have desired revolutionary change, but in practice most appeared reluctant to use revolutionary means to achieve their goals.

For Melchiorites in Holland, the success or failure of Münster would determine the outcome of their particular enterprise. When Münster was taken in June of 1535, Holland Melchiorites, like their fellow believers elsewhere, undertook a significant reappraisal of their faith. What were the viable options for urban Anabaptists? Of the six main directions which Melchiorites took after Münster, the Spiritualism or Nicodemism of Obbe Philips and David Joris offered the least danger of detection by the authorities. The radical militancy of Jan van Batenburg and the continuation of Münsterite radicalism under Heinrich Krechting could only lead to self-destruction.[102] The peaceful sectarianism of Menno Simons and Dirk Philips was to prove the most enduring of the options, but involved dangerous levels of visibility to a hostile government. It made much more sense then to take the approach of David Joris, and it is to this important Anabaptist leader that we now turn.[103]

Notes

1. Originally Grebel and the Zurich radicals had merely aimed at a faster paced reformation of the entire civic community. When this was rejected by Zwingli and the city council, the Grebel circle went ahead and attempted to replicate the apostolic church. See Heinold Fast, "Conrad Grebel: The Covenant on the Cross," in Hans-Jürgen Goertz (ed.), *Profiles of Radical Reformers* (Kitchener: Herald Press, 1982), pp. 118-31.
2. For Sattler see C. Arnold Snyder, *The Life and Thought of Michael Sattler* (Scottdale: Herald Press, 1984). For the writings of Sattler, see John H. Yoder (ed.), *The Legacy of Michael Sattler* (Scottdale: Herald Press, 1973).
3. Snyder, *Michael Sattler*, 114-23.
4. The authoritative formulation of the polygenesis model is in James M. Stayer, Werner O. Packull, and Klaus Deppermann, "Monogenesis to Polygenesis: The Historical Discussion of Anabaptist Origins," *MQR*, Vol. LXIX, 1975, pp. 83-121.
5. See Gottfried Seebass, "Hans Hut: The Suffering Avenger," in Goertz, *Profiles*, p. 55. In Müntzer's scheme, the ungodly were specifically identified with the clergy. For anticlericalism in the revolt, see Peter Blickle, *The Revolution of 1525* (Baltimore: Johns Hopkins, 1981), p. 138, and Henry J. Cohn, "Anticlericalism in the German Peasants' War, 1525," *Past and Present*, Vol. LXXXIII, 1979, pp. 3-31.
6. Stayer has recently argued that the Peasants' War "was significantly connected with the beginnings of Anabaptism," including both the Swiss and the South and Central German variants ("Anabaptists and Future Anabaptists in the Peasants' War," *MQR*, Vol. LXII, 1988, pp. 99-139).

7. For Müntzer, see Goertz, "Thomas Müntzer: Revolutionary in a Mystical Spirit," *Profiles*, pp. 29-44. The Grebel group had also looked to Müntzer for advice, as seen in a 1524 letter to the radical. See "Letters to Thomas Müntzer By Conrad Grebel and Friends," translated by G.H. Williams in *Spiritual and Anabaptist Writers* (Philadelphia: Westminster Press, 1957) (hereafter *S.A.W.*), pp. 73-85.

8. Seebass, "Hans Hut," p. 56.

9. "We conclude that Hut's baptism by Denck did not constitute a break with his Müntzerian past. On the contrary, an analysis of his ideas indicates a strong dependence on Müntzer. Hut, even as an Anabaptist, was but a foiled revolutionary" (Packull, *Mysticism and South German Anabaptist*, p. 64).

10. Hut's version of baptism involved no water, but the marking of the sign of the cross on the forehead (Packull, "The Sign of Thau: The Changing Conception of the Seal of God's Elect in Early Anabaptist Thought," *MQR*, Vol. LXI, 1987, pp. 363-74).

11. This discussion on Hoffman is based on the study by Klaus Deppermann, *Melchior Hoffman* (Gottingen: Vandenhoeck and Ruprecht, 1979) and his summary in "Melchior Hoffman: Contradictions between Lutheran Loyalty to Government and Apocalyptic Dreams," in Goertz, *Profiles*, pp. 178-90.

12. Hoffman made his prediction in 1526 in his commentary on the book of Daniel, *Das XII Capitel des propheten Danielis aussgelegt*.

13. Obbe Philips remarked that Hoffman was as devoted to Leonard Jost "as to Elijah, Isaiah, Jeremiah, or one of the other prophets." See his "Confession," *S.A.W.*, p. 211. The Strasbourg prophets in turn regarded Hoffman as the second Elijah (*S.A.W.*, p. 212).

14. See Deppermann, "Melchior Hoffman," pp. 186-7.

15. Krahn, *Dutch Anabaptism*, pp. 91-101.

16. Packull ("Melchior Hoffman — A Recanted Anabaptist in Schwäbisch-Hall," *MQR*, Vol. LVII, 1983, pp. 83-111) discusses Hoffman's imprisonment in the light of his discovery of evidence that a recanted Anabaptist named Melchior Hoffman appeared in Schwäbisch-Hall after the Anabaptist prophet's supposed death.

17. The name Trijpmaker means a wooden shoemaker. Williams (*S.A.W.*, p. 209, note 18) identifies Trijpmaker as a weaver of tripe-de-velours.

18. From Philips' "Confession," pp. 209-10. There is evidence that Hoffman himself proselytised in Amsterdam. Deppermann (*Melchior Hoffman*, p. 284) states that Hoffman was in the city in the summer of 1531. This evidence, however, is not overwhelming, for it consists primarily of two summaries recounting the rise of Anabaptism in Amsterdam which were composed in 1536 for the magistrates of that city. One of the accounts makes the mistake of claiming that Hoffman baptised Trijpmaker in Amsterdam in 1531, when it is known that he was baptised in Emden in 1530 (*DAN*, Vol. V, p. 252). The other places Hoffman's visit to Amsterdam in 1529 (ibid., p. 264). It is quite possible, therefore, that government officials simply erred regarding Hoffman's whereabouts. It is also difficult to comprehend why not one of the nearly two hundred interrogated Anabaptists mentioned Hoffman's presence in Amsterdam. The only reference to Hoffman in these documents was the comment of Elbert Martsz on May 16, 1535: "Seyt dat Henrick voors. [de Varckendrijver] mit hem heeft gesproeken van Munster ende dat die coninck van Munster zoude Melchior selfs uuyter gevanckenisse verlossen" (ibid., p. 150). Martsz confessed that he had been baptised by Trijpmaker in 1531, but did not mention Hoffman in this connection.

19. Philips, "Confession," p. 211.

20. Dietrich Kuyper, Bartholomeus Boeckbinder and Peter Houtsager were also important leaders in Amsterdam, although they were arrested for having marched through

the city waving unsheathed swords. According to the account of the incident, they had proclaimed that "in the name of the Lord: God's blessing over the new side, God's curse over the old city!" (Williams, *S.A.W.*, p. 219, note 47).

21. Albert Mellink has more than adequately proven the interconnections between Anabaptist activities in Münster and those in the Low Countries. See his *De Wederdopers in de Noordelijke Nederlanden*, 2nd ed. (Leeuwarden: Uitgeverij Gerben Dykstra, 1981) and "The Beginnings of Dutch Anabaptism in the Light of Recent Research," *MQR*, Vol. LXII, 1988, pp. 211-20.

22. Stayer, "Christianity in One City: Anabaptist Münster, 1534-35," in Hillerbrand, *Radical Tendencies*, p. 118.

23. This tract of Rothmann's was in the peaceful Anabaptist tradition. It later formed the basis for the *Vermahnung* of Pilgram Marpeck, a pacifistic South German Anabaptist (Frank J. Wray, "The 'Vermahnung' of 1542 and Rothmann's 'Bekenntnisse,'" *ARG*, Vol. XLVII, 1956, pp. 243-51; see also Stayer, "Christianity in One City," p. 121).

24. See Philips' "Confession," p. 214.

25. Münster Anabaptists came to regard the events of February as a miracle that confirmed the veracity of Matthijs' prediction that Christ would establish his kingdom in the city in Easter of that year. See Taira Kuratsuka, "Gesamtgilde und Täufer: Der Radikalisierungsprozess in der Reformation Münsters. Von der reformatorischen Bewegung zum Täuferreich 1533/34," *ARG*, Vol. LXXVI, 1985, pp. 233-61.

26. While Matthijs may have been hoping to force God's hand by his action, it amounted to little more than an act of suicide.

27. These tracts are in Robert Stupperich (ed.), *Die Schriften Bernhard Rothmanns* (Münster: Aschendorffsche Verlagsbuchhandlung, 1970).

28. For more on Münster and the "Great Trek," see Stayer, "Was Dr. Kuehler's Conception of Early Dutch Anabaptism Historically Sound? The Historical Discussion of Anabaptist Münster 450 Years After," *MQR*, Vol. LX, 1986, pp. 261-88. Participants in the "Great Trek" had planned to gather under the Münsterite banners in Overijsel before continuing to Münster.

29. Regarded as "the most important outbreak of militant Anabaptism in the Netherlands," the capture of Oldeklooster, a wealthy Cistercian monastery, was directly related to the arrival of emissaries from Münster seeking "to raise new centers of Anabaptist resistance." Jan van Leiden was planning to break through the siege forces surrounding Münster and to establish his reign in a Dutch city, possibly Deventer, by Easter (March 28), the new prophesied day of divine deliverance (James M. Stayer, "Oldeklooster and Menno," *SCJ*, Vol. IX, 1978, p. 52).

30. The first attempt occurred during the procession of the "Miracle of Amsterdam" on March 18, 1534. The radicals had planned to use the confusion surrounding the procession to surprise the authorities. The city chronicler recorded that "when the procession passed by, [the Anabaptists] would create a riot in the streets, putting to death all the monks and priests and treading upon the sacrament with their feet. Then they would drive the whole community out of the city and take possession of their goods" (*DAN*, Vol. V, p. 23). The Amsterdam magistracy was warned in advance and dispersed the attackers.

31. For the revolt in Amsterdam, see Mellink, *Amsterdam en de Wederdopers* (Nijmegen: Socialistiese Uitgeverij Nijmegen, 1978). Moreover, the remainder of the incumbent magistrates, whose tolerance of religious dissent was now regarded as duplicity, were unceremoniously thrown out of office and others, more staunchly Catholic, took their places (Dudok van Heel, "Katholiek Amsterdams regentenpatri-

ciaat ten tijde van de Hervorming; werd de Familie Huynen door het wederdopersoproer van 1535 gedeclasseerd?'' unpublished Ph.D. diss., University of Amsterdam, 1978 [from Gemeente Archief Amsterdam, H 1018]).

32. Several other groups of Anabaptists arrived from outside the city too late to take part
    in the revolt.

33. As seen in the number of Anabaptists who recanted and returned from exile to
    Deventer and Zwolle between 1536 and 1538 (J.G. de Hullu [ed.], *Bescheiden
    Betreffende de Hervorming in Overijsel* [Deventer, 1897], pp. 237-42).

34. For a period of about three years, some Melchiorites attempted to restore the original
    vision of the movement. These included a dissenter from England by the name of
    Henry, who financed the Bocholt conference of Anabaptist leaders in 1536 (see
    below, chapter 7), and Jan Matthijs van Middelburg, who arranged the meeting
    between Joris and the Melchiorite refugees in Strasbourg in 1538 (see below, chapter
    8). Neither of these, however, can be said to have won a major following.

35. For Simons, see Christopher Bornhauser, *Leben und Lehre Menno Simons*
    (Neukirchen-Vluyn: Neukirchner Verlag, 1973); Cornelius Krahn, *Menno Simons*
    (Newton: Faith and Life Press, 1982); and Irvin B. Horst, ''Menno Simons: The
    New Man in Community,'' in Goertz, *Profiles*, 203-13. For the dispute between
    Simons and Joris, see Stayer, ''Davidite vs. Mennonite,'' *MQR*, Vol. LVIII, 1984, pp.
    459-76, and Samme Zijlstra, ''Menno Simons and David Joris,'' *MQR*, Vol. LXII,
    1988, pp. 249-56.

36. While much research has yet to be conducted on the Dutch practitioners of Nicodem-
    ism, there is considerable literature on John Calvin's response to French Nicodem-
    ites. See Carlos M. N. Eire, *War Against the Idols. The Reformation of Worship from
    Erasmus to Calvin* (Cambridge: Cambridge University Press, 1986), pp. 234-75.

37. As late as 1538 Münsterites and Batenburgers plotted together to recapture Münster.
    For both of these groups, see chapter 6 below.

38. See Packull, ''Peter Tasch: From Melchiorite to Bankrupt Wine Merchant,'' *MQR*,
    Vol. LXII, 1988, pp. 276-95.

39. His disillusionment is clearly evident in the ''Confession.'' For Franck's view of the
    Anabaptists, see Gary K. Waite, '''A Recent Consultation of Lucifer': A Previously
    Unknown Work by Sebastian Franck?'' *MQR*, Vol. LVIII, 1984, pp. 477-502.

40. Claus-Peter Clasen, *Anabaptism: A Social History, 1525-1618* (Ithaca: Cornell Uni-
    versity Press, 1972). By neglecting northern Anabaptism, Clasen was able to argue
    that Anabaptism was a numerically insignificant movement. Karl-Heinz Kirchhoff
    has produced an admirable social history of Anabaptist Münster in *Die Täufer in
    Münster 1534/35* (Münster in Westfalen: Aschendorfsche Verlagsbuchhandlung,
    1973). R. Po-chia Hsia has recently provided an insightful discussion of the
    Münsterite adoption of community of goods and polygamy in the light of the social
    and political tensions within the city (''Münster and the Anabaptists,'' in R. Po-chia
    Hsia [ed.], *The German People and the Reformation* [Ithaca: Cornell University
    Press, 1988], pp. 51-69).

41. Mellink (*De Wederdopers*, p. 102) remarked: ''Amsterdam neemt van de aanvang af
    een centrale plaats bij de Anabaptistische beweging in Holland, ja in heel de Neder-
    landen.''

42. Of the total of 332 known Anabaptists providing the sample for this study, 242 are
    from Amsterdam. The primary sources used were *DAN*, Vols. I and V and Grete
    Grosheide (ed.), ''Verhooren en Vonnissen der Wederdoopers, Betrokken bij de
    Aanslagen op Amsterdam in 1534 en 1535,'' in *Bijdragen en Mededeelingen van het
    Historisch Genootschap*, Vol. XLI, 1920, pp. 1-231, hereafter ''Verhooren.'' Con-

temporary accounts were also found in all three volumes. An earlier version of this portion of the chapter appeared in *SCJ*, Vol. XVIII, 1987, pp. 249-64.

43. Based on *CDI*, Vols. I-V.
44. From "Verhooren," pp. 1-198.
45. Jacob van Bommele, a schoolmaster of Leeuwarden, who was exiled from Friesland for using his position to spread Anabaptist doctrine (*DAN*, Vol. I, p. 14). Also identified were: 2 bricklayers, 1 schoolmaster, 1 bookbinder, 1 barber, and 1 shoemaker. Most of those in the records were women captured at the attempt to capture Oldeklooster.
46. Nicolaas Meyndertsz van Blesdijk wrote that while Dirk "was skillful in the Greek and Latin languages, the other [Obbe] was clearly unskilled, but well-spoken with the people" (*Historia vitae, doctrinae ac rerum gestarum Davidis Georgii haeresiarchae* [Deventer, 1642], p. 6).
47. It might be possible to assume that at least a good number of those Anabaptists whose occupations were not listed had no particular skills or were ordinary journeymen. These unskilled workers usually made up 20-30% of a sixteenth-century city's population.
48. From "Verhooren," pp. 1-198, and *DAN*, Vol. I. All of the Frisian leaders were listed on a government missive of 1533. Goldsmiths, bakers, master builders, bookworkers, surgeons and the like were all regarded on a higher level than those labourers in the textile or similar trades.
49. The Amsterdam Anabaptists can thus be contrasted dramatically with their fellow dissenters in the South. Clasen's findings indicated that the early Anabaptist movement in the Southern Empire had, for the early decades of the sixteenth century at least, a fairly high proportion of leaders with intellectual or pastoral backgrounds (*A Social History*, pp. 309-10). The backgrounds of leaders changed significantly after 1550.
50. From *CDI*, Vols. IV-V. Others include one each of brewer, steward, servant, linguist, cardmaker, advocate, platemaker, knight, and several others whose occupation was difficult to identify.
51. He was one of those later beheaded for leading the 1534 revolt in the city.
52. The actual number is probably much higher. See also de Hoop Scheffer, *Geschiedenis*, pp. 618-23.
53. See de Hoop Scheffer (ibid., p. 356), who says that two sermons of Wouter, one on Psalm 1 and the other on Luke 10:42, "had, at any rate, an overwhelming and deep impression on one of his hearers, David Joris."
54. He was reported to have said: "These false hypocrites, monks and priests, have made us believe that the [images] were the books of the unlearned, but the Spirit of the Lord says that [they] are snares to the falling of the unlearned and are the tempters of the souls of men" (*CDI*, Vol. IV, p. 349).
55. Also indicated were: Frederik Hondebeke the rector of the Latin school (ibid., p. 336); the Pastor of the Old Guesthouse (ibid., Vol. 5, pp. 77-78); and an Augustinian monk who had preached a heretical sermon in the city in the New Church and elsewhere on Ascension Eve, 1526 (ibid., pp. 133-35, 168). Another lay-member, Gijsbrecht Aelbrechtsz, a tailor from Delft, had publicly denounced the Sacrament on Corpus Christi Day, 1528, in front of the door of St. Peter's Church in Leiden and had thrown blasphemous letters into the church where the service was being held (ibid., p. 353).
56. See de Hoop Scheffer, *Geschiedenis*, pp. 611-13, and James M. Stayer, *Anabaptists and the Sword* (Lawrence: Coronado Press, 1976), p. 207 for a confirmation of this.

57. "Menno Simons," in Goertz, *Profiles*, p. 207.
58. Hans-Jürgen Goertz (*Die Täufer. Geschichte und Deutung* [München: C.H. Beck, 1980], p. 23) on the other hand has argued that what the various currents of Anabaptism had in common was anticlericalism. In spite of the regional differences, all the Anabaptist groups organised themselves as alternatives to both the sacerdotal system and the "new clericalism" of the magisterial Reformers. Anticlerical sentiment, in the case of the Low Countries, however, also held together otherwise diverse reform movements such as the general reform and Anabaptist traditions. Anabaptism was simply one stream of the popular reform movement which as a whole was motivated by anticlerical sentiment. Goertz's evidence is mainly from the South.
59. Deelen was appointed to his post by the city magistrates in 1533 (*DAN*, Vol. V, 145, note 348). He later became librarian for the King of England.
60. "Seyt dat hij gehoert heeft dat Jan Mathijsz. mede es geweest in Spaengnen bij meester Wouter ende meester Peter ab Hovia, nyettegenstaende datter hier gelt was geset op zijn lijff" (ibid., p. 145). A price was placed on Matthijs' head on March 2 of that year.
61. *DAN*, Vol. V, p. 257: "Ten regimente van der scole wairen genoemen twee suspecte persoonen als meester Wouter omme te leeren Griecxs ende gaven hem weden ende meester Jan Certorius omme te leeren Latijn, wiens discipulen veel blasphemie dagelicxs zeyden ende suspecte boecken leerden ende die de principaelste vant verraedt naderhandt gebeurt wairen."
62. From *CDI*, Vols. I-V.
63. The authorities were particularly concerned about Amsterdam and Delft, see *CDI*, Vol. I, nos. 134, 149, 175, 196 and 336. Frederik Hondebeke likewise reported the quick spread of the Reformation at Delft (ibid., no. 18).
64. Ibid., nos. 149-52, 161, 167.
65. Ibid., Vol. V, pp. 350-51.
66. See Audrey M. Lambert, *The Making of the Dutch Landscape* (London: Seminar Press, 1971), pp. 173ff.; and Jan de Vries, *The Dutch Rural Economy in the Golden Age, 1500-1700* (New Haven and London: Yale University Press, 1974), p. 99.
67. De Vries, *Rural Economy*, pp. 87-90. The population of Amsterdam stood at 13,500 in 1514 and 30,000 in 1565. Amsterdam may have been the only city in Holland to have sufficient resources and economic diversification to resist the prevalent economic malaise. See R. van Uytven, "What is New Socially and Economically in the Sixteenth-Century Netherlands," *Acta Historiae Neerlandicae* (hereafter *A.H.N.*), Vol. VII, 1974, p. 23.
68. See Jan Paeuw's testimony (*DAN*, Vol. V, pp. 85-90).
69. W.P. Blockmans and W. Prevenier remarked that poor relief became intensified in urban centres at this time and that the poor tended to abandon the countryside to seek more effective relief in better organised urban *dessen* ("Poverty in Flanders and Brabant from the Fourteenth to the Mid-Sixteenth Century: Sources and Problems," *A.H.N.*, Vol. X, 1978, p. 28).
70. *DAN*, Vol. V, p. 158.
71. Ibid., p. 171.
72. Walter Klaassen, personal communication, Conrad Grebel College, February, 1984.
73. *DAN*, Vol. V, p. 88.
74. Ibid., p. 65.
75. Ibid., pp. 225-26, testimony of Harmon Hoen.
76. Mellink, *De Wederdopers*, p. 109.
77. "Verhooren," p. 8.

78. *DAN*, Vol. V, p. 117.
79. Ibid., p. 89.
80. Most of these immigrants had been dispossessed of their money and possessions by the authorities before their arrival in Amsterdam, so regardless of their previous standing, they were certainly impoverished upon their arrival. See S. Zijlstra, *Nicolaas Meyndertsz. van Blesdijk* (Assen: Van Gorcum & Co., 1983), p. 155.
81. De Vries, *Rural Economy*, p. 80. De Vries mentions that the rural non-agricultural sector was the only sector to experience a high rate of natural increase.
82. J.A. van Houtte, *An Economic History of the Low Countries 800-1800* (London: Weidenfeld and Nicolson, 1977), p. 125.
83. Ibid., and de Vries, *Rural Economy*, pp. 87-88.
84. De Vries, *Rural Economy*, p. 96. According to N.W. Posthumus (*Inquiry into the History of Prices in Holland*, Vol.II, [Leiden: E.J. Brill, 1964], pp. li and 527), Amsterdam's rapid commercial rise came at the expense of Utrecht.
85. From "Verhooren," pp. 1-198.
86. See the researches of N.W. Posthumus, *An Inquiry*, p. lxiii; J.A. Faber, "Dearth and Famine in Pre-Industrial Netherlands," *A.H.N.*, Vol. XIII, 1980, pp. 51-64; van Houtte, *An Economic History*, pp. 123-36; and P.J. Blok, *Geschiedenis Eener Hollandsche Stad* (The Hague: Martinus Nijhoff, 1912).
87. Blok (*Geschiedenis*, p. 12, and *History of the People of the Netherlands* [New York: AMS Press, 1970], p. 327) notes that from 1500 to 1543 Holland was in a continual state of war. In particular, the countrysides of Utrecht, Overijsel, Friesland and Groningen were frequently devastated by the armies of Emperor Charles V and Duke Karel van Gelder as they battled over the political control of the Low Countries. Those who suffered most were commoners. Destruction of homes and crops, plunder, piracy, high taxation (not to mention the pervasive lack of domestic order associated with these conflicts), could only increase the desperation and dislocation of the third estate. Although dealing with a later time period, Myron P. Gutmann's *War and Rural Life in the Early Modern Low Countries* (Princeton: Princeton University Press, 1980), provides a good description of the devastating effects of even limited-scale warfare on the early modern countryside.
88. Posthumus (*Inquiry*, pp. xcvi and 245), where it is noted that wheat prices jumped from 47.19 stuferi in 1527 to 67.50 in 1528, and remained high until 1533 in Utrecht. See also van Uytven ("What is New," p. 28) who notes the loss in buying power of wages between 1500 and 1540.
89. They created a more liberal and better organized distribution of bread because of the "tegenwoordelicken groet duerte es ende een wile tijts geweest es in den koorne, daerduere de scamele gemeente ende arme persoonen grootelicken belast zijn" (J.G. van Dillen [ed.], *Bronnen tot de Geschiedenis van het Bedrijfsleven en het Gildewezen van Amsterdam*, Vol. I: *1512-1611* [The Hague: Martinus Nijhoff, 1929], p. 100).
90. According to de Vries (*Rural Economy*, p. 81), Holland's population at this time was 50% urban; that of Frisia 23% and Overijsel 38%.
91. Blockmans and Prevenier, "Poverty in Flanders," pp. 22-23.
92. Faber, "Dearth and Famine," p. 52
93. As a result of the war with Lübeck. See Blok, *History*, p. 327.
94. Reportedly said to Harman Hoen in Groningen (*DAN*, Vol. V, p. 226).
95. "Dit is een enorm aantal (3500), gezien de totale bevolking der stad, ook als men rekening houdt met de vele gevluchten van elders. In maart 1534 was er nog gesproken over 3000 herdoopten in heel Holland samen!" (Mellink, *Amsterdam en de Wederdopers*, p. 42).

96. A certain Thijs to Evert Aertsz van Utrecht (ibid., p. 136).
97. *DAN*, Vol. V, pp. 37-38. This act was passed on April 29, 1534, the month after the trek.
98. Ibid., p. 131.
99. Ibid., p. 156. "By holding back their followers from joining the Anabaptist rebellion, Obbe and Jacob van Campen ultimately determined the failure of the abortive revolution in Amsterdam" (Williams, *S.A.W.*, p. 222, n. 53).
100. *DAN*, Vol. V, p. 155.
101. See Kuehler, "Anabaptism in the Netherlands," in Stayer and Packull, *Anabaptists and Thomas Müntzer*, p. 97.
102. While revolutionary Anabaptism did not die out as quickly as formerly thought, there was no chance of ultimate success (Stayer, *Anabaptists and the Sword*, p. 297).
103. All of these possibilities had been latent in early Anabaptism, but the failure of the kingdom of God in both Münster and Amsterdam ultimately placed the spiritualist and sectarian responses in priority positions (Zijlstra, "David Joris en de doperse Stromingen [1536-1539]," in M. G. Buist, et al. [eds.], *Historisch Bewogen* [Groningen: Wolters-Noordhoff, 1984], p. 126).

PART II

DAVID JORIS:
LIFE, THOUGHT AND
FOLLOWING, 1501-43

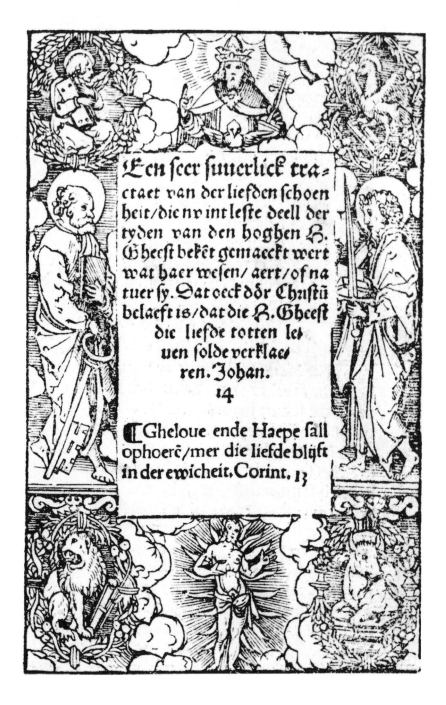

Title page: David Joris, *A Very Lovely Tract on the Beauty of the Beloved* (Deventer: Albert Pafraet, 1539). Courtesy The Mennonite Library, University of Amsterdam.

CHAPTER THREE

From Sacramentarian Lay Reformer to Melchiorite Sympathiser, 1501-33

Many details of David Joris' early life remain shrouded in obscurity. His mother, Maritje Jans de Gortersdochter, belonged to the social elite of Delft.[1] Maritje married a man of lower standing. The marriage apparently led to dissension in the family, and she was forced to leave Delft with her husband, Joris de Koman or Joris van Amersfoort, a lesser merchant from Amersfoort.[2] His merchant activities and more likely his involvement in the Chambers of Rhetoric acquired for him a reputation as an adventurer. Maritje may have been enamoured by the excitement and glamour of marriage to the sixteenth-century equivalent of a modern "movie star." As a *rederijker* actor, Joris senior would have been involved in acting out the satire directed against the Church, priests, and images for which the Chamber plays had become famous. It is no wonder then that Maritje's upper-class parents were offended at her marriage to this lower-middle-class merchant. The young couple moved to Flanders, perhaps to the city of Brugges, where Maritje gave birth to a son. As best as can be determined, this must have been in 1501.[3] Joris senior was able to set up a small shop and he and Maritje settled down to raise a family. Significantly, their first-born was not named after any of his immediate relations, but was given the name David after the Israelite King David, because this was the leading role played by his father in a performance by the Rhetoricians.[4] This selection was to have far-reaching significance after the infant grew up.

Presumably David spent at least part of his childhood in Flanders. From all accounts he was a well-behaved, sensitive but frail child, tending towards melancholy, "always in sorrow and maintaining a humble nature." His education and strict upbringing betrayed the social background of his mother. "All silliness was driven out of him," not only by maternal concerns, but also by his teachers. David's impressionable personality and later fits of depression and neurotic fears suggest a rather insecure early childhood, which may have had some relation to the familial disputes.

David's schooling was typical for children of his mother's social standing. He first attended a junior grammar school where he would have learned to read and write in the vernacular Dutch.[5] He then graduated, probably at the traditional age of eight or nine years, to a senior or Latin school. These schools were usually attended by the children of more socially ambitious

---

Notes to Chapter Three are found on pages 59-63.

middle or upper class families. The curriculum of Latin schools concentrated on the learning of Latin grammar, progressing from the ABC books
and primers of the beginning seventh class to a more sophisticated study of
syntax and readings from Cicero, Horace, Virgil and Livy by the fourth and
third classes.[6] Also included in the curriculum was the study of hymns and
music, readings in the catechism and gospels, and perhaps a little logic and
arithmetic. Although we are told that the young David lacked interest in the
Latin curriculum, spending his time instead sketching or day-dreaming, he
clearly retained much of his musical training and many of the memorised
proverbs, phrases, Scripture verses and catechism would reappear in later
writings. He emerged, however, from the fourth class, likely at the age of
twelve or thirteen, with only a limited ability in Latin.[7] He would later prove
his considerable rhetorical skills in his native Dutch while displaying a fash-
ionable disdain for formal learning.

Sometime around 1513 when David was twelve or thirteen years old, the
youth was confirmed by a suffragan bishop and given the name of his grand-
father Johann. This may have taken place in Delft, and it is possible that the
family had already moved back to that city. When Joris later joined the Reformation, he returned to using David, although for his trips to Germany and
Switzerland he appears to have used the appellative Johann van Brugge. Johann
was also the name used when his marriage banns were read in Delft.[8]

For the next two or three years David worked in his father's shop.
Then, when the boy was a young teenager, his father, two brothers and four
sisters died of the plague within a few days of each other.[9] David, as the
eldest, assumed responsibilities for his mother and remaining siblings. His
vocational training was delayed while he was apprenticed to a wealthy merchant. Meanwhile the family had returned to Delft where the widow pos-
sessed considerable property.

The account of Joris' apprenticeship with this rich merchant provides
some interesting details. According to the well-informed biographer, the
merchant was without male heir, living alone with his daughter and servants.
Presumably he grew so fond of David that he offered him the hand of his
daughter and with her his inheritance. If this was not merely wishful thinking on Joris' part, then his rejection of the proposal must be admired.[10] That
this offer was a considerable temptation to the boy may be gleaned from the
rest of the story, which could only have come from David himself. He had
been entrusted with recording all of the merchant's accounts. One morning,
around four o'clock, David was left unattended in the room where the merchant kept his money chest. Curiosity must have gotten the better of him
and what he saw remained vividly fixed in his mind:

> There was in the chest a corner, which was divided by a shelf, which
> was so tightly packed with great pieces of gold, that one could look at
> but could not examine any single piece. I believe they could not have
> been more tightly packed together with a hammer. All that was pure

gold. The silver pieces were of even greater number, probably worth more than 100,000 florins if as tightly packed together to the bottom as the gold pieces.[11]

No wonder David found the alleged choice between marriage and his interest in an artistic career a difficult one. According to his later recollections, we are led to believe that young David was wary of the temptations that came with Mammon. He felt constrained to leave the man's employ because of his offensive wealth. On the pretext of having to take care of his mother's business, David requested and received a leave of absence until he could find another master to work under.

What consumed the young David's energy beside his love for art was an absorbing passion for true religion. According to the anonymous biographer, he belonged to "one in a thousand" in his devotion to the Catholic faith and practice. We can perhaps speculate that this side of Joris' interests reflected the maternal influence on the "young man" David. Surprisingly, this devotion did not lead to the life of a religious. Instead David chose the vocation of glasspainter. His mother had desired for him to become a goldsmith and his grandmother wanted to see him as an organist. These choices were considered "harmless to the soul," for both involved lay service to the Church. David's choice was apparently influenced by a friend who had made a similar decision. The craft of glasspainting provided not only an artistic outlet, but also promised aristocratic patronage. Material considerations may also have played a role in his decision.[12]

At age eighteen or nineteen, David began his glasspainting apprenticeship in earnest, possibly in Antwerp which had become the artistic capital of the Netherlands. Joris learned quickly and became a successful journeyman. He set out around 1520 with some companion glasspainters from Antwerp on a journeyman tour to sharpen his skills in northern France. At Calais they were approached by King Henry VIII's Treasurer, Lord William Sandys, to do some work in Basingstoke (Lasing) some twenty-five miles from London.[13] With the promise of being able to "earn as much as they wanted" in one year, the artisans journeyed to England with Sandys. The climate or the working conditions were apparently not ideal for Dutch glasspainters. Later Joris claimed that "not one in ten wanted to stay there."[14] After several months, and some disputes that are no longer clear, David and several of his companions returned to London in search of their employer, who actually had returned to Calais.[15] Renewed hostilities with France delayed David's immediate return to the Netherlands until health problems made his continued residence in London impossible.

Available evidence suggests that Joris did indeed return to the Netherlands in 1522, for he was commissioned in that year to paint several windows in a church at Enkhuizen.[16] David moved gradually back to Delft, finding employment as he went. His artistic skills were such that seventeenth-century historians found his works worthy of citation.[17]

The Delft Reformer

In 1524 the young glasspainter returned from his vocational journeys ready to establish his own craft shop in Delft as a "young master."[18] In this year he married Dirkgen Willem (little is known of her background). By this time, however, the teachings of Luther had already reached the Netherlands and formed the agenda for all religious discussions. Delft became a centre for discussion of Luther's ideas and an early centre of iconoclastic activity. Some members of Luther's own order were the first to spread reformation ideas in this territory, and one is known to have preached at two Delft churches as late as Ascension Day, 1526.[19] But the Augustinians were not the only ones receptive to Luther's program. One of the key figures in Delft was the Dominican Wouter, who had become the mentor of an "evangelical discussion group" in that city. David Joris was drawn into this circle upon his return. He may have been predisposed to the reform movement by his father's involvement in the anticlerical and iconoclastic rhetoric notable in the Rhetoricians' Chambers.[20] The anonymous biographer recorded two sermons as particularly influential on the young artisan. The first, based on Psalm 1, admonished the hearer not to walk "in the counsel of the ungodly" but to delight "in the law of the Lord." The second, using as its text Luke 10:42, contrasted the attitudes of Martha and Mary. Mary "had chosen the good part." Struck by these passages, David became more and more inflamed with a reforming zeal for "the house of the Lord." He turned to the study of the Scriptures.[21]

Between 1524 and 1528 David Joris was increasingly drawn into the religious reform vortex while at the same time becoming more and more critical of what he considered religious malpractices. According to Anonymous, Joris visited imprisoned religious dissenters, and "in the streets and alleys, wherever the images of Mary or other wooden idols were honoured or worshipped," he spoke against their veneration.[22] Joris also fought against the evil of idolatry by means of printed pamphlets which he distributed throughout the city. Some were fastened to church doors, others were scattered in the streets during processionals or placed in the confessionals for the clergy to read.[23] The artistically inclined Joris also spearheaded the poetic campaign for religious reform. According to his future son-in-law, Nicolaas Meyndertsz van Blesdijk, his spiritual songs gained great popularity throughout Holland.[24]

The written sources for Joris' religious ideas can be inferred from the available data. Certainly the *Theologia Deutsch* was influential for Joris as it was for other Dutch reformers.[25] This work stressed the inward, spiritual meaning behind the sacraments and was translated into Dutch in the early 1520s. Popular pamphlets on anticlericalism and iconoclasm were also widely read in the Netherlands.[26] One of these may have been Andreas Bodenstein van Karlstadt's *Van abtuhung der Bylder*, which circulated widely after its publication early in 1522 and which promoted the removal of images from churches. At least one of Karlstadt's arguments may in fact have been influential upon Joris, as shall be seen below. Some of Luther's devotional tracts were popular in the Netherlands and Joris' anonymous biographer affirmed that Luther's writings were influential for the young reformer.[27] Another important source must have been the *rederijker* plays. Joris quite naturally would have attended at least some performances, and the anticlerical rhetoric expressed in them would certainly leave its mark.

The actions of other popular reformers in Delft sheds some light on Joris' own activities. The Delft reform party included several laymen of artisan rank who gained a measure of notoriety by their iconoclasm. In November 1526, two weavers of Delft smashed the monstrance in one of the churches and physically threatened an observant priest of the old order.[28] Several iconoclasts were arrested in 1527, including Jan Joestez, a book-binder and his apprentice, Adriaan Jansz van Blenckvliet.[29] Jan van Hae-strecht, Jan van Schoonhoven and Gijsbrecht Aelbrechtsz, a tailor, were arrested in 1528.[30] We assume that these, and others, were the brethren vis-ited and comforted by Joris.

On May 21, 1528, as a result of an iconoclastic speech during the Ascension Day procession, Joris was arrested and imprisoned for eleven weeks. Court records indicate that he had situated himself in front of the New Church at around 10 a.m., the time when "the common people were passing with the procession of our beloved Lady" and publicly, "as if he were a preacher," spoke to the crowd, decrying their idolatry. Emotions were running high, and had the sheriff, Jan de Heuter, not taken Joris into protective custody, the old believers might have beaten Joris to death.[31] Some insight into Joris' religious ideas of this period may be gleaned from the summary of one of the anticlerical pamphlets presented during his trial on July 30. About the use of images in the Church, Joris apparently had written:

> These false hypocrites, monks and priests, have made us believe, that [images] were the books of the unlearned, but the Spirit of the Lord says, that they are snares to the falling of the unlearned and are tempters of their souls.[32]

This rationale for the use of images as the books of the laity was one of the major points that Karlstadt argued against in *Van abtuhung der Bylder.*[33] Second, Joris had abominably injured the religious professions, by writing that:

> the religious, having preached that the images were the books of the unlearned, are themselves false hypocrites, and had been against . . . the holy Scriptures, for the people, seeing the images of the saints, are moved to suffer a similar life [to that of the saints].[34]

Joris had also denigrated the priestly state by writing that those whom Christ had intended to be the guardians of the sheep have instead become the stranglers and persecutors of the flock. This argument is reminiscent of the language of the *rederijkerscamers*. Of special significance is that already at this early stage we find the identification of the old Church with the Babylonian Whore and of the papacy with Antichrist. De Heuter noted that this point had particularly inflamed Joris' followers. The key charge was that Joris had blasphemed the Holy Sacrament, calling it "the whitewashed God, by which the Zealanders swear,"[35] and had denied the presence of the true body and blood of Christ in the consecrated host. According to de Heuter, this scandalised the common people. Moreover, Joris alleged that the common people had been forbidden by Imperial mandate to read the Holy Scriptures, a charge emphatically denied by de Heuter.[36] Thus it can be seen that Joris' reformed ideology contained all the ingredients of Dutch lay reform noted earlier — anticlericalism, iconoclasm, the rejection of the physical presence and an appeal to the vernacular Scriptures as the authority in religious matters. Also notable is an incipient Dutch patriotism reflected in two of his hymns, which are entitled "A Refrain to the Praise of the Netherlands and of the Dutch Language" and "Concerning the plain Dutch Language." The Netherlands, in these songs, would soon be exalted above all its neighbours and the sower's seed, presumably the gospel, would find fertile soil in the Low Countries. The gospel had in former times been proclaimed in Hebrew, Greek and Latin tongues, but now the Spirit communicated in *"den Duytschen Woorden."*[37] It is ironic that while Joris showed an evident disinterest in his Latin schooling, he would not have been able to compose these songs without it.

In spite of his actions and his written attacks on the religious establishment, Joris' initial sentence, passed probably after his arrest in May, was quite lenient. Joris' sympathisers had influence with the magistrates of Delft and may have included de Heuter himself.[38] Thus Joris was sentenced only

> to march in his linen clothes before the procession with a burning candle in his hands, to offer the same before the holy Sacrament, having the aforementioned libellous pamphlets tied around his body or neck. After this was done, he was to remain inside his house for six weeks and inside the city for one year, on pain of having a piece of his tongue cut off.[39]

However, the inquisitor found this sentence too lenient and demanded the death penalty. Upon his instigation a more severe sentence was handed down, which included a severe whipping, the boring of his tongue and a three-year period of banishment.[40] However, even this stiffer sentence was made more bearable by the intervention of Joris' sympathisers. The flogging was scheduled to take place at an untimely hour so as to mitigate against it becoming the public spectacle it was intended to be. The city fathers feared that such a public display would prove counter-productive and increase their own unpopularity. Apparently a sizeable faction in the city supported the cause of the radical lay-preacher.[41] It is not clear whether

Joris was ever required to recant, for it appears that his relatives secured his release early in August without a written recantation.[42] The fact that the Inquisitor-General failed to procure the death sentence and the confiscation of Joris' property indicates how influential were Joris' family connections.

The Melchiorite Sympathiser

Joris and his family spent the day after his banishment at the home of Dirck Willemszoon in Pijnakker, which had been used as a meeting place for Delft "evangelicals." From there Joris bade farewell to his family and travelled to Rotterdam.[43] As best as can be determined Joris spent part of 1529-30 in East Frisia. It is known that around 1529 Joris carried on some discussions with Jan Volkerts Trijpmaker who was in East Frisia until late 1530.[44] Also, some time in 1530 Joris resided in Emden, where he disputed with a preacher referred to as Henricus N.[45] This disputation illustrates that Joris had not given up his religious convictions. Large numbers of Joris' fellow religious dissenters from Holland and the Southern Netherlands had also fled to East Frisia. Melchior Hoffman, who brought Anabaptism to this region, made his first converts among these refugees in May-June, 1530. Trijpmaker himself was one of these early converts, and as Hoffman's messenger travelled to Amsterdam by December 1530 to establish an Anabaptist congregation there. Did Joris hear or even meet Hoffman in Emden? Unfortunately all extant sources are silent on this intriguing question. Given Joris' interest in religious reform, there seems no valid reason why he would not have attended Hoffman's preaching if Emden was indeed Joris' home at this time.

Although the account of Joris' discussions with Trijpmaker in 1529 is sketchy, it does shed light on Joris' religious concerns and activities during this period. The central issue disputed was that of the nature of Christ. Apparently Trijpmaker, before his subsequent baptism by Hoffman, had denied the deity of Christ, claiming "Christ as only a mere human or servant of God." Joris later claimed that with the help of his associates he was able to convince Trijpmaker of his error. Trijpmaker confessed to Joris before his execution on December 5, 1531:

> "Were you not he, with whom I formerly disputed of Christ?" "Yes, I am," replied David. "Indeed," spoke the bishop, "now I am completely free and delivered from it, and believe in Christ my Saviour."[46]

While Joris may have helped to convert Trijpmaker to an "evangelical" understanding of the nature of Christ, Trijpmaker was probably alluding to his later Melchiorite Christology in these remarks. Joris' zeal on behalf of the deity of Christ provided the other side of the coin to his disdain for the Mass and the devotion to Mary and the saints. Joris and other lay reformers viewed Christ as the sole mediator between God and man, thereby leaving little room for the mediatrix or for the Mass.[47]

During his residence in East Frisia between 1529 and 1530, Joris wrote at least four songs which provide some clues about his state of mind. All four reflected both his personal experience of persecution and a familiarity with the Penitential Psalms, perhaps as interpreted by Martin Luther.[48] Briefly, they constituted a plea for deliverance and comfort. A full year after his trial and banishment, Joris wrote of the ''trembling and fear which now fiercely shake me'' and of the enemy who ''desired to make me faithless.'' Joris felt that a ''cross of suffering'' had been laid upon him and his ''frail flesh'' could endure it only through the hope that the oppression would soon ''be driven away.''[49] In another song of 1529, ''I lift up my heart, O God, to you,'' Joris cried out to the Lord for protection, for his many enemies opposed and cast derision upon him because of his faithfulness. He felt that his soul was on the verge of ''smothering'' and that his strength had completely departed, and so he called upon the

> Prince whom I kiss, come quickly to my aid
> Bring forth your spears against my persecutors
> Break their position
> Which is buttressed
> For above all you are my chosen one.[50]

There were two hymns written the following year. The first, penned in the New Year, 1530, was a song celebrating the coming of the Saviour into the world. In the first verse, Joris noted the humble nature of Christ's birth. The second and third stanzas reflect much more confidence than the earlier hymns:

> You poor come forth in one accord,
> Christ's birth is revealed.
> Hear South and North,
> the Word of God has become flesh in the New Year.
>
> You Christian folk will now rejoice
> Your King comes riding, uniformly meek:
> To fight for you without any shunning
> In order to deliver you in the New Year.[51]

While this may indicate that Joris had already some interest in the eschatological return of Christ, it is not particularly apocalyptical and is more a celebration of the incarnation. The final song of these four probably reflects most clearly Joris' spiritual preoccupation at this point in time. The song, entitled ''Wake up, all you people,'' is a call for men to awake, to forsake evil, sins and the world with its wealth, to follow God's teachings, to put on the armour of the heart and to fight with the sword of the Spirit.[52] One can easily imagine Joris exhorting his listeners with the very words of this particular hymn. While the first three songs reflect Joris' inner struggles and longings, this last seems a poetical reformulation of his early reformation preaching.

Joris' falling out with the Emden preacher and his return south probably took place near the end of 1530 or at the beginning of 1531. Trijpmaker was likewise driven away from Emden at about the same time, again raising the question of Joris' interest in the Melchiorite program. From East Frisia Joris moved to The Hague, where he spent most of 1531. Here he supported himself and his expectant wife (she had evidently joined her husband some time earlier) by his vocation, but likely because of his newness to the city he found little work. While decorating two large windows for a city magistrate, he came down with a fever which forced him to cease work for six to eight weeks and to rely on the donations of his "brothers in the gospel." Presumably these were persons with similar religious inclinations.[53] What is interesting about this incident is that Joris, a previously sentenced and unrepentant heretic, could not only stay for several months at the seat of the Imperial Court, but that he was given work by one of the city magistrates. This suggests that Joris had toned down his reformation activity and was engaged already in a form of Nicodemism, while continuing to meet with fellow reformers and to write several more hymns.

Four hymns from this period are included in Joris' *Songbook.* Although they continue the themes from his earlier hymns, a new element presents itself. Two hymns in particular continue the earlier ascetic themes of denying the "old man" and his sinful intentions and clinging more fervently to the Lord.[54] The new element is a more pronounced apocalypticism, illustrating again that Joris had probably come in contact, sometime before 1531, with some Melchiorite apostles (if not Hoffman himself) who were proclaiming Hoffman's eschatological message throughout the Netherlands beginning in 1530. This element went even further than the identification of the pope with the antichrist, seen in his pamphlet on idolatry. A hymn from the New Year, (January) 1530, shows traces of this apocalyptic message, particularly with its references to Jerusalem and its call for

> You Princes, Knights, Kings, Lords
> Clothed with good and blessed clothes,
> Change them for truth like the Angelic multitude
> Rejoice in this sweet New Year.[55]

The most clearly apocalyptic song by Joris in this year was "The Day will not be concealed." Joris speaks of the revelation of the Day of the Lord which will separate the good from the evil and will bring the triumph of the oppressed.[56] Although the nearness of the end is not as pronounced as in songs produced in the next few years, it has definitely come more into the centre of Joris' awareness.

Joris' contacts with Anabaptists increased from this point on. On December 5, 1531, Joris in fact witnessed the execution of Trijpmaker and nine other Anabaptists at The Hague. Trijpmaker was considered an Anabaptist bishop and a principal baptiser in Amsterdam during 1530. At least one of the martyrs (Trijpmaker), and probably more, were already familiar with Joris, for "they spoke to the same David Joris, and called to him:

'Brother, are you here? See, we ... testify to our faith for the name of the Lord Jesus Christ.' "[57] Their reference to Joris as a "brother" suggests a close relationship between Joris and at least some Melchiorites. The martyrdom left a deep impression not only upon Joris but also upon Hoffman, who, as noted above, declared a two-year suspension of baptism to avoid further executions.[58]

The question of how long Joris remained in The Hague before returning to Delft is no longer clear, although we do know he returned to his mother's city sometime between 1532 and 1534.[59] Joris may simply have returned to Delft after the expiration of his banishment to find a better market for his skills. The year following Trijpmaker's death, Joris wrote a song which alluded to this execution and which called on God's children to suffer persecution patiently, "until their time is fulfilled." The first verse reflects Joris' reaction to recent events:

> Blow the horn, and make a shout,
> The Lord is set as King over the earth,
> Raise your voice, shout everywhere,
> The Kingdom has been given to Christ,
> Dear ones pay heed,
> God's children in the Spirit,
> Against whom the world sharpens its sword,
> Yes, bear suffering with patience,
> until its time is fulfilled,
> Pure, without guilt, clean and clear,
> With this more, rejoice in this sweet New Year.[60]

If Joris cannot be called an Anabaptist or Melchiorite at this time (the evidence is inconclusive), the lines between Anabaptism and other reform manifestations were not sharply drawn. Joris had clearly imbibed of Hoffman's central tenets. Another song written by Joris in 1532 continued the apocalyptic theme. Indeed, it is improbable that this hymn, "Hear all who have ears to hear," would have been written any differently by an Anabaptist. The theme was that in light of the nearness of the Day of the Lord, his hearers must repent and shun the world and its vanity. Joris wrote:

> Separate yourselves from everything that makes you err
> Separate yourselves,
> I say it is more than time:
> The Lord is coming to pay vengeance
> To subjugate the world with her followers.
> But will you then conceal your face
> When you stand before the severe Judge:
> When the stones are rent, hide behind the rocks,
> For you will receive wages according to your work.[61]

Joris' continued preoccupation with apocalyptic judgement confirms again Melchiorite influences. It is known that he held several discussions with groups of covenanters (as the Melchiorites were called) through 1532 and 1533. According to the extant account, Joris showed a decided reluctance to throw in his lot with them completely. Perhaps his own experience with the Inquisition and witness of the death of several Anabaptists help to explain his caution. Attempts by the Melchiorites to convince Joris to submit to baptism were terminated because he seemed to be one "who is against God."[62] Apparently Joris was able to hold his own when it came to interpreting Scripture. Nevertheless, this did not prevent Anabaptist apocalyptical ideas from influencing his own thinking. It appears that Joris adopted Hoffman's prediction that 1533 marked the end of the current age and the coming of the kingdom of God. This aspect of Joris' thought is naturally absent from the anonymous account, but is plainly seen in one of the songs from 1533:

> Let not yourselves sorrow
> When God's strong hand appears:
> We will receive his Kingdom coming in its pure glory:
> For God is our fire
> Why should we grieve:
> It is the last year
> It shall not endure forever.[63]

Despite his caution, Joris was caught up in the eschatological excitement which was sweeping the Low Countries in the early 1530s and was at the very least a Melchiorite in sympathy and ideology well before his baptism in 1534.

Notes

1. Friedrich Nippold ("David Joris von Delft. Sein Leben, seine Lehre und seine Secte," *Zeitschrift für historische Theologie* [Gotha: 1863], pp. 23-24) remarked: "Seine Mutter ist nach den besten Nachrichten von guter Familie." David Joris' well-informed anonymous biographer affirmed this contention, mentioning that when Joris' mother was arrested in 1539, the sheriff confiscated her "houses and inheritance, also her and his [Joris'] possessions." Furthermore this author remarked that after her execution, her body was buried behind the altar in the church "because she was one of the upper class of the city" ("David Joris sonderbare Lebensbeschreibung aus einem Manuscripto," in Gottfried Arnold, *Unparteiische Kirchen- und Ketzerhistorie*, Bd. 1-4, Frankfurt Ausgabe, 1729 [reprinted Hildesheim: Georg Olms, 1967], p. 727). Hereafter Anonymous. The fact that Joris' mother was allowed to choose her form of execution, including "bleeding to death," in the Cellebroeders' Cloister, also suggests upper-class status. One of Joris' uncles was apparently night watchman and hour-caller at Delft (Nippold, "David Joris," p. 24).
2. He may have been from Bruges instead. See Nippold, "David Joris," p. 24. The family disagreement is mentioned by Anonymous, p. 704. This account of Joris is so detailed, both in regards to historical information and insight into Joris' state of mind, that it must have been penned with at least Joris' cooperation, if he in fact did not write it himself. See Waite, "Spiritualizing the Crusade," pp. 48-50.
3. The evidence for Brugges as David's birthplace is circumstantial, but not without merit. This would account for his use of the name Johann van Brugge when he moved

to Basel in 1544. Since Johann was his confirmation name, it may also be the case that the appellative "van Brugge" was likewise accurate. For the evidence regarding his birthdate, see Bainton, *David Joris*, p. 1.

4. Anonymous, p. 704.
5. These schools were often free and promoted literacy in the towns and cities of the Low Countries. See Post, *The Modern Devotion*, pp. 406-26, and especially his *Scholen en Onderwijs in Nederland Gedurende de Middeleeuwen* (Utrecht: Uitgeverij het Spectrum, 1954), pp. 83-85, where he describes the daily curriculum of these schools as beginning with the *pater noster* and continuing through the ABCs, morning prayer, noon prayer, prayers for each hour and the evening prayer.
6. Post remarks that often less than one half of students graduated from the fourth class (quarto) to the third. Graduation from the third class prepared a student for University. Few cities would have had demand for a second or first class (Post, *Scholen*, pp. 92-99).
7. Anonymous, p. 704. Gerald Strauss describes the impact of the Latin school methodology: "Children listened to a sentence spoken by the teacher and repeated it aloud while looking at the written syllables in their ABC book or tracing the letters on a wax tablet or scrap of paper. The rote memorization encouraged by this procedure seems to have left many youngsters less than fluently literate" (*Luther's House of Learning* [Baltimore: The Johns Hopkins University Press, 1978], p. 189).
8. Anonymous, p. 704 and "Teghenbericht Op een Laster unde Scheltboecxken," translated into High German in Arnold, *Ketzerhistorie*, p. 768.
9. Anonymous, p. 705. De Hoop Scheffer (*Geschiedenis*, p. 356) says that David was fourteen years old at the time. This is assuming that he was twelve years old at his confirmation and that he worked at his father's shop for two years. The destruction of relevant source material in the great fire of Delft in 1536 makes the dating of the family's return to Delft difficult. They may have moved back earlier, as David's confirmation may indicate the end of the family dispute.
10. Anonymous, p. 705. He offered his daughter and his inheritance to David once he had turned eighteen or nineteen. The man later became burgomaster of the city. Hans Koegler argues that this merchant clearly lived in Delft ("Einiges über David Joris als Künstler," *Öffentliche Kunstsammlung Basel*, Jahresberichte 1928-30, p. 165).
11. Anonymous, p. 705. This passage is uncharacteristically in the first person, and indicates that Joris was involved in the authorship of his biography. See Waite, "Spiritualizing the Crusade," pp. 48-50.
12. Anonymous, p. 705. He would be "able to wear gold, silk and jewels." In the early sixteenth century, the craft of glasspainting was still regarded as a highly skilled art. It later degenerated to a level little higher than that of a house painter (A. van der Boon, *Monumentale glasschilderkunst in Nederland* [The Hague: Martinus Nijhoff, 1940], p. 19). See also Koegler, "Einiges über David Joris," p. 162, where he describes Joris' talents as being superior to a mere technician's. For later examples of Joris' glasswork, see illustrations 3 and 4.
13. Henry's Treasurer was in Calais during the negotiations there between Henry and Emperor Charles V in 1521. A treaty was signed, one that the English hoped would gain for them a greater share of the Netherlands cloth market (C.S.L Davies, *Peace, Print and Protestantism, 1450-1558* [London: Hart-Davis MacGibbon, 1936], p. 161, and A.F. Pollard, *Henry VIII* [New York: Harper Torchbooks, 1966], p. 104).
14. Anonymous, p. 705. Bainton (*David Joris*, p. 3) identified one window in the Chapel House of "The Vyne," a manor in Hampshire, as Joris' work. The brochure concerning this window confirms that the glass is of Flemish design and manufacture and must have been installed between 1518 and 1527. See *The Vyne* (Hampshire: The

National Trust, 1976), p. 24. Koegler ("Einiges über David Joris," pp. 167-68), argues that the style of the window was influenced by Joris himself, while K.G. Boon ("De Glasschilder David Joris, een Exponent van het Doperse Geloof. Zijn Kunst en Zijn Invloed op Dirck Crabeth," *Mededelingen van de Koninklijke Academie voor Wetenschappen, Letteren en Schone Kunsten van België*, XLIX [1988], esp. pp. 119-21) believes that the master craftsman was the Brussels glasspainter Bernard van Orley.

15. They believed Sandys to be in London because the Emperor Charles V arrived in that city in the spring of 1522 (Anonymous, p. 705). See Roger Lockyer, *Tudor and Stuart Britain, 1471-1714* (New York: St. Martin's Press, 1964), p. 44.

16. Koegler, "Einiges über David Joris," p. 169.

17. Nippold, "David Joris," p. 27, foonote 50, cites van de Hoof (*Histoire van Enkhuyzen* [n.p., 1666], p. 19) who knew of works at Enkhuizen and Dordrecht. Van der Linde (*David Joris*, p.xi) has the following quotation from van den Hoof: "In den jaere 1522 syn 'er noch eenige glasen in de Norderkap [der Westerkerk] geset, ten koste van de gilden gemaekt door David Joris, glassshrijver of schilder van Delft."

18. Koegler, "Einiges über David Joris," p. 169.

19. *CDI*, Vol. IV, pp. 133-35.

20. Although not himself a known member of a *rederijker* chamber, he had received the name David because his father was at the time acting the part of the Israelite king. F.C. van Boheemen and Th. C.J. van der Heijden (*De Delftse rederijkers 'Wy rapen gheneucht'* [Amsterdam: Huis aan de drie Grachten, 1982], p. 41) remark: "David Jorisz. wordt in het algemeen beschouwd als de eerste Delftse rederijker, die fel getuigt van een nieuwe geloofsrichting. Nu is er geen enkel bewijs voorhanden, dat hij lid zou zijn geweest van de Delftse kamer. Veel waarschijnlijker is het, dat hij tijdens zijn jeugd toneelspeler was bij de troep van zijn vader; hij trok immers met zijn vader door het land. Dergelijke zwervende *beroepsvertoners* treden vaak tegen betaling binnenskamers op en worden veelal *kamerspeelders* genoemd. Zij hebben meestal niets met de rederijkerskamers te maken." Boheemen and Heijden's contention that Joris Sr. was a "wandering entertainer" and not a *rederijker* lacks evidence. In David's youth his father was a merchant with a shop, located, it appears, in a city in the Southern Netherlands.

21. "For quite a while, there was not a sermon preached which did not cause him to receive an increasing love for knowledge in his heart, which consumed his mind, just as occurs with physical love" (Anonymous, p. 706). De Hoop Scheffer identifies the preacher of these two sermons as Wouter (*Geschiedenis*, pp. 356-57).

22. Anonymous, p. 706. It may not be coincidence that anti-Mary sentiment came on the heels of the institution of the "feast of the Seven Woes of Mary" (1503) and the erection of several monuments or chapels dedicated to Mary at the Old Church in Delft (1510-1522) (G. Berends en R. Meeschke, "De Bouwgeschiedenis van de Oude Kerk," *De Stad Delft. Culture en Maatschappij tot 1572*, ed. R. A. Leeuw [Delft: Stedelijk Museum Het Prinsenhof, 1981], p. 36). According to Huizinga (*Waning of the Middle Ages*, pp. 148-49), one of the more prominent features of late medieval religious life was the growth of observances, images and special masses devoted to the Virgin Mary, threatening to trivialize the holy and pious character of these observances.

23. Anonymous, p. 706.

24. See Zijlstra, *Blesdijk*, p. 5 ("Volgens Blesdijk kreeg hij door die lideren bekendheid in geheel Holland"). It is probable that the desire of Anabaptist leaders to gain Joris as a recruit may be accounted for partly by the popularity which these songs gained

their author. See below, chapter 4.

25. A few days after Joris' stay at Dirck Willemszoon's house in 1528, the authorities found in his premises a copy of the *Theologia Deutsch* and also the *Gulden Onderwysinge* (De Hoop Scheffer, *Geschiedenis*, p. 544).

26. See Moxey, "Image Criticism," pp. 148-61. Several of these early pamphlets are included in the *BRN*, Vol. I.

27. Anonymous, p. 706. Luther's works were popular in the Netherlands only until 1525 and generally only his devotional tracts were printed there. Wouter Nijhoff and M.E. Kronenberg, *Nederlandsche Bibliographie van 1500 tot 1540* (The Hague: Martinus Nijhoff, 1923+1963), 3 vols., see numbers 1419-28 and 3457-63.

28. Duke, "Popular Religious Dissent," p. 46; *CDI*, Vol. V, p. 170.

29. *CDI*, Vol. IV, pp. 259-60.

30. Ibid., pp. 375-76 and 353.

31. Ibid., p. 349; Anonymous, p. 706. The de Heuter family was one of the most prominent in Delft. See J.J. Raue, *Vorming en ruimtelijke ontwikkeling in de late middeleeuwen de stad Delft* (Delftse Universitaire Pers, 1983), p. 83. His house still stands in the city.

32. *CDI*, Vol. IV, p. 349. While there is no direct evidence that Joris wrote the pamphlet (it is presumably not extant), the court officials identified it as his.

33. *Van abtuhung der Bylder/Und das keyn Betdler unther den Christen seyn soll* (Wittenberg, 1522, available in H.J. Khler, *Flugschriften des frühen 16. Jahrhunderts* [Microfiche Serie, Zug/Schweiz, 1978-, Microfiche 434, #1175]), fol.B(r) to Ciii(r). Karlstadt argued "Drumb ists nit war / das bilder / der Leyhen bucher seind. Dan sie mogen kein seligkeit aus yhn lernen / und gar nichts aus bildern schepffen / das tzu der seligkeit dienet / oder tzu Christlichem leben notlich ist." See Calvin A. Pater, *Karlstadt as the Father of the Baptist Movements* (Toronto: University of Toronto Press, 1984), p. 130, on the influence of this pamphlet.

34. *CDI*, Vol. IV, p. 350.

35. The meaning of this phrase is unclear, although it may refer to the belief that the inhabitants of the province of Zealand, less urbanised than Holland, were particularly materialistic in their devotion to the Catholic *cultus*.

36. He remarked that the mandate had intended only to inhibit meetings and disputations about the Scriptures (*CDI*, Vol. IV, p. 350).

37. *Een Geestelijck Liedt-Boecxken*, Mennonite Songbooks, Dutch Series, I (Amsterdam: Frits Knuf, n.d.), fols. 85v-92r (hereafter *Liedt-Boecxken*). The songs are undated but possibly belong to his pre-Anabaptist phase.

38. It is clear that de Heuter was being pressured by the Procurator to proceed with this trial. Ten years later de Heuter and Joris met again; this time de Heuter refused even to arrest the radical. See below, chapter 4.

39. *CDI*, Vol. IV, p. 350.

40. Bainton (*David Joris*, p. 4) discusses whether Joris' tongue was actually bored. De Hoop Scheffer (*Geschiedenis*, p. 543) mentions that the Prosecutor had written a half year later that "David Joriszoon zijne correctie ontfangen had." A similar sentence was passed against Dieuwer Reyersdochter, mentioned above, who was to have her tongue bored on the same scaffold in Delft. She was banned from the city of Münster (*CDI*, Vol. IV, p. 348).

41. Anonymous, p. 706. The author says that Joris had become a friend of the common folk because of some "small outdoor worship services."

42. Ibid. They apparently provided the authorities with a written guarantee of good conduct.

43. Nippold, "David Joris," pp. 33-34.
44. Anonymous (p. 707), mentions that these disputations had occurred two years before Trijpmaker's execution on Dec. 5, 1531.
45. Zijlstra, *Blesdijk*, pp. 6 and 179, note 26. Possibly this preacher was Heinrich, the Evangelical preacher of Oldersum, just outside of Emden (Ubbo Emmius, *Friesische Geschichte*, Vol. VI, translated by Erich von Reeken, from Latin original of 1615 [Frankfurt: Verlag Jochen Worner, 1982], fol. 837).
46. Anonymous, p. 707.
47. This is also illustrated in the confession of another early Dutch reformer, Wendelmoet Claesdochter, who replied when questioned on the Sacrament of the Altar, "I hold your sacrament to be bread and flour, and if you hold it as God, I say that it is your devil." She refused to take comfort in the proffered crucifix, remarking instead "this is not my Lord and my God, my Lord God is in me, and I in him" (Williams, *The Radical Reformation*, pp. 345-46; from Thielman van Braght, *The Bloody Theatre or Martyr's Mirror* [Scottdale: Herald Press, 1951], p. 422ff.).
48. Luther's commentaries on these Psalms were published in Dutch in 1520 and became some of his more popular works in the Netherlands (Nijhoff and Kronenberg, *Nederlandsche Bibliographie*, no. 1426). See *Luther's Works*, Vol. 14, pp. 137-206.
49. "Ach kranckelijcke Vleysch/noyt heb Ich u beth bedacht," July 1529, in *Liedt-Boecxken*, fols. 1r-2v.
50. Ibid., fols. 3r-5r.
51. "Die Salichmaecker pleyn/is gheborn kleyn," ibid., fols. 6r-6v.
52. "We'l op wacker alle Menschen," ibid., fols. 6v-8r.
53. Anonymous, p. 717. The source is unclear as to whether these were early reformers or Melchiorites.
54. *Liedt-Boecxken*, "Fy olden Mensch," fol. 68v and "Nu holdt aen wel," fols. 14v-15r.
55. "Ontwaeckt ghy wtvercoren droevighe Geesten Kleyne," ibid., fols. 8v-10v. The verse refers to Rev. 7:14.
56. Ibid., fols. 11r-14r.
57. Anonymous, p. 706. The others were: Vrank Willemszn van Amsterdam, Evert Janssen van Koesvelt, Jan van Delft (whom Joris presumably knew), Jan Hermanszn, Thomas Janszn, Jan Thomaszn, Jan Gouwenszn, Geryt Meynertszn, and Frans Willemszn (from Grete Grosheide, *Bijdrage tot de Geschiedenis der Anabaptisten in Amsterdam* [Hilversum: J. Schipper, Jr., 1938], p. 302).
58. Obbe Philips, "Confession," p. 211.
59. Anonymous is silent about his departure from The Hague. We know that he was ordained in Delft in the winter of 1534 (Philips, "Confession," p. 223).
60. *Liedt-Boecxken*, fols. 15v-17v. If New Year was regarded as January 1, this song would have been composed scant weeks after the execution. The medieval calendar generally regarded December 25 as New Year, but many regions had switched to January 1 by the first quarter of the sixteenth century. The Estates of Holland officially adopted the use of January 1 in 1532, although it was most likely common practice well before that date. See Reginald Poole, *The Beginning of the Year in the Middle Ages* (n.p., 1921), p. 25.
61. *Liedt-Boecxken*, fols. 20v-21r.
62. Anonymous, p. 707.
63. *Liedt-Boecxken*, fol. 23r "Die tijt van onsen Jaren/Is weynich Kort unde Kleyn."

Een feer goede Reden berft my ter herten wt, Pfalm.xlv.

David Joris, "The Fountain of Life" from *Wonder Book* (Deventer: Dirk van Borne, *c*. 1543), fol. iiiv°. Courtesy The Mennonite Library, University of Amsterdam.

CHAPTER FOUR

From Anabaptist to Nicodemite, 1534-39

In December 1533 Jan Matthijs declared the reinstatement of baptism in Amsterdam and later emissaries from Münster spread the news throughout the Netherlands.[1] Throughout that year Melchiorite sympathisers were called upon to submit to baptism and to come to the support of Münster, now under siege. David Joris was confronted directly with this issue. Given his sympathies and the fact that many of his friends and acquaintances were heeding the call of the Münsterite apostles, Joris must have been sorely tempted to join the "Great Trek" to Münster in March of 1534. He not only knew many of the leaders captured by the authorities, but several of his relations were among their number. He highly esteemed the participants, for they included "the best, most innocent, faithful and honest, who sought after God and his kingdom."[2] While he applauded the intentions of the covenanters, he was still hesitant about the whole enterprise. Given the treatment he had already received at the hands of the authorities for his Reformation activity, Joris' cautious attitude is not surprising, although his reluctance to join the Trek illustrates as well the ambivalent relationship between Dutch reformers, Melchiorites or Melchiorite sympathisers, and Münsterites immediately following the end of Hoffman's *Stillstand*. The lines between the camps must have been fluid.

Throughout the summer of 1534 several important Anabaptist leaders passed through or baptised in Delft, including Jacob van Campen, a major leader of the Amsterdam community. Jacob Symons, a citizen of Delft, was active on behalf of Anabaptism in Joris' home town, and may have been one of the captured trek leaders with whom Joris was familiar. Joris included a song written by Symons (under the date January 1534) in his published collection of hymns.[3] Joris most certainly had contact with these and other Anabaptist leaders after his return to Delft and may have been closer to the Melchiorites than the anonymous biographer admits. At any rate, Joris continued his contacts with the Anabaptists throughout 1534.

Joris' decision to submit to baptism came some time during the winter of 1534-35. It seems that he first attended a number of Anabaptist gatherings as a sympathetic observer. The Anabaptists in turn must have been flattered to count a man of Joris' stature among their sympathisers. Discussions came to a head at a gathering of eight or ten Anabaptists led by an

---

Notes to Chapter Four are found on pages 81-87.

unidentified teacher.[4] He held a private discussion with the teacher in the back of the room so that "the other simple, poor sheep would not worry themselves about it and despair." Among the questions he sought to have answered was the basis or authority for rebaptism. It appears that Joris was opposed to the reinstitution of baptism. The teacher responded with a 'literal' exposition of the last chapter of the Gospel of Mark, concluding that "the Lord had commanded such, that he would risk it, and would confirm such with his blood." The reference to martyrdom perhaps reminded David of his own torture and the martyrdom of Trijpmaker. Moved by the courageous faith of these simple believers, Joris returned (with three or four others) to the Anabaptist meeting a short time later and "surrendered himself to the Lord, requesting to be received into their fellowship."[5] We are told that his "conversion" brought great rejoicing on the part of the Anabaptists, and many other hesitant sympathisers now became more receptive to rebaptism. Joris' baptism, however, was less a "conversion" than a coming out of hiding; if his songs are reliable guides to his ideas, he had months before adopted the beliefs of the covenanters.[6]

Joris' Early Leadership Role

Because of his reputation, Joris was almost immediately recognised as a potential leader in the movement. Thus, shortly after his baptism he was commissioned a bishop or teacher by Obbe Philips and a certain Damas, most probably Damas van Hoorn, with the assent of the *gemeine*.[7] In spite of the new role, Joris did not feel himself compelled to evangelise or to baptise others. He recounted later that he lacked the "inner confirmation" which he regarded as necessary before he felt competent to take on the mantle of leadership.[8] It is possible that this attitude reflected also a certain depreciation of external ceremonies, including baptism, an attitude he developed from his knowledge of Sacramentarian ideas and which was reinforced by Hoffman's prudent *Stillstand*. It also made concealment from the authorities much easier.

During the next few years, however, Joris' reluctance to assume religious authority disappeared, particularly after he experienced a set of visions in December 1536. Confidence in his leadership qualifications also developed as a result of Joris' participation in several important conferences of Anabaptists, particularly meetings in Waterland (winter of 1534-35); at Bocholt, Westphalia in 1536; and at Oldenburg, Westphalia and in Strasbourg in 1538.[9]

Upon his return home from the Waterland conference in January or early February 1535, Joris was faced with a less tolerant magistracy. Several incidents, such as the Harmen Schoenmaker affair at 't Zandt in Groningen in mid-January 1535, had caused the Imperial government to apply more pressure on local administrators to deal with the Anabaptists.[10] The authorities tried a period of grace extending from February 13 to 26,

1535, but cracked down with increased severity after its expiry. The harsh measures came into effect in Delft by March of that year. Joris and other Anabaptists were soon affected. By April Joris was again absent from Delft looking for a more tolerant residence, for on the seventeenth of that month the sheriff of Delft informed the court of one

> David Jorissen, glassmaker, who is contaminated with the aforementioned sect and is baptised, keeping himself fugitive, and on whose cause the aforementioned sheriff did register exile on April 17, 1535.[11]

Joris had in fact left, with wife and child, for Strasbourg, hoping to find lodging, work and tolerance. He may also have chosen Strasbourg because Hoffman himself was there and had proclaimed this city the New Jerusalem. If this is the case, Joris as an Anabaptist may have considered himself a supporter of Hoffman's rather than of Matthijs' program. According to his anonymous biographer, Joris and his wife had to sell some of their clothes and jewelry in order to finance the trip.[12] It appears that other Anabaptists were making the same journey, for they found company on the way. If they were hoping to find the New Jerusalem they were in for disappointment. They arrived at Strasbourg in June (at about the time of the fall of Münster), and were met by another Anabaptist, Leenhardt the butcher, who expressed shock at Joris' presence in this "godless city."[13] Understandably, given the turn of events in Münster, the authorities in Strasbourg were in no mood to welcome heretics. Joris found his lodging full of mercenaries and other "dissolute people." He and his family left two days later. Joris and his companions then returned to the Netherlands in order to set sail for England, where they hoped to find refuge.

Joris arrived at the port of Vlissingen in Zealand later in the summer. He was dissuaded from the attempt to reach English refuge by a storm and by some travellers who had just arrived from England with the news that no one could enter that country without being first interrogated.[14] Joris and his family therefore headed home, staying at Gorkum on the Waert where Joris found work as a journeyman. His wife's pregnancy forced them to return to Delft around December of 1535.[15]

The fact that Joris could return to his home city despite the actions taken against him by the city fathers indicates again the measure of support he still had among the residents. As the leader of the Delft Anabaptists he was forced to remain in hiding, but managed to find employment with a master craftsman. Under these conditions Joris wrote another hymn, which reflected a growing pessimism concerning any fleshly or human aid. Beneath this pessimism there still seethed an undercurrent of desire for retribution (the kingdom of Münster had only recently been crushed), which becomes evident in the last verse of this song:

The Prince should well consider,
Grasp aright in his understanding:
Unlearned and all clerics
With all the wise in the land,
Stick out, cut off your hand
Which draws on you the anger of God,
So that you might not be burned with it,
eternally tormented in the lake of Hell.
Keep your spirit undefiled
or it will cause you to mourn.
Do not trust in any flesh.[16]

Joris' preoccupation with the mortification of the flesh was no doubt reinforced by his physical difficulties. The poor living conditions in Delft had
brought on a severe illness.

Joris and Anneken Jans

In the spring of 1536 the authorities again began to take stronger measures
against heretics, no doubt the result of the activities of radical Anabaptists
such as the Batenburgers and the Münsterites who attempted to capture the
village of Poeldijk at the end of 1535.[17] Joris in turn began a search for a
more secure hiding place, a search which would occupy him for the next
several years. Only days before the great fire which destroyed much of
Delft on May 3, 1536, Joris again left his home city and headed by boat to a
nearby town, most likely Den Briell. He and a companion stayed in the
home of a female resident, presumably Anneken Jans.[18] Events which
occurred in Den Briell proved to have future significance. Joris received
new understanding from the Scriptures and "divine dreams." Evidence
suggests that these were the first visions Joris experienced. Thus it seems
that Joris had at least "night visions" prior to the better known December
visions of 1536. Moreover, it is possible that Anneken, who scholars
assume to be the inspiration for the later visions, was the catalyst for his
aspirations to prophetic status. Joris and his female supporter fell in love
here, although the relationship appeared from all accounts to have been of a
platonic nature. According to our source they prayed together whenever
tempted by the flesh. The hostess seemed taken by Joris' spirituality and she
knew not "how to praise God enough about this man's gifts."[19] Not only
did Joris have a strained marriage as a result of his frequent absences, but his
hostess had been separated from her husband for some two years. That
Joris' prophetic ecstasy seems to have increased during his time with the
woman is an intriguing aspect of this relationship and one that may prove
enlightening if examined more fully.

The woman's husband, presumably the barber/physician Arent Jans,
returned home unexpectedly from his refuge in England. Because the
woman wanted nothing to do with him and refused to be defiled by what she
considered his dissolute lifestyle she departed, leaving Arent alone with

Joris. The husband, unconvinced by Joris' arguments, returned to England where he spread the rumour that his wife and Joris were lovers. Sometime thereafter two or three other Anabaptists arrived from England to investigate the matter. Joris and the investigators met and discussed this situation and from all accounts came to a favourable understanding of the incident. A few days later the covenanters from England escorted David back to Delft.[20] The investigators, satisfied that David was now out of danger of temptation, presumably returned to England.

In November 1536, Joris wrote a song which reflected the abiding influence of Anneken. This song bears striking similarities with one written by Anneken herself.[21] Joris in this composition reasserted many of his eschatological motifs, which were perhaps strengthened by his contacts with this spiritual woman. With the apocalyptical preoccupation he here combined an increasingly intense flesh-spirit dichotomy. In brief, this long and complex song has to do with the unregenerate, earthly seed destined to perish, while the reborn, heavenly seed will tread upon the serpent and gain the kingdom of Christ. This victory is achieved by the Word of God, Christ, who "became flesh and for us has suffered, The Son of Man Named. His flesh has come from heaven."[22] Joris maintained both the evil nature of the flesh and the sinless purity of the Son of God by adopting Hoffman's doctrine of the Heavenly Flesh of Christ.[23] He continued that believers must at the moment go through the oven of persecution to become pure as gold, to forsake all flesh and to prove their faith. Then they can rejoice in the Day of the Lord, when Christ shall return, establish his kingdom and judge all unbelievers. There are, in this hymn, some references which could refer to a re-establishment of an earthly kingdom of God. Joris wrote of the purified believers:

> Who will endure in the House of God
> Which shall be established.
> That is the Mountain of the Lord,
> Zion, the prepared City.
> Which now suffers to be trod upon.
> Thereto shall Israel turn,
> And desire to be in it:
> To praise and honour God in her,
> As his kings and priests:
> Who will reign with Christ
> and drink the new wine.[24]

More than a year after the fall of Münster, Joris adhered to an eschatological hope, still centred on the regenerated city, which further intensified his ascetic tendencies.

During this time Joris was also forced again to look for work in Delft. He occupied himself as well with corresponding to the covenanters, particularly concerning what he regarded as their misuse of the name of God. Joris may, in this instance, have attempted to provide his supporters with another means for elite group identification.[25]

Joris' Visions

Two events at the end of 1536 pushed Joris into the forefront of the Anabaptist movement. The first was his participation in the Bocholt conference in which he managed to mediate a settlement between the radical and pacifist participants.[26] Then, in early December, Joris experienced his climactic visions which were inspired by a letter he received from a sister in the faith.[27] Anneken may have indeed been the author, so that the impact of this letter is not difficult to comprehend. Unfortunately the contents of this letter are not known; a letter previously assumed to be the one was more likely written two years later.[28] It can be assumed, however, that the letter enthusiastically praised Joris' gifts and office, and probably proclaimed him as the prophet of God. Thus inspired, Joris became entranced while standing before his workbench, and saw several visions which greatly influenced his later career.[29]

In the first vision, Joris witnessed a great tumult and uproar upon the earth. There was a gathering together of all the authorities, both secular and spiritual, who fell down in fear before a group of small and innocent children. This vision certainly accorded well with Joris' eschatological framework where the upright believers (whom he elsewhere called little children)[30] would judge the world, including the authorities. The vision therefore dealt with the pressing issue of vengeance and confirmed in his mind the ultimate victory of the oppressed Anabaptists over the authorities.

Immediately after this vision there was another, in which he saw himself surrounded by naked women and men, in various shapes and postures. At the end of this scene, Joris cried out "Lord, now I may indeed see everything!" He interpreted this latter vision to mean that "his eyes must be so pure and clear, that he cannot be tempted or be made impure by any created work of God."[31] This then was an encouragement to one who was struggling against the temptations of the flesh. Coming as it did just a few months after the temptations experienced, we presume, at Anneken's house, this vision likewise could provide relief to an overburdened conscience. Perhaps, too, Anneken's letter had made some reference to past events.

Joris awoke exhausted from his visions, but immediately took up his quill and began to write while still in this state of inspiration. Apparently an inner voice dictated to him, but it spoke far faster than he could write. The work which resulted was entitled *Hear, Hear, Hear, Great Wonder, Great Wonder, Great Wonder*, and an analysis of this booklet shows that it was indeed written in great haste and with tremendous prophetic excitement and fervour. It is highly repetitive and redundant, akin to the modern "stream of consciousness" technique. It consists of loosely-strung together admonitions, of which the following quotation will suffice as an example:

See to it, see to it, heed what I say to you, and taste from this fruit, and become healthy and praise the Lord. Become seeing, become seeing, become seeing through the true man, his eyes, his eyes, his eyes, they are light, light, light, for no darkness is in him, not in him. See to it that you do it quickly, do quickly. Neglect not yourselves, see to it, see to it. Become childlike, without guile, simple, simple in your eyes, simple and right, simple and right. Spirit, spirit, spirit, without flesh, that is, without sins, without spot or wrinkle, innocent, innocent as little lambs.[32]

It is also clear from this work that Joris now had a very exalted view of his calling and authority, and he found it necessary to conclude with these words:

I pray for you all through the merciful God and our Lord Jesus Christ, that you will not be offended by any lofty words which have been written by me in this book. Though they appear to be from me ... See, they have flowed out of the pen through the Holy Spirit which has spoken in me.[33]

The lofty words which Joris alluded to were probably his claim to being the third David. He argued that like the triune God, everything has its perfection in "three" and since the first David was a figure of God Almighty, then it is possible that there are also three Davids. The first was the Israelite King, in whom was the Spirit and power of God; the second was Christ, in whom was the entire Godhead; and the third, "upon him the Spirit of Christ shall abide. He is the least, although he shall appear as the greatest." This third David would complete the work begun by the first two, but only through the power of the second, who "remains the most and greatest." While the middle David is the Lord, the third is a servant who will cut off the head of the last great enemy, death and its works. There is little doubt that throughout this lengthy pamphlet Joris is referring to himself at this point. In fact, he tells his readers and followers to "observe that you, small children and young Davidites, ought to be as strong as David, in order that you might stand against Goliath, the death in the flesh."[34] What other Anabaptists saw as arrogance and presumption, Joris saw only as fulfilling the call of the Lord. From this point on, Joris' previous doubts about his religious vocation seem to have vanished.

For the next three months this confidence of spirit remained with the prophet. His acquaintances were amazed at the change, and no wonder, for Joris remarked to one brother "I have been afraid now for a long time of everyone, but now I am no longer afraid, be it of Emperor or King. Let them be ashamed before me, I have no need to be ashamed before them!" He further remarked, on the basis of his first vision, that these authorities would not obtain peace, until they had made peace with Joris himself.[35]

As a result of his visions, Joris spent the first few months of 1537 attempting to detach himself entirely from the desires of the flesh. He lived so frugally and ate so little that he became dangerously weak and was finally forced to eat by his companions. By denying his physical needs and becoming totally resigned to God's will, he believed he could become divine in spirit. The account of this period in Joris' life is in fact similar to the accounts of medieval ascetics and mystics. There seems little doubt that Joris aspired to a rigorous asceticism based on late medieval models.[36] The physical and psychological effects of these practices on Joris are aspects of his personality at this stage of his life that have not been fully accounted for and which may shed new light on his later career.

Leadership and Persecution

In the light of this high calling, Joris found it increasingly difficult to continue to perform the menial task of glasspainting. His vocation was also a dangerous one, requiring the use of a shop and, more importantly, a clientele which normally consisted of members of the aristocracy or church hierarchy.[37] He had in fact experienced difficulties with his profession since he became an iconoclast in 1524, for much of his work would be displayed in churches as "the books of the unlearned." The anonymous account of Joris' life described this dilemma as "a fire in his body" which entered him whenever he sat down to work.[38] Financial necessity however forced him to continue glasspainting until he arrived at the belief that he was no "longer to be the servant of men but of God." Giving up his livelihood was no easy matter, for his wife had obtained several rather lucrative jobs for him and his glasswork was apparently quite popular. Finally in 1537 he decided to rely solely on God and to abandon his craft. Living upon donations was for Joris very trying at first, for in addition to small sums of money he received gifts of dubious worth.[39]

As a result of the inner confirmation of his spiritual calling provided by the visions, Joris' self-conception as a prophetic leader of the Anabaptists increased dramatically. He directed his energies to the unification of Melchiorite and Münsterite groups both by means of a vigorous writing campaign and by participation in several crucial meetings of Anabaptist leaders, particularly conferences in Oldenburg and in Strasbourg in 1538.

Joris' activities gained for him a number of followers from the other Anabaptist camps. Among Joris' followers were ex-Batenburgers such as Heinrich Kaal, who brought with him a number of supporters to Delft when he joined Joris late in 1538. This influx of suspected radicals into the city caused a number of local citizens to fear an attempted revolt. The nervous burghers may have remembered the attempts at nearby Hazerswoude and Poeldijk, a mere three years before. An attempt to root out the radicals was unsuccessful and Jan de Heuter, the sheriff of Delft, allowed a one-week period of grace in December to permit all Anabaptists to leave the city without prosecution. When most of Joris' followers, including Kaal, refused to comply, several were arrested and executed in January and February 1539.

In total, in this year twenty-seven of David's followers were executed in Delft alone[40] and at least seventy-three more in other parts of The Netherlands. This particular inquisition was a result of pressure from the Court at The Hague and from the church authorities. Joris himself managed to escape detection, primarily because his courageous followers refused to divulge their leader's whereabouts under torture. Some information got out, however, including word that Joris had been awakened by God as their prophet and that he was divinely inspired.[41] Of those captured and questioned, several confessed to practising polygamy, and one, Geertgen Cornelis, reputedly testified that communal nakedness was also practised in order to mortify the flesh as Adam and Eve had done in Paradise.[42] Although the evidence is controversial, it seems plausible that some Davidites practised communal nudity until 1545.[43]

Two women very close to David were also arrested and executed. Joris' own mother was put to death on February 21, 1539 in a cloister of the Cellebroeders.[44] According to one account, she could have escaped execution except for having publicly embarrassed de Heuter, accusing him of embezzlement. De Heuter, otherwise neutral, therefore joined with Joris' detractors in pushing for her execution. Joris' mother professed that her son had done nothing wrong, and was as true as the biblical prophets and apostles.[45] Another woman who, like Joris' mother and wife, figured significantly in his life was also arrested. Anneken Jans had returned from England late in 1538 to speak with Joris and was arrested on December 20 before she could visit him. She was sentenced and drowned on January 24, 1539 at Rotterdam.[46]

After his mother's death, Joris fled with wife and child to Haarlem.[47] From Haarlem, he travelled to another place where he was able to hide in a boarding house.[48] Joris and his fellows, having settled temporarily in their new locale, went through some rather fascinating spiritual experiences. Joris on his part said he received a "heavy spiritual burden" which often forced him to either fall prostrate or to stumble. With this he felt that he had received "five new senses" through which he had become totally renewed or divinised. Joris believed he could now see, hear, feel, taste and speak in a totally different and spiritual manner. With this experience he reported he had another vision, in which he believed "that not John the Baptist nor any creature on the earth, yes, not even Stephen . . . had seen Jesus Christ more lovely than he had."[49] Shortly afterwards, on Easter morning (April 6, 1539), Joris heard a voice commanding him to "rise up and write." He obeyed, and the results were published later in the *Wonder Book*. The theme was the coming of the kingdom of God and the destruction of the Devil's kingdom, which is "upheld with force and injustice."[50] Again the eschatological vengeance motif is central, as would be expected after he had lost so many beloved friends to the authorities. Joris reasserted his calling, to proclaim as a "certain witness" before all the world of the "hiddenness of the kingdom of life and light in the truth."[51] It is fascinating that during this time Joris and indeed his companions continued to experience visions. Most of these reaffirmed Joris' calling and authority.[52]

While Joris was in hiding, several more of his followers were arrested in Haarlem, including a thirteen-year-old youth by the name of Aelbrecht van Breuchel. Under torture Aelbrecht allegedly confessed the names of several other Davidites.[53] Aelbrecht's confession forced Joris' wife to flee Haarlem and she sought haven in Utrecht.[54] Joris himself was no longer safe and he was advised to flee. David's hopes of joining his wife in Utrecht were dashed, however, when Dirkgen herself and thirteen other disciples were captured in Utrecht in June. While her companions were executed, Dirkgen managed to be released on June 18.[55] When the prosecutor and suffragan bishop both died shortly after these executions, the Utrecht magistrates decided they had had enough of bloodshed.[56] The summary of Dirkgen's confession is worth noting here:

> The woman asked leave from the good lords and mayor at Utrecht, if she might be able to speak freely and respond.... She was so enraged and angry about the great public lies, that had been spread behind his [David's] back, publicly shaming him, and she insisted that he [the prosecutor] prove his allegations ... and she had seen nothing but virtue, honour, faithfulness and total piety among the brothers.

The authorities could not expect her to give up her husband. Besides, no one knew better than Dirkgen that "he feared the Lord and loved the truth of Christ, sought to do good to all men, and not to conceal the blessedness which was revealed to him by God."[57] Although Dirkgen did defend her husband, she was eventually released.

Joris then attempted to find refuge in Deventer. While in this city he was able to write down his thoughts on "the heavenly stream," later to become a major theme of the *Wonder Book* (see above, p. 64). Angered by the deaths of his followers, he also wrote a letter to the Court of Holland at The Hague. In this letter Joris admonished the Court "to cease from the great bullying persecution of his companions and not to join with the Roman Antichrist in the shedding of innocent blood."[58] He defended the victims as "the least prompted to revolt, but instead [were persons who] lived innocent, gentle and quiet lives."[59] He asked that the Court assemble a general council against the Romanists and Evangelicals so that David could show that he was indeed sent by God. For Joris, there was nothing to fear from the mighty, for God had shown his might in him. Joris furthermore believed that the time was near when God was to vindicate the innocent blood, for the letter is full of apocalyptic foreboding with respect to the authorities. The missive, abounding with defiant language, was to be delivered to The Hague by an unfortunate courier who was caught and executed by the magistrates in Leiden.[60] Some time after sending this letter, Joris read a distressing news sheet reporting his disciples' executions at Utrecht. Even though this news was later softened when he read of his wife's release, the emotional trauma of the executions must have had a considerable effect on Joris, who was already prone to anxiety. It can only be surmised that the loss of supporters furthermore heightened Joris' inclination and development to Nicodemism.

Escaping Persecution

One of the questions raised by a biographical study of David Joris is how, as one of the most wanted Anabaptists in the Netherlands, he managed to survive.[61] For as long as she was still alive, Joris' wealthy mother must have had some influence on the Delft council on behalf of her son. After her death, Joris had to rely on others to counteract the often ingenious methods used by the authorities.

One of the most widely used procedures for locating fugitives was the provision of financial remuneration for those who informed upon or captured Anabaptists. On January 2, 1539, a price of one hundred pounds was placed on Joris' head, while other Anabaptist teachers garnered forty pounds and ordinary Anabaptists were worth twenty.[62] This was a tremendous incentive to would-be informants and "bounty-hunters" of which there were a considerable number. The authorities seem to have supported a "career infiltrator" by the name of Adriaen Ariaensz van Dordrecht. Ariaensz had been arrested as a Anabaptist in March of 1534, but was released so that he could aid the government in capturing other Anabaptists. Five years later, he was brought into Haarlem by the sheriff of that city and placed in a prison cell containing several followers of David Joris. He managed to win the confidence of these Davidites and the incriminating statements he garnered were used to hasten guilty pleas.[63] The authorities also used torture to extract incriminating evidence. Occasionally this method bore fruit for the prosecutors, as in the case of the young Aelbrecht van Breuchel. The government's use of torture made the finding of safe refuge extremely difficult. It is recorded that, leaving Delft after his mother's execution in 1539, Joris departed "with great expense, because no one would conceal him or do him good, because it was forbidden upon the neck [i.e., beheading]." Nevertheless, a few supporters risked aiding the fugitive.[64]

Another method, which was used in particular against David Joris, employed family members as bait or hostages to force the leader to turn himself in to gain the release of his loved ones. Both David's children and his wife were exploited in this manner. In each case the method was nearly successful. After his mother's death, David's children remained in Delft, and de Heuter distributed them throughout the city, forbidding anyone to help them. Thus they could be carefully watched, and any would-be rescuers could be followed to discover their leader's whereabouts. One of Joris' young followers, Jan Jansz van den Berch, went to Delft to check on the whereabouts and well-being of the children. While he was there, one of the girls recognised him and pleaded for Jansz to take her to her mother. He agreed, but was followed by an informant. This *"ertz-schalk"* had been waiting for such an opportunity to cash in on the lucrative reward on David's head. Pretending to be a fellow Anabaptist, he joined the two young travellers, gaining Jansz's confidence by speaking well of Joris and talking in an "evangelical" fashion.[65] When the "bounty-hunter" realised that Jansz was not taking the girl to Joris himself, he decided to take the loss and turned Jansz in to the Amsterdam authorities for the lower twenty-pound reward. Jansz was cruelly tortured and executed, but he refused to reveal Joris' whereabouts.[66] The daughter was handed over to the burgomaster's wife for "friendly" interrogation. When she still refused to divulge the required information, the magistrate tried threats, but to no avail. Frustrated, he handed the girl over to a convent, from which she was later released and returned to her mother by a sympathetic nun.[67]

A similar tactic was used by the authorities after they had arrested the Davidites in Utrecht. No doubt Dirkgen, Joris' wife, was kept alive while the rest were executed because the authorities believed she could be used as bait to attract the prophet himself. The ploy nearly worked, for when Joris, who was travelling to Deventer at the time, heard of his wife's capture,

> the good man was so troubled and oppressed, that he wanted to jump out of the wagon . . . and actually did jump off once, in order to go to Utrecht to give himself into their hands in place of his wife and remaining children.

His companions, however, managed to convince their leader against this action.[68]

The authorities occasionally used other methods. City magistrates, for example, could place extra guards over the main gates. This was done by the Leiden authorities from December 30, 1538 to June 6, 1539, and is probably the reason why Joris showed great reluctance to enter that city in 1539.[69]

Joris' survival depended to a great extent on the devotion, courage and inventiveness of his followers and supporters. They developed a network of contacts which may be likened to the nineteenth-century American "underground railroad" which was used to aid the escape of fugitive slaves. The Anabaptist version was successful in keeping Joris' whereabouts unknown. Secrecy and courage on the part of the network's contacts were crucial to counteract the use of torture in extracting confessions. Clandestineness included not only the concealing of information from the authorities and strangers, but also involved a rather complex system whereby "guides" in one region were kept ignorant of the identities of their fellow workers in neighbouring territories.[70]

The other ingredient for success, courage, was noted several times. Joris' followers showed remarkable courage and devotion, even under torture. Jan Jansz, for example, had remarked to his captors, "Why should I lead my brother to execution. . . . I know indeed where he is, but I will not tell you, do what you may, you will not force it out of me."[71] Courage was also displayed by two of David's top lieutenants, Jorien Ketel and Leonard van Dam, who time and time again travelled to different towns and regions in order to secure a safe hiding place for their leader. Names of potential protectors included several nobles, although, more often than not, these sympathisers experienced a change of heart when the fugitives actually arrived.[72] Even when a benefactor remained willing, the fugitives themselves often turned down prospective lodging. For example, while a Junker in Guelders was willing to house Joris and van Dam, the fugitives refused, because they found the place crawling with soldiers.[73]

The network of supporters also displayed a measure of creativity. In 1539, Joris and his wife were finally reunited in Delft. Word leaked out, however, that the notorious heretic was again in the city, and Joris' supporters devised a plan to distract or mislead the attention of the authorities. It was arranged in this instance, that David would head south and Dirkgen north in the city, and in the ensuing confusion, Joris could escape once again.[74]

An infrequently used but rather dramatic function of the underground network was the rescue of imprisoned Anabaptists from jail. Although the usefulness of this procedure had been disputed by Joris himself at the Waterland conference, some of his own followers were the beneficiaries of such action in Leiden in 1539. On April 1541 Frans Jansz confessed to his actions of a couple of years earlier: "With his accomplices [he] had broken open the prison in Leiden, where some Anabaptists were imprisoned, and released these same prisoners, and had kept them in his house for some time."[75]

Despite the precautionary measures of the underground network, survival as an Anabaptist fugitive in the towns and cities of the Netherlands was no easy matter. And yet, even in cities such as The Hague, the seat of the Imperial Court, Joris was able to hide quite successfully. This success involved several precautions. First, open proselytising was of course out of the question. Second, a safe hiding place had to be secured. This was usually in the lofts or attics of the homes of trusted sympathisers. This procedure was common practice for most Anabaptist fugitives, and during 1535 the Amsterdam authorities had noted their consternation at the difficulty in flushing the covenanters from the "lofts and concealed places" in their city.[76] Hiding in attics required complete quiet and lack of movement during the times that strangers were in the lower levels of the house. The effects of this form of concealment will be discussed later. Third, because travel inside the city could be hazardous, movement was restricted, usually to the nighttime.

Perhaps the most difficult part of living in the city was making it through the city gates in the first place. These were usually guarded, but often fortuitous circumstances were a great assistance to the fugitives. For instance, fog conditions occasionally concealed Joris' identity.[77] Other times the watchman could be persuaded to look the other way, as when van Dam bribed a Delft gatekeeper. Usually, however, fugitives and their accomplices needed to plan carefully to escape detection. Normally they tried to arrive at the gates before daybreak or join a crowd going to market when recognition would be less likely.[78] If all else failed, the main gates could be by-passed completely, with the aid of some supporters who presumably lived next to the walls. In April 1536, Joris was forced to leave Delft in broad daylight, and he escaped by being "placed in a basket just like a dog, and covered with other furs and rags and . . . a beloved servant let him down in a sack into a small boat." Joris remained inside the sack for this trip on the canal and nearly drowned when the boat overturned. The concealed fugitive was rescued by strangers, who may have wondered about the value of the sinking sack.[79] In all of this, the fugitive was again at the mercy of his supporters, who themselves faced execution if it became known that they had harboured an Anabaptist leader.[80]

As difficult as it was to remain undetected in a city, travelling as a fugitive brought its own set of dangers. There were, of course, the normal hazards of the road to contend with. After he accepted the call to come to Oldenburg, Joris journeyed there with four or five of his followers. On the way David contracted "scarlet fever" which slowed their progress considerably. They also encountered a persistent "*schnapphahn*" or highwayman. The story of this encounter is fascinating. While the highwayman's appearance was frightening enough, his possession of four or five muskets and remarkable mastery over his horse must have struck terror into the hearts of Joris' followers. They therefore split up to throw the highwayman off Joris' trail, leaving their leader with two companions. The other two or three departed that same evening, causing the highwayman to remark that "they were accompanied by many devils, because they would not remain until the morning, and he could not follow them with a weary horse." The next morning Joris' small company left "before the *schnapphahn* knew it," but before they had travelled far, "he was instantly at the wagon, riding with us, behind us, ahead of us and circling around us." He then rode next to the wagon, looking at the enfeebled David, as if measuring his prey. He told David "I will have you soon," but for some reason he took no further action, except to accompany the group to Stecklenburg. Paradoxically, his presence with the company may have given second thoughts to a disgruntled Batenburg terrorist who apparently had designs of his own on Joris' life.[81]

Travelling by boat could be equally difficult. In order to avoid detection, Joris was forced to stay in the lower decks or locked in small compartments in the larger vessels.[82] Because he was a fugitive, Joris had to find a skipper willing to take on "secretive" cargo. This often meant travelling in less than seaworthy craft. On their return from Breda, Joris and some travelling companions hired a boatman to take them to Dordrecht. His boat was "so full of water, that one must go from the sides to the middle. . . . They pumped very hard, so that the ship would not sink, because it was leaking all over, and was not at all seaworthy." When the passengers expressed their desire not to enter the city of Dordrecht (presumably because it was still daylight), the skipper replied "What kind of people are you, that you do not desire to be in the city?" At this the Anabaptists acquiesced.[83] In spite of occasional difficulties, the water was often a safer place for Joris to hide, whenever the "land became too narrow for him."

An important precaution, regardless of the mode of travel, was to plan the route so that no one place was visited twice. Finding a safe hideaway during a trip required great discretion as well. Frequently inns were used — a sacrifice of caution for comfort. Such places were scouted first, in order to discover the attitude of the host or hostess towards strangers. Several times the travellers refused proffered lodging because they were not sufficiently convinced of its safety. Retiring early and departing before sunrise also reduced visibility in public lodgings. While in one particular inn, David recognised a former acquaintance who could identify him. He and his companions therefore went to bed early. When the acquaintance retired, the hostess refused to give him a candle, and he stumbled about cursing until he could find an empty bed. The fugitives left before daylight and hence avoided identification. If Joris' identity was in danger of detection, he would often be forced to camp out in the open while his companions enjoyed the comfort of an inn. For example, in the summer of 1535 when returning from Strasbourg, Joris was forced to stay in the bush behind an inn. In 1539, Joris was even forced to hide "under the earth" near Deventer until his followers could find better lodging.[84] Understandably then, travelling as a fugitive involved its own set of dangers and anxieties, and Joris frequently showed reluctance to leave the relative security of Delft for the unknown hazards of the road.

By 1537, Joris was a seasoned veteran of detection avoidance and could therefore advise his followers in the art of survival. His advice is seen clearly in letters to his followers and in particular in a work from 1537. In it, Joris counsels against unnecessary speech, and admonishes his fellows to keep quiet unless words were absolutely essential.[85] This advice was necessary because the road on which they travel is narrow, "full of thorns and snares, full of danger." His advice for them is to "look ahead," to guard themselves, to "watch out for the questioners or the accusers who seek to kill you." Therefore, be afraid and "be suspicious" at all times.

The Effects of a Fugitive Existence

In a letter written to an unknown follower, shortly after more than two dozen of Joris' adherents were executed in January 1539, Joris found it necessary to defend himself against the charge that he was promoting the avoidance of martyrdom. He stated

> that I advise no one that he should seek to keep his own life here, or that
> he should run from death or from his enemy or to be frightened of him,
> but instead to desire to stand against him . . . ready to be delivered up as
> sheep to the slaughter.[86]

Joris, as leader of a movement formed largely in the context of martyrdom, did not always feel at ease with his own survival. This tension between martyrdom and survival might have produced symptoms of "survivor's guilt," the hallmarks of which have been described as ambivalence (feeling guilt for surviving but wanting to stay alive), a numbing of the senses to the pain and suffering of others, intense guilt and shame, the suppression of anger, preoccupation with death imagery and, frequently, manifestations of psychosomatic ailments.[87] This was only one of the many stresses and strains which greatly affected the fugitive Joris, and we turn now to a brief consideration of them.

The physical effects of a fugitive lifestyle were often extreme. Joris and his companions suffered frequently from fevers, dysentery and similar illnesses. At least on two occasions, Joris himself lay so still from sickness that his companions were not sure if he was alive or dead.[88] Attics and shops were poorly heated and ventilated and when combined with the lack of movement could result in conditions similar to hypothermia. One incident is worthy of note:

> He was here [Delft, in 1536] nearly through the whole winter, and sat
> upstairs under a low ceiling, and also worked and slept there. He suf-
> fered much cold and much sighing, and it was a wonder, that he did not
> die at this time. . . . And nevertheless he had to be quiet and hide him-
> self, as much as he loved his life and the lives of those with whom he
> was concealed. He lay in great pain, flat as a worm upon the earth, and
> was cast up and down by his loins, without his co-operation, from one
> end to another, just like a worm . . . and was by himself as dead. There-
> fore he was placed at the fire, where he came to himself again, and
> became healthy again.[89]

These conditions were harsh enough on a person with a strong constitution, but Joris was "frail" and his proclivity to a physically rigorous form of asceticism increased his susceptibility to illness.

The psychological effects were even more dramatic. The ever-present anxiety and fear could lead to an emotional or mental breakdown. Although it is nearly impossible to accurately assess the mental health of a person dead for over 400 years, at the very least Joris' frequent visionary episodes can be seen as an emotional outlet for his anxiety. Conditions in the enclosed attics, where several of Joris' visions occurred, may have acted similar to those in "sensory deprivation chambers," where the deprivation of light and/or sound over several hours can frequently result in hallucinations.[90] The deprivation of sleep, dietary factors, and the constant tension therefore contributed to his susceptibility to visions. It seems also that Joris' emotional anguish led to physical convulsions. In 1536, Joris appears to have suffered from an affliction for which he had to quiet himself completely and take some kind of medication.[91]

Naturally the fugitive lifestyle did not lend itself to a good family life or husband-wife relationship. David was frequently separated from his wife and his several children. This of course added to his emotional distress and anxiety. After her release from the Utrecht prison in 1539, Dirkgen returned to Delft. Here she spent two weeks with her husband, but at the end she returned to her children who were situated in another residence for safety. This separation continued for a while, and David became troubled and wrote to her. Dirkgen responded that "she was advised not to journey, until he had obtained a place, then she would come again to him as a good wife is responsible to her husband."[92] David therefore had to find a secure place to re-establish his family. It may have been anxiety over the survival of his family, more than any other factor, which caused him to take temporary refuge in Antwerp in 1539 and then to move permanently to the city of Basel four years later.

Notes

1. Stayer, "Was Dr. Kuehler's," pp. 273-74. The resumption of baptism began with the publication and dissemination of Bernhard Rothmann's *Confession of the Two Sacraments*, starting on November 8, 1533. Matthijs himself was baptised in December of that year in Amsterdam and the practice spread quickly. A portion of this chapter appeared as "Staying Alive: The Methods of Survival as practiced by an Anabaptist Fugitive, David Joris," *MQR*, Vol. LXI, 1987, pp. 46-57.
2. Anonymous, p. 707.
3. "Hoort Broeders int gemeyne/Die mit sonden sijt belaen," *Liedt-Boecxken*, fols. 72r-74r. For Symons, see Mellink, *De Wederdopers*, pp. 209-10. Symons was arrested during the Great Trek and executed on March 30 as one of its leaders.
4. Mellink, *De Wederdopers*, p. 245, suggests Obbe Philips, but the only source, Anonymous, does not provide the identification of the teacher. Anonymous does mention that Obbe had a hand in Joris' ordination and there seems no reason why Anonymous would not name him here if the teacher was indeed Obbe. Another Anabaptist present, N. Kniepers, a woman from Rotterdam, also impressed Joris.
5. Literally *gemeine*. Anonymous, p. 707.
6. There is some debate as to whether Menno Simons had his own covert "Melchiorite period" before his baptism in 1536. See W. Bergsma and S. Voolstra (eds.), *Uyt Babel ghevloden, in Jeruzalem ghetogen* (Amsterdam: Doopsgezinde Historische Kring, 1986), pp. 27-31.
7. Anonymous, p. 709. Philips confirms his involvement in his "Confession," *S.A.W.*, p. 223. The involvement of Damas has generally been ignored by scholars. Obbe Philips was in Delft during the fall to early winter 1534 and Damas van Hoorn may have been in the city on his way from Monnikendam to Middelburg, where he proclaimed the Münsterite message around Christmas, 1534 (Mellink, *De Wederdopers*, pp. 165 and 168). The possibilities of cooperation between Damas and Obbe could indicate that there were no clear distinctions between "radicals" and "pacifists" at this time.

8. Anonymous, p. 709.
9. All of these conferences will be discussed in detail below.
10. For details of these events see below, chapter 5.
11. Zijlstra, *Blesdijk*, p. 6; from A. Matthaeus, *De iure gladii* (Leiden: 1689), p. 663.
12. P. 717.
13. Ibid., p. 708. Strasbourg had been regarded as one of three cities which God had intended to give to the Anabaptists. See "Meister Heinrich Gresbeck's Bericht von der Wiedertäufer in Münster," in C.A. Cornelius, *Geschichtsquellen des Bisthums Münster*, Vol. II (Münster, 1853; new photo-duplicated edition, Münster: Aschendorffsche Verlagsbuchhandlung, 1965), p. 23. Seeing that attempts to establish the kingdom at Münster and Amsterdam, the other two cities, had failed, Strasbourg may have provided the last hope. Leenhardt told Joris that no strangers could stay in the city without the consent of the city fathers. In fact, because of its treatment of Hoffman, Strasbourg soon received the brunt of pessimistic prophecies. See Deppermann, *Hoffman*, p. 311.
14. Anonymous, p. 708. In fact, twenty-five Anabaptists had been arrested there in the late spring of 1535, and over half of them were executed (Irvin B. Horst, *The Radical Brethren: Anabaptism and the English Reformation to 1558* [Nieuwkoop: B. de Graaf, 1972], p. 77). Horst writes that "The report of these three strangers at Flushing, it appears, was greatly exaggerated."
15. Dirkgen, staying at her mother-in-law's, gave birth on February 2, 1536 (Candlemas).
16. *Liedt-Boecxken*, fol. 40v.
17. See below, chapter 6.
18. Neither the city nor Anneken are actually identified by Anonymous. The description of the trips to and from Delft, and of the events themselves, leave little room for doubt about the identity of either. See Packull, "Anna Jansz of Rotterdam, a Historical Investigation of an Early Anabaptist Heroine," *ARG*, Vol. LXXVIII, 1987, pp. 147-72. See Anonymous, pp. 711-12. One of the other believers here was presumably a member of Joris' Delft fellowship, Anthon.
19. Anonymous, p. 719. While the author conceded that Joris fell on occasion just like any other man, he denied that he went about looking for such relationships. This account's denial of any immorality with Anneken seems therefore to carry weight.
20. Ibid., p. 712. Packull suggests that because Joris and his companions wanted to arrive in Delft before sunrise, at 4 a.m., but instead arrived at the gates after the sun had arisen at 5 a.m., that this must have taken place in late April or early August. Packull argues for the former date, while this author contends that the latter time period fits in better with Joris' known activities. See Packull, "Anna Jansz," pp. 153-54.
21. Perhaps she composed this with Joris' poetic help. Joris' hymn is seventeen stanzas long, fols. 44r-57r; Anneken's is thirteen, fols. 80-85r in the *Liedt-Boecxken*.
22. Ibid., fols. 46v-47r.
23. S. Voolstra's contention in *Het Woord is Vlees Geworden: De Melchioritisch-Menniste Incarnatieleer* (Kampen: J.H. Kok, 1982), p. 51, that "David Joris' menswordingsleer vertoont meer overeenkomst met Sebastian Franck, dan met Melchior Hoffman" is based on his reading of Joris' later *Twonder-Boeck*. By the time of the publication of the *Twonder-Boeck* in 1543, however, Joris had become more of a Spiritualist than Anabaptist, while his earlier writings, such as the song cited above, indicate that his early Anabaptist understanding of the Incarnation was formed within the context of the prevalent Melchiorite conception.
24. *Liedt-Boecxken*, fols. 49r-49v.
25. Anonymous, p. 713. Seen also in a 1537 work, *Eene onderwysinge ofte raet / omme die gedachten in den toem tho brengen* (n.p., 1537), fol. 86r-v. The subject of the cor-

rect name of God was to become a topic at the Strasbourg disputation. See the "Twistreden oder Was David Gerg zu Strassburg mitt Melcher Hoffman vnd andern gehandlet," fols. 28v-29r. The original of this document is in the *Jorislade*, Vol. I, *David Joris. Aus eigenen Schriften*, in the manuscript department, Universität Basel. A critical edition by Annette Gottwaldt, is found in Marc Lienhard, Stephen F. Nelson and Hans Georg Rott (eds.), *Quellen zur Geschichte der Täufer*, Vol. XV, *Elsass 3, Stadt Strassburg 1536-1542* (Gerd Mohn: Gutersloher Verlagshaus, 1986), pp. 156-231. The original folio page numbers will be used here.

26. The conference will be discussed in detail below, chapter 6.
27. "At this time, there came to me a letter from a sister, concerning what office I held, or should hold" ("Twistreden," fol. 29v).
28. Included in van Braght, "Het Offer," *BRN*, pp. 70-75, and dated there, by her son, as 1538. On the evidence presented by Nippold ("David Joris," pp. 56-61), Bainton and others have assumed that this letter was the 1536 one instead. See Packull, "Anna Jansz," for the contrary evidence. The 1538 letter called Joris "the winnow in the hands of the Lord," a "knightly leader of Israel," "the beloved of the Lord."
29. The accounts of the vision are included in Anonymous, p. 713, and Blesdijk, *Historia vitae*, pp. 18-20. Like the Anonymous, most of the *Historia vitae* appears to be reliable on questions of historical detail. Interpretation of Joris' teachings in this source, however, must be viewed with caution. If Anonymous wrote with affection to defend Joris, Blesdijk wrote to uncover his father-in-law's shortcomings. Zijlstra's conclusion (*Blesdijk*, pp. 165-71) that Blesdijk's earlier Davidite writings provide more reliable summaries of Joris' doctrine than the *Historia vitae* (written, after all, to distance Blesdijk, now a Reformed Preacher, from his former heresy), ought to be kept in mind.
30. For example, *Hoert, hoert, hoert, Groot Wunder, groot wunder, groot wunder* (n.p., n.d.), fol. 30v.
31. Anonymous, p. 713. According to Blesdijk's account (*Historia vitae*, p. 19), the women turned into doves, as did Joris, and he then mated with them.
32. *Hoert, hoert, hoert*, fol. 1v. Portions of this tract are in Anonymous, pp. 713-714.
33. *Hoert, hoert, hoert*, fol. 62v.
34. Ibid., fol. 30r-v.
35. Anonymous, p. 714.
36. Ibid., pp. 715-16. This is confirmed by a few vision accounts not contained in Anonymous but found in Ubbo Emmius, purportedly from Blesdijk. In one, God embraced and kissed David and said the words "Kiss me, my beloved, with the mouth, for your love is as lovely as wine to me. You are my servant, yes my son, who fulfills my will, and shall lead out my work from beginning to end." See Nippold, "David Joris," p. 73; from Emmius, *Den David Jorischen Gheest in Leven ende Leere* (The Hague: 1603), pp. 54-56. The fact that Joris had been reading the *Canticum Canticorum* in December 1536, as seen in *Hoert, hoert, hoert*, fol. 2, may confirm the validity of this testimony.
37. In 1535, for example, while working in a shop, Joris was nearly identified by members of the court. He took refuge in a thatched shed, which had previously accommodated a victim of the plague (could a safer hideaway be found?). He returned only when he was assured that the coast was clear (Anonymous, p. 719).
38. Ibid., p. 716.
39. Anonymous goes into considerable detail describing an already putrefying cow head which he received on one occasion (p. 719). It appears, however, that this financial support increased with time until in 1544 he could pass himself off quite successfully to the Basel magistrates as a wealthy Dutch merchant.

40. Blesdijk's statement that 27 were executed in 1538 and 31 in 1539 is a result of confusion in dating. Mellink, *De Wederdopers*, p. 203.
41. Nippold, "David Joris," p. 90.
42. Gerard Brandt, *The History of the Reformation*, Vol. I (translated from the Dutch original of 1674, London: 1720-23, reprinted A.M.S. Press, 1979), p. 75; Nippold, "David Joris," p. 92; Blesdijk, *Christlijke Verantwoordinghe ende billijcke nederlegginge des valschen onghegrondeden oordeels, lasterens ende scheldens, by Menno Symonsz in eenen Sendt-brief . . . niet bevonden werden als hy* (n.p., 1610), pp. 29-30.
43. Zijlstra, *Blesdijk*, p. 32.
44. Little is known of this Cloister. Apparently they were a "free brotherhood which lived according to the third Rule of St. Francis." They tended the sick and buried the dead for the city. The Cloister itself was situated in the middle of the city until its destruction in 1578 (H.C. Brouwer, "De verdwenen Kloosters uit de Delftse Binnenstad," in Leeuw, *De Stad Delft*, p. 56).
45. Anonymous, p. 727.
46. Packull, "Anna Jansz," and Anonymous, pp. 728-29.
47. There is in the *Hydeckel* (fol. 135v) a letter written by Joris from Haarlem and dated March 29, 1539.
48. The actual town or city is not known, although circumstantial evidence suggests Groningen. Zijlstra (*Blesdijk*, p. 18) mentions a report there of an Anabaptist who had drawn up some "selsame figuren." Considering Joris' artistic talents which he used to illustrate his own works, this could have been him. One of his companions was Leonard van Dam.
49. Joris described this vision in a written statement which he gave to a follower. Apparently it was later confiscated (Anonymous, p. 729). There is an interesting parallel from the Inquisition against Johannes Becker, burned at Mainz in 1458 as a Free Spirit. Apparently Becker confessed that the Holy Spirit had descended on him "seizing him so that he felt a great pain within. After that time the Spirit often carried him away to the degree that he could do nothing without its guidance and he believed that no man before or after him was or could be so illuminated" (in Robert E. Lerner, *The Heresy of the Free Spirit in the Later Middle Ages* [Berkeley: University of California Press, 1972], p. 178). There were, however, no known Free Spirits by the sixteenth century and the causes for the similarity of experience can only be a matter for speculation.
50. *Twonder-Boeck* (Deventer, 1542-43), fol. lxxxv(r), (chapter 130). He also described this particular inspiration here: "What punishment it be, how and what, the Lord has revealed and given knowledge to me, through his Holy Spirit, early Easter morning 1539. And it spoke to me in this way: 'Write what you hear said.' Yes, I was impelled inwardly thereto. And behold, I wrote, how and what. It will at its time be well revealed, it will now, however, be received with derision (fol. lxxxv[v])."
51. Ibid., fol. lxxxv(r).
52. For example, see Leonard van Dam's vision (Anonymous, pp. 730-31) discussed in detail below, chapter 8 and translated in Appendix IV. Another vision related to Joris: "Look, even in this way will I from henceforth awaken the hearts of Princes, Lords, Kings and mighty ones all against each other, and there will be no end or rest, until they have all perished."
53. A. Hulshof (ed.), "Extracten uit de Rekeningen van het Schoutambacht van Haarlem Betreffende Wederdoopers (1535-39)," *Bijdragen en Mededeelingen van het Historisch Genootschap*, Vol. XLI, 1920, pp. 217-18; Mellink, *De Wederdopers*, pp. 183-85; Anonymous, p. 732.

54. According to Nippold ("David Joris," p. 83) Dirkgen and her child had been banned from the city of Delft on May 20, 1539.
55. De Hullu, *Bescheiden*, p. 276. Anonymous (p. 734) points to the conflict between the Imperial representatives, the Prosecutor-General from The Hague, Reinier Brunt and the Suffragan Bishop on the one side, and the local authorities, especially the sheriff Jan Sondersyl, on the other, for the reason behind Dirkgen's survival. Because Utrecht was a bishopric, such overlapping and competing jurisdictions were a commonplace.
56. They in fact executed only one more Anabaptist, a Münsterite woman whose execution had been delayed until she had given birth. Reinier Brunt, the Prosecutor-General of the Court of Holland, died on October 15, 1539. His death therefore occurred after Dirkgen's release, although he may have been suffering from a prolonged illness. For Brunt's enthusiastic persecution of Anabaptists, see I.H. van Eeghen, "De inquisitie in Amsterdam," in Margriet de Roever and Boudewijn Bakker (eds.), *Woelige tijden: Amsterdam in de eeuw van de beeldenstorm* (Amsterdam: Gemeentearchief Amsterdam, 1986), pp. 73-82.
57. Anonymous, pp. 734-75.
58. Available only in Blesdijk, *Historia vitae*, pp. 81-84; summarised in Nippold, "David Joris," pp. 115-16. See also Anonymous, p. 735.
59. Blesdijk, *Historia vitae*, p. 82.
60. Nippold, "David Joris," p. 117.
61. This was in spite of the ease with which he could be identified, on account of a distinctive long red beard.
62. Meynart van Emden was also worth one hundred pounds. Mellink, *De Wederdopers*, p. 215; Karel Vos, "Kleine Bijdragen," *Doopsgezinde Bijdragen*, Vol. LIV, 1917, p. 106. In 1537-38 two women received twenty-five gulden for informing the sheriff of Haarlem where Jan van Batenburg had stayed in the city (Mellink, *De Wederdopers*, pp. 182-83). On January 9, 1535, the Leiden authorities had also promised the same amount for information leading to the capture of Anabaptists (ibid., p. 195).
63. "Aan hem schonken zij hun vertrouwen en zij bekenden toen allen, zodat de schout later uit zijn mond alles voor burgemeesters en schepenen kon optekenen" (A. Hulshof, "Extracten," pp. 208-10 and 218; Mellink, *De Wederdopers*, p. 184).
64. Anonymous, p. 728.
65. This may have included using recognised code words, such as "The Lord be with you," to which the other Anabaptist would respond, "And with you" (de Hullu, *Bescheiden*, p. 264), from the confession of Johan Morveldinck, a Batenburger (he also called himself a Davidite) in 1542.
66. Anonymous, p. 733; *DAN*, Vol. II, p. 13. Jansz had only been baptised the previous year by a "Claes with a lame hand." Joris had, according to the account, warned Jansz against attempting to rescue the children.
67. Anonymous, p. 728. She was apparently a sister of the Magdalene Order who was related to the family. The *Magdelenzusters* were not a true order, but a group of sisters united by the loose band of a common lifestyle, according to the Third Order of the Franciscans. Most were connected to hospitals and guesthouses, to help travellers and the sick (Brouwer, "De Verdwenen Kloosters," p. 55).
68. Anonymous, p. 734.
69. Mellink, *De Wederdopers*, pp. 182-83, Anonymous, p. 736. This latter source describes an incident, when, on a trip to Breda (South Netherlands) in 1539, the driver of Joris' hired wagon and Joris got into a shouting match because the former wanted to drive through Leiden, not through The Hague. Joris threatened to return by foot if the driver insisted on passing through Leiden.

70. Anonymous tells us, "they must entrust everything to unknown people, who themselves did not know one another, so that no harm could have occurred, as might have happened if they were known by the others. They might have indeed guessed or thought it out for themselves, but they desired not to know" (p. 728).
71. *DAN*, Vol. II, p. 13, Anonymous, p. 733. "One has seen openly, in city and lands, that his disciples so loved and valued him, that they suffered the pains of martyrdom on his account. They would not tell where he was, saying that they knew where he was, but would not tell" (Anonymous, p. 723).
72. See Anonymous, pp. 736-37, where several instances are described, including when a potential wealthy benefactor in Breda was dissuaded from his planned support by his wife.
73. Ibid., p. 737. The Junker apparently had helped to besiege the Anabaptist kingdom at Münster in 1535, but later felt remorse for his participation.
74. Ibid., p. 735.
75. Mellink, *De Wederdopers*, pp. 204-205. Jansz was evidently a Batenburger. Reported briefly in Anonymous, p. 732, where these prisoners were identified as Davidites who were "rescued at night through the help of a courageous man." There is also evidence that Obbe Philips had also escaped from a prison in Groningen (*DAN*, Vol. I, p. 175).
76. *DAN*, Vol. V, p. 45.
77. Returning from Breda, Joris and van Dam stayed in Rotterdam, where a fog concealed their identity from some Rotterdam magistrates. A similar incident occurred shortly afterwards in Delft (Anonymous, p. 737).
78. The anonymous account describes two incidents when these attempts nearly backfired, pp. 712 and 735.
79. Ibid., p. 711.
80. This likewise occurred to those who harboured Menno Simons. In January 1539 Tjaard Renicx was executed for hiding Menno (Krahn, *Menno Simons*, p. 58).
81. Anonymous, pp. 720-21.
82. Ibid., p. 711. On arrival at one town, perhaps Den Briell, in 1536, an older sympathiser had a great deal of difficulty prying off the lock to Joris' hiding place, although he eventually succeeded.
83. Ibid., p. 736.
84. Ibid., p. 735. The exact meaning of this phrase is not clear.
85. *Eene onderwysinge*, fols. 86v-87r.
86. Karl Vos (ed.), "Brief van David Joris, 1539," *Doopsgezinde Bijdragen*, Vol. LIV, 1917, pp. 164-65.
87. Robert J. Lifton, *Death in Life: Survivors of Hiroshima* (New York: Random House, 1967), pp. 480-541. Extreme forms of survivor's guilt could lead to depression and/or paranoia, the latter representing "a struggle to achieve a magical form of vitality and power over death" (ibid., p. 514). Joris frequently referred to a personal mastery over death in his writings. For Joris, "death is now the last terrifying enemy, which shall be brought to nothing or slain in the victory of the man Jesus Christ" (*Hoert, hoert, hoert*, fol. 30r).
88. For example, during the trip to Oldenburg, it was recorded that "In the bed he was so quiet, that no one knew, if he had lain as a dead man the whole night, without any knowledge, thought, sight, hearing or understanding" (Anonymous, p. 720).
89. Ibid., p. 709.
90. M. Zuckerman, "Reported Sensations and Hallucinations in Sensory Deprivation," in Wolfram Keup (ed.), *Origin and Mechanisms of Hallucinations* (New York: Plenum

Press, 1970), pp. 133-45. See, in particular, van Dam's and Joris' visions, recounted by Anonymous, pp. 730-31 (see Appendix IV).

91. Anonymous, pp. 711-12. Joris' convulsions may also have been the result of some form of physical ailment, or again a psychosomatic symptom of "death anxiety" or "survivor's guilt." Many herbal remedies were hallucinogenic, although there is no way to identify the ingredients referred to here.

92. Ibid., pp. 735-36. In a work written in 1539, Joris in fact complained, "SJet / des menschen vianden synt sijn huysgesin / sijn eygen vrienden ende gebroders, Naesten / end die oeck in sijn schoot slaept en liefft heeft" (*Een seer schone tractaet off onderwijs van mennigerley aert der menschen vianden* [Deventer: Albert Pafraet, 1539], fol. A3r).

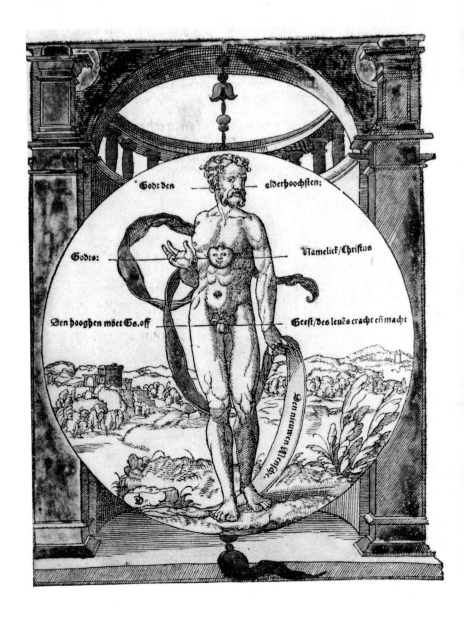

David Joris, "The New Man" from *Wonder Book*, Part II, fol. 211v°. Courtesy
The Mennonite Library, University of Amsterdam.

CHAPTER FIVE

Joris' Early Theology, 1534-36

Before examining David Joris' later life, we should consider his thought and career as an important Anabaptist leader in the Netherlands. Among the more important issues is Joris' position with respect to events in Münster, particularly his thoughts regarding the radical program as spelled out by Bernhard Rothmann. While no evidence exists to confirm that Joris was ever in Münster, there is no doubt that he had knowledge of the Münsterite program, for in the winter of 1534-35 he participated in the Waterland conference where Rothmann's tracts *On the Restitution, On Vengeance*, and possibly *Concerning the hiddenness of the Word of God* were discussed.[1]

The limited evidence available indicates that Joris opposed aspects of the Münster program from the beginning. Moreover, his hesitancy to accept rebaptism in 1534 can be interpreted as an indication of his opposition to Jan Matthijs' usurpation of Melchiorite leadership and reinstatement of baptism following Hoffman's two-year suspension. Furthermore, despite his sympathetic attitude, Joris had also refused to join in the "Great Trek." Münsterites elsewhere in the Netherlands at this time were more and more participating in senseless actions which could only lead to failure, and this situation in general may very well have contributed to Joris' opposition to Münster radicalism. A Münsterite emissary, for example, in the winter of 1534 had gathered a group of several hundred Anabaptists at 't Zandt (in Groningen) to march under Anabaptist banners in support of Münster. Leadership of the crowd was taken over by Harmen Schoenmaker, who zealously raved "Beat to death, beat to death monks, priests and all authorities across the whole world, and especially our authorities! Better yourselves, better yourselves, your redemption is now at hand!" While Schoenmaker enraptured these potential Münsterites, his invective directed their energy away from Münster itself.[2] When Münster finally fell in the summer of 1535, Joris stepped in to raise a "new banner" around which all Anabaptists could rally.

In order to comprehend Joris' position regarding Münster more fully, it is necessary to compare his early writings with those of the principal exponent of Münster Anabaptism, Bernhard Rothmann. As background to this, Joris' relationship to the early Melchiorite movement can be clarified by an overview of Melchior Hoffman's teaching on subjects relating to Münster.

Notes to Chapter Five are found on pages 106-11.

89

These avenues of investigation are necessary to a clearer conception of both the Münster debacle as a whole and Joris' role in this movement in particular.[3] The relationship between the Dutch Melchiorites in the Netherlands and the Münsterites may be clarified[4] by considering, first, hermeneutics; second, the concept of Restitution and the Sword; and third, polygamy.[5]

Hermeneutics

Melchior Hoffman's hermeneutic informed the Scriptural reading of the entire Melchiorite movement. According to Klaus Deppermann, Hoffman stood as "the prophet against the learned." As an artisan and lay-preacher, Hoffman found himself in conflict with formally educated theologians and reformers. Unlike the learned, he emphasised spiritual discernment by disparaging educated opinion, for "God's wisdom is not perceived with fleshly eyes, but only with spiritual eyes, which do not look upon the person, nor upon the position of rank."[6] In short, Hoffman's interpretation of Scripture assumed a sharp distinction between letter and spirit, where "the spiritual meaning lay concealed under the letter." The thrust of this approach meshed well with popular anticlerical sentiment, a fundamental feature of the early Dutch Reformation. For Hoffman a true understanding of Scripture came only by means of the Spirit active in the hearts of the children of God.[7] In practice this meant Hoffman and his followers must look beyond the literal meaning of individual texts to a comprehension of the spiritual meaning as a whole. For Hoffman then, the entire enterprise was the mystery of Christ's work in history as revealed in Scripture, particularly its prophetic passages depicting the course of events, past, present and future. The Old and New Testaments presented a mine of allegory, spiritual types, symbols and images for Hoffman. His Christocentric hermeneutic was at root oriented toward expectations of a return of Christ and the coming kingdom. This, when viewed in apocalyptic terms as the coming judgement on the evils in the church and Christendom, is the key to his theological stance.[8]

Related to this spirit-under-the-letter motif was Hoffman's use of the "Cloven Hoof." The "Cloven Hoof" analogy provided a key to go beyond outward contradictions in Scripture.[9] It permitted a retention of the essential unity of the Word of God despite the many opposing statements within it. Therefore, in order to understand the Bible correctly, one must "let both parts of the Hoof [i.e., the contradictory statements] stand and find the middle."[10] To do this, one needed the apocalyptical "Key of David" which was given to all those who lived in the pure fear of God.[11] This tool meant spiritual illumination for unlocking the secrets of Scripture, especially the apocalyptical passages.[12] With the Key of David, one could both explain the apparent contradictions between the Old and New Testaments and discover the fulfillment of Scriptural images in the present age.

Unlike Hoffman, Rothmann approached the Scriptures as a trained theologian and preacher. Although he must have read and understood

Hoffman's tracts and hermeneutic,[13] it is evident that the propagandist for the Münster kingdom altered them to suit the changing circumstances in that city. Above all the situation in Münster seemed for Rothmann analogous to the situation of the Israelite kingdom as depicted in the Old Testament. One therefore finds in Rothmann's works a peculiar Old Testament "realism," particularly in its application to a theocratic state.

Rothmann stated that neither human wisdom nor the traditional commentaries were adequate to understand the true meaning of Scripture. Because of this notion the Münsterites burned all books save the Bible.[14] Rothmann moreover agreed with Hoffman that the true meaning of the Word of God lay hidden under the letter, as if in a locked cabinet:

> However the Sanctuary and treasure of his [God's] wisdom he has so concealed in the Scriptures, that no one can come to it through any kind of strength, understanding or wisdom, but only if he opens and enters the chest with the dual keys of the keeping of the commandments and of the fulfilment of the will of God.[15]

The keys were given to those "who fear God with all their heart, who do his will and are always so inclined."[16] So far, then, Rothmann followed Hoffman in that the Scriptures were unlocked not in intellectual study but in seeking to live according to the commands of God.

The major difference between Rothmann and Hoffman lay in the questions of the relationship between the Spirit and the Letter and of the "Cloven Hoof" motif. Although Rothmann affirmed that neither vain philosophy nor the dead letter were in themselves sufficient to interpret Scripture, he defined the "living understanding of the Spirit" rather differently than Hoffman. Specifically, Rothmann disavowed the use of the spiritual meaning of Scripture, for he believed it could be used to spiritualize the Kingdom of God and to deny the validity of the physical restitution of that kingdom on earth.[17] Therefore the key to understanding the Word of God was not in a spiritual meaning which could negate its application to the socio-political arena, but in finding the "inward meaning" which brought out the truth of the letter.[18] What was central in Rothmann's thought was the applicability of the Scriptures to a concrete social, economic and political situation in the present age.

Rothmann's handling of Hoffman's "Cloven Hoof" analogy was equally adept. He discarded Hoffman's exegetical usage and instead reshaped the "Cloven Hoof" notion into a tool to divide history. The one side of the Hoof signified the time of Christ's incarnation and suffering and the suffering of his people. The other side was a metaphor for Christ's resurrection and ascension and the deliverance and victory of his people over their enemies. The "two-edged sword" was therefore used to so differentiate the two periods in history and this act was the "noblest art in the Scriptures."[19] Presumably a correct application of this "Cloven Hoof" analogy would for Rothmann lead to the conclusion that the time of suffering was past and the period of deliverance was at hand.

Much of David Joris' hermeneutic was formed within the context of the popular reform movement in the Netherlands of the mid-1520s. The anticlericalism of that movement served to reinforce Joris' disavowal of clerical monopoly over religious truth and bolstered his acceptance of the responsibility of the common man or artisan to read the Scriptures for himself.[20] Joris approached the Scriptures as a theologically untrained artisan, in much the same way as Hoffman himself.[21] Hence traditional exegetical tools do not enter consciously into Joris' hermeneutic. Like Hoffman and Rothmann, he too rejected the place of human wisdom in Bible study. Presumably Joris reflected the prejudices of the artisans when he turned against the usefulness of classical languages in the study of the Scriptures. In a song which may belong to his early reform period, Joris remarked that the languages of Hebrew, Greek and Latin had come under the judgement of God, as seen in their inclusion in the sign placed upon the cross of Christ.[22] The Holy Spirit had now come for all contemporary believers to sow the seed of the Word of God in the Dutch language:[23]

> But just as with its advent in the East,
> God gave the first faith to the Hebrews,
> Which gave way to the advent in the South,
> Through the Apostles to the Greek people,
> And again gone down in the West,
> Through the Latin, the Roman nest,
> So it stands to expect it in Dutch words,
> Which shall shine eternally,
> Dutch must be highly praised.[24]

The goal of Joris' hermeneutic was from the beginning directed toward a form of personal perfection. Emphasis on the mortification of the "old man" (inclinations to sin) was a prominent feature of early reform writers and Joris maintained this perspective throughout his career. Scriptural truths in Joris' early hermeneutical framework were applied to the mortification of the flesh and spiritual renewal, not for piecing together the eschatological puzzle and its meaning for reform in society at large.

As an Anabaptist leader, Joris insisted on the need for spiritual discernment when reading Scripture. Like Hoffman, he believed that the written word concealed the mystery of God's revelation. After the fall of Münster, Joris devoted himself to maintaining the charismatic leadership of the early Melchiorite movement, believing it to be an organising principle for the scattered and disunited movement. The whole tenor of Joris' writings is therefore quite distinct from Rothmann's trained exegesis and contains more claims to charismatic authority than even Hoffman's prophetic stance. This is clearly evident in the treatise dated before his vision episode of December 1536. Joris' sense of prophetic calling therefore was at the very least already present in seminal form several months before the climactic vision of 1536.[25] His hermeneutic was to a large extent shaped within this increasing sense of divine calling.

Joris concurred with both Hoffman and Rothmann that human wisdom or learning was inadequate to promote the goal of the Scriptures:

> The Lord give you much wisdom and power from above, in order to obtain the victory, which must take place not with knowledge of the letter but of the Spirit.[26]

Where Hoffman and Rothmann had restricted this belief largely to the use of commentaries in the study of Scripture, Joris took the concept a step further. He wrote that believers were to "stand still," for "your perfection"

> has begun without your wisdom, will or resolve, it shall also be completed indeed without them. Stand fast on this, fit that you merely fulfill the Word, and the same Word, which he, blessed, has commanded, that is to keep the faith, hope and love with patience; to become humble, meek and longsuffering, simple, poor and innocent as children. Work to this end, hunger, thirst and study to this end. Further, let go all other wisdom of the letters or intelligence. Only be obedient and faithful in the least as in the greatest.[27]

While similar to Rothmann's idea that obedience was the key that unlocks the Scriptures, Joris' language approaches the medieval mystics' concept of *Gelassenheit*.[28] In Joris' perspective, the intellect of the believer was to become passive when reading or hearing the Word of God. The believer was instead to become as a child, intent only on obeying the message. Joris' hermeneutic, therefore, primarily had a personal or psychological meaning.

Joris' stress on spiritual authority led him to downplay the use of proof-texts as supports for his teaching, for not everyone would agree with their interpretation. The Spirit of God, however would overcome such disagreements.

> See, I began to set the texts in the margins as evidence. But the Spirit was adverse to my doing any more of this, therefore I stopped. Besides, there came on me a fatigue in my body which has not improved to this time. Each one be careful that he has the Spirit, through which he will be able to judge best. For although I have after all set up some texts here, the first ones that have occurred to me, they surely will not be received by everyone to the same end. Therefore receive the Spirit, and pay attention indeed to him.[29]

Joris' skepticism about the use of proof-texts may have come about as a result of his experience at the Waterland Conference. When Joris tried to counter the whole program behind the Münsterite experiment with his contention that "it was against the Word of God," Damas van Hoorn (a supporter of the radical approach) simply responded that the Münsterites had just as much Biblical authority on their side.[30]

After the destruction of the Münster experiment, Joris redefined the

"Cloven Hoof," Keys of David and two-edged sword within his prophetic and lay-mystic context. The two-edged sword was not to be applied to the text of Scripture to divide the letter from the spirit as in Hoffman; nor to history to discern the time of suffering from the time of victory as in Rothmann. Instead, the sword was to be turned inward to the hearts of his readers to "cut them free from all lusts."[31] The key of David performed the same function for the mind of Joris' contemporary associates as the final revelation of Christ in the eschatological drama:

> See, the books will be opened before the face of the firmament and they will see everything, that is, the veil over their minds will be removed. It [the veil] had covered over and concealed the fleshly eyes because of the darkness or roguishness of the world. This must once more be known, it must happen to us first through the key of David, blessed is he who has found it.[32]

The key of David was the supra-rational illumination which Joris himself had received. This work of the Spirit was the only basis for true unity among the children of God, for, as Joris saw it, the Spirit alone could overcome the many differences in Scriptural interpretation. Therefore, while Joris was willing to accommodate himself to others' interpretations on nearly every other issue, his own inspiration was not a matter for discussion.[33] In Joris' scheme, one could understand the "letter" only if one experienced the enlightenment of the Spirit of God, but someone who did not "have the Spirit, . . . also does not have the letter."[34] Joris' hermeneutic, therefore, was based on an experience that relied on a passive (*gelassen*) reception of the Word of God without necessarily engaging the rational thought processes. Those with the same Spirit would of necessity listen to and obey the human vessel through whom God chose to communicate. On the basis of this brief summary of Joris' position, it is clear that he went beyond Hoffman's claims for authority and stood more squarely in the line of Jan Matthijs rather than in the more trained approach of Bernhard Rothmann.

As we will presently see, while Joris applied Hoffman's "Cloven Hoof" method in a manner consistent with Hoffman's usage, he did so with a different corpus in mind. Rather than using this idea to find a middle ground between two opposing statements in Scripture, Joris applied the "Cloven Hoof" to find a middle position between the teachings of the two main Melchiorite exegetes, Hoffman and Rothmann. This is illustrated in Joris' position on the restitution and the sword.

The Restitution and the Sword

While the theme of the restitution, the "restoration of all things," was a central *leitmotif* for many radical Reformers and Anabaptists, this was especially significant for the followers of Melchior Hoffman in the Low Countries. Hoffman's expectations of reform of church and society were based

Uoozbeelt / Beeldt oft Letterlijcke figuer des Bzuyts Chziſti.

Engraving by Hieronymus Wiericx, after David Joris, ''The True Restoration or Restitution, the Image of the Bride of Christ'' from *Wonder Book*, 1551 edition (n.p., [1584]), Part III, fol. iiiv°. Courtesy The Mennonite Library, University of Amsterdam. This illustration was not included in the first edition.

on his apocalyptic conception of history, and his hermeneutic was inextrica-
bly interwoven with it, serving to illuminate future apocalyptic events.[35]
Hoffman divided history into three ages: (1) the Old Testament Age of the
Law (Father); (2) the New Testament Age, when Christ brought a higher
spiritual law and restored man's freedom of will; and (3) the present age,
when the power of the Holy Spirit has broken through in the hearts of believers.[36] The second and third ages were further subdivided into seven periods, corresponding to the visions of sevens in the Apocalypse.[37] Although
Hoffman did not in any of the available sources use the term "Restitution,"
it is nevertheless clear that he expected the Church of his own day to be
restored to a condition more like that of the New Testament.[38] It is important
to understand that Hoffman saw the blowing of the sixth trumpet as stated in
Daniel to refer to 1526. The following seven years, Hoffman believed,
would therefore involve the preaching of the two witnesses, "Enoch and
Elijah" and the great persecution of believers. At the end of this period of
persecution — in the year 1533 — would be the final judgement.[39]

Unfortunately for Hoffman and his followers his views on resisting
ungodly authorities or the taking of vengeance on the persecutors of Christ's
true followers were ambiguous. While Hoffman in contrast to Jan Matthijs
desired "a revolution from above [which involved] a military breakthrough
with the help of the ruling magistracies of the free Imperial cities,"[40] at the
same time there seemed to be a tendency that could lend itself to a theocratic
interpretation in his writings. In particular, if Anabaptists managed to gain
lawful control over a city government (as happened in Münster), then they
would find themselves as the legal magistracy. There was in Hoffman's
writings no effective brake to hinder Anabaptist magistrates from imple-
menting the restitution by force of arms.

Although Rothmann was familiar with Hoffman's works, his concept
of restitution was uniquely designed to suit the needs of the kingdom of God
in Münster. For example, while Rothmann maintained the tripartite schema
of history, he realigned this historical outline so as to emphasize the Old
Testament theocracy. Rothmann's first age went from Adam to Noah, the
second from Noah to the present, and the third age began with the creation
of the New Heaven and New Earth.[41] The second age was the "time of
Esau" or the time of suffering for the saints.

For Rothmann, a part of the Restitution actually had already taken
place in Christ who had restored everything lost by Adam. This restitution,
however, was incomplete for Rothmann, for after his ascension Christ ruled
merely "inwardly in the Spirit's power and under the cross" while the
powers of evil continued to rule the world.[42] Restitution therefore meant for
Rothmann that the kingdom of Christ and his saints would only become visible once the "Palace of David which had fallen is restored and rebuilt." If
the "time of reviving and deliverance of the true Israelites from the violent
and murdering Babylon and the retribution of the same" took place, "then

shall the Lord come."[43] For the Münsterites, the Restitution involved the physical restoration of the Kingdom of God on earth as it had been displayed in Israel. This implied judgement of the godless but for Rothmann this would not necessarily occur at the end of time.[44] With this argument in mind Rothmann, fully believing in the viability of Münster, found a way to rationalise the taking up of arms for the defense of the kingdom.

According to Rothmann, therefore, Anabaptists had not only the right to defend themselves, but were assigned the role of vengeance,[45] as he explained:

> It was . . . the intention of our hearts in our baptism, that we would suffer for Christ, whatever men did to us. But it had pleased the Lord, and still pleases him, that now we and all Christians at this time may not only ward off the force of the godless with the sword, but also, that he has put the sword into our hands to avenge all injustice and evil over the entire world.[46]

Believers were therefore to "let the apostolic weapons fall to the ground" and take up "the armour of David" in order to establish "the future peaceful Kingdom of Solomon" by cleansing the earth of all unrighteousness.[47] The Restitution was then the reign of Christ and his saints, once "unrighteousness had been eradicated by the righteous David."[48] Then God's people would possess the earth and all creatures "shall be freed to the glory of the children of God." What had been lost with the coming of sin and Adam's fall would be restored and all material wealth could be used in the service of the children of God.[49]

Joris, like the rest of the early Melchiorites, was caught in an apocalyptic vortex resulting from both socio-economic conditions and the preaching and writing of Hoffman and apostolic emissaries from Münster. From about 1531, Joris' songs reflect contact with a strong apocalyptic message, one that was proclaimed most vociferously by the Melchiorites. Considering that Hoffman's suspension of baptism blurred the lines between his followers and non-Anabaptist Reformers, Joris' apparent acceptance of Hoffman's apocalyptical message indicates that Joris had already become an Anabaptist sympathiser by 1531. Joris wedded the Melchiorite eschatological scheme to his previously formed framework of reform thought, with the apocalyptic message adding urgency to the earlier theme of the mortification of the flesh. His adoption of early Melchiorite apocalypticism was thorough and extensive and can be traced in his writings from 1531 to at least 1539.[50]

It is telling in this context that Joris' songs from 1533 to 1535 reflect both a pronounced apocalyptical theme and a continuation of his early reform pietism.[51] The nearness of the end, the judgement of God against the godless, and the restoration of the children of God to their rightful place of glory were prominent themes. Indeed, Joris may have accepted the Melchiorite prediction that 1533 would witness the return of Jesus Christ.

It is of interest too that during the final weeks of the siege at Münster,

Joris wrote two more songs while hiding near Strasbourg, and these serve to underscore Joris' attitude to the failure of the Kingdom. At the end of June, 1535 he wrote:

> These are now truly dangerous times,
> When the elect of God stand in worry,
> But God will justly fight for them.
> Their days will be shortened according to his promise.
> Oh, that the disciples would joyfully consider this . . .
> All the blessed of God must drink
> the clear red wine from the cup of bitterness;
> But God shall pour out yeast for the godless,
> Which they will spit out, vomit and fall to eternal death.
> Grasp understanding, O beloved of Christ,
> Hold fast your faith and spread God's honour. . . .[52]

A few days later Joris repeated his musical plea, this time to encourage his brothers in the light of an apparent victory of wickedness:

> The Lord is King in Israel,
> Of this we rejoice from full hearts,
> He will quickly come to us soon,
> To leave us nevermore . . .
> You poor of this naked world,
> Do not become faint-hearted.
> You will yet reign with great might,
> You will tread down the Serpent,
> Your eyes will yet see the proud, godless lion
> which was one with Babel,
> trod down on the earth as dung.
> When their time is ended,
> Then you will greatly rejoice.[53]

In 1535 after the fall of Münster Joris composed a tract reflecting on the meaning of true restitution. This treatise, entitled *Of the Divine and Godly Ordinance*, represents an attempt to reinterpret Münsterite expectations of restitution under new, drastically altered circumstances. He began this work with the tripartite scheme developed by Hoffman and Rothmann, affirming that "God has created all things in three according to his image" and that "all things have their perfection in threes."[54] However, Joris took this notion from the historical-social-political plane to the arena of individual minds and hearts.[55] In Joris' thinking there were three interpretations of the restitution, the first of which incorporated the belief that everything had been restored at the time of Christ and his apostles and that all the images and figures of the Old Testament had been fulfilled or established in the apostolic church of the first century. In this view Joris expected the final restitution to be nothing more than the restoration . . . of what has fallen and crumbled away through the fall produced by the Antichrist. The same [i.e., the apostolic church of Christ] must yet be re-established now, but only in the same nature and ordinance as had happened with the Apostles.[56]

The second view of Restitution for Joris was similar to that held by the Münsterites, and particularly by Rothmann. Münster, in Joris' mind, had been a "great light and joyous brilliance" and its inhabitants

all believed it to be the restoration, and they also thought that they were to exercise it entirely outwardly in full power and might over the whole earth, ruling over all powers and forces of the world, which they thought indeed to bring under themselves in the name of Jesus. And they had faith in God, blessed in Eternity, hoping for freedom, space, refreshment and mercy.[57]

This excerpt confirms Joris' empathy with the motives of the Münsterites. As a post-Münster leader, then, Joris' task was to find a way to account for the downfall of the kingdom and to maintain what he believed to be the essential features of Melchiorite faith. He did this by focussing on the concept of the "Cloven Hoof," in other words by taking a mediatory position between the views of Hoffman and Rothmann. As Joris put it,

There are many who have written concerning the Restitution, who indeed have come to two parts, although one has run southward and the other northward and they fight against each other. I wish to join these together in a true middle way, so that we might have one mind and have peace. In this way is Satan excluded. This is surely the will of the Lord.[58]

Joris argued that his concept of Restitution had formerly been ignored and as a result the Münster attempt "had no full power nor might, nor could it survive."[59] He disagreed with Rothmann on the importance of the Old Testament images in the Restitution. Where for Rothmann the images of the Old Testament kingdom contained in themselves hidden truth which would be restored literally at the last day,[60] Joris countered that these images (Adam, Noah, Abraham, Isaac, Jacob, and of course David and Solomon, of whom much was made in Münster) had no "true nature or perfection" in themselves and therefore could not produce a restoration. They, for Joris, merely pointed, imperfectly, to Christ.[61] The true or third restoration must therefore be based on the first, that

everything that we have lost through Adam's disobedience by the devil has been restored through the obedience of Christ. . . . Whoever now believes in the name of Jesus, that he is Christ and calls upon him as his head and Lord and shows himself obedient, in this same person all things shall be restored and renewed and changed out of flesh into spirit, out of death into life, out of the earthly into the heavenly nature, until he has become again the true likeness and image of God through Christ

Jesus by grace, just as God had made Adam in the beginning as an image of God.[62]

For Joris, then, the most important restitution involved the return of individual believers to a pre-fall Adamic purity and innocence which could be neither exclusively the Melchiorite vision of the New Testament Church nor the Münsterite conception of an earthly kingdom. Once this state of Adamic innocence had been achieved in all believers and they donned the "pure Bride's garment," then and only then would the second restitution in its glory be realised.

> See, this [the putting on of the Bride's garment] must be completely fulfilled in us before the promise of the Father or the blessedness can be openly seen and all things be restored in their first condition.[63]

Joris, like Rothmann, expected the physical restoration of the kingdom to take place when "we will receive the glorious divine freedom of the children of God." Münster's defeat was rationalised by Joris as the failure of its inhabitants to fully incorporate the "spiritual restitution" so that in his view Jan van Leiden's kingdom crumbled more from internal spiritual decay than by external siege.[64] Joris could therefore also take a stand against those who criticised the concept of a physical restitution. These critics he described as

> the counter-spirits or opponents who must hold their proud tongues here and no longer oppose the promise and glory of God or the kingdom of our Lord Jesus Christ in its power. For only the saints or little ones can judge, as it is written. Yes, only they will inhabit it, for to no other is it given.[65]

Joris therefore added to contemporary thought an element of postponement. Before the final restitution of the children of God to their earthly reign he believed a delay was necessary to allow the third or spiritual restitution to take place. Joris set forth the implications of this for his fellow Melchiorites in the following statement:

> I say to you once more, although the whole earth and everything that is in the world and all its fullness belong to the Lord and to his anointed ones or children, nevertheless, we must forego all of it and be dead and resigned in everything . . . until the time of the renewal and restoration which first must be renewed and restored in all of us together.[66]

Considering the failure of the attempt to reform society in Münster and the dangers inherent in a visible dissenters' church in a hostile society, Joris eventually arrived at a third option, the renewal of the inner man.[67]

Joris, within this context and because of his further actions, can perhaps be best understood as one of the few consistent advocates of pacifism among early Melchiorite leaders. That his notion of inner renewal was one of the initial stages of his developing ethic of non-violence is clear from the anonymous biographer's account of the 1534-35 Waterland Conference. There is a definite self-serving tone, an "I told you so," in the Waterland account and moreover no hint to contradict its main contention that Joris opposed the Münsterite representatives' program of violence. When the question of the use of the sword was initially raised, Joris likely deferred to the more experienced leaders of the movement because he had been ordained just prior to the meeting, and not because he was in any way non-committal. When he did voice his opinion it was that "he could not agree that one should smite with the sword." As to the problem of freeing the imprisoned brethren — a situation analogous to that of Münster — Joris answered that "such was not in accordance with the example of the Lord Jesus, nor was it taught by the Apostles. Instead [we are] to bear the cross and suffer every injustice."[68]

Most likely Joris' response reflected his own fear of being drawn into hopeless and dangerous plots. This can be clearly seen in the verbal confrontation between Joris and a certain Damas at the conference.[69] Damas responded to Joris' initial remarks by claiming that Rothmann's position was based on God's word (and vindicated by means of direct revelations in Münster) "which is spoken as well from the prophets as from the apostles, and abides just as certainly in eternity, what do you say to this?" Joris in turn replied, "I say nothing against it [Münster], except that I have to study it first, and will let it take its course."[70] Joris could ultimately not agree with the final conclusion of the conference, which evidently supported Münster, but he was willing to keep quiet as long as everyone involved agreed to pray for a deeper understanding of this issue.

Curiously, Joris' pacifistic stance was not deemed by his contemporaries as contradictory to the apocalyptic expectations that influenced Joris' thinking throughout this period. Like many others, Joris believed that ultimately the blood of the saints would be avenged. If nothing else the evidence suggests that apocalypticism in itself was not thought of as violent or revolutionary, although it was at the same time probably considered volatile and unstable in its ideological function for Joris. In 1531 after the martyrdom of Trijpmaker, for example, he stressed the ideal of patient suffering. By 1535 after the slaughter of the Münsterites, Joris had so intensified the vengeance motif in his songs that the theme of patient suffering was largely discarded or barely visible. The shift of thinking from peaceful martyrdom to concerted revenge is clear for example in the following Joris text:

> Complaint, mourning and woe will you eternally receive,
> The judgement of hell, which you have not feared.
> The end comes over the four corners of the earth,
> The end, yes, the end falls on you with might.
> The righteous will be snatched out of this evil generation.
> Oh Behold, God's scythe will strike all of you
> And it shall violently cut you down to the earth,
> So that neither branch nor root will remain.

The Day of wrath, [and] complaint, the Day of Vengeance,
Has come now over Zion, God's beloved City.
It will, however, cast its shadow over the Lord's enemies,
His burnished sharp sword will cut, yes indeed,
it is grasped to hew, to strike all who are drunk,
and who are unconcerned and glad.
You who have loved your life above God,
The burnished sharp sword will cut through . . .
For God will avenge the death of the saints.[71]

This excerpt suggests that Joris was writing his verses from the broad context of the Münster experiment. With this in mind, Rothmann's *On Vengeance* serves here as a comparison piece and possible inspiration for Joris' song text.

Joris' unique approach to the question of vengeance is perhaps best seen in his reflections on the Münsterite call that Anabaptists meet at designated places under "banners of righteousness" which were to have proclaimed the start of the Restitution. As Joris remarked,

But we thank God through Jesus Christ, who has given us victory in his name. Namely, to prove obedient to the death of the cross and proceed to the perfection or victory. With that have the flags or banners of righteousness been raised up, under which we all must be gathered before they shall be unfurled visibly over all in full power and majesty, to the punishment of all disobedience, disbelief and evil.[72]

Only after believers had gathered under spiritual banners and achieved personal perfection could they hoist the flag proclaiming the final vengeance and societal purification, Joris maintained.

After the fall of Münster, Joris was prompted to perform an act of intellectual gymnastics on the question of vengeance similar to that on the Restitution. He affirmed the positions of both Hoffman and Rothmann by applying the "Cloven Hoof" exegesis. Attempting to maintain the unity of opposites, Joris once again preferred a conciliatory stance. He therefore affirmed both patient suffering and the taking of vengeance by the saints by postponing revenge tactics until such time as believers had attained the internal restitution, which he viewed to be a state beyond their current condition.[73] In his words,

When you are advanced enough and know that your flesh is dead so that it seeks nothing for itself, nor has any will nor work in you; then [you may] burn with wrath as Moses, Phyneas, Ehud, Jahel, David, Christ etc., [burn] against the evil ones and the contumacious proud enemies of God and the opponents of the truth who also deserve the perfect, jealous, burning love, and such earnest, zealous love shall be aroused.[74]

In the meantime Joris cautioned that believers were to suffer "violence and injustice on account of the faith of Jesus," because "they will receive again a hundredfold when they come into the glorious freedom of the children of God."[75] Although their suffering at the hands of the godless would indeed be avenged, Joris, addressing believers, warned "you must not threaten your enemy as long as (I say) you have not overcome your flesh to the point that there is none of it intermingled with [your anger]."[76] Believers were encouraged therefore to turn their sword upon their own souls to eradicate all fleshliness. This was the sword of the Spirit, which, if successful, could then and only then be turned on the external enemies. Here Joris may have assumed that the achievement of spiritual perfection on the part of the Melchiorites would coincide with the Lord's return, although he is in this characteristically unclear. In any case the actual result of internalising the apocalyptic crusade was a further negation of the concerns with social justice of the early Melchiorite movement.

It would appear, then, that Joris' middle-ground approach allowed him to take further liberties with his choice of words, liberties which he later regretted, especially after the forming of Jan van Batenburg's revolutionary group. His anonymous biographer explained in retrospect that

> in the first editions of his writings ... one might discover two or three statements which could be misconstrued to signify that God and his saints execute the vengeance and will hold the Judgement. But against this he taught also that they ought to look out, that they do not proceed before the time, because there must [first] be angels.[77]

One example of Joris' ambivalent position is sufficient to demonstrate the conflicting notions he encountered and had to ameliorate. In *The End is Coming*, he remarked that believers were to take up the sword of faith. Shortly thereafter Joris composed this enigmatic passage:

> But be foresighted and watch and guard your house well with every weapon. Sharpen your sword, burnish and wipe it until it glistens. And gird it onto your side, because of the terrors of the night. And guard the bed of Solomon well. Keep robbers from the house, so that tormenting spirits will no longer come in and out or run through it. And be of good courage, oh you strong ones in Israel.[78]

Revolutionary-minded supporters with more concrete concerns might be excused for not understanding the finer points of Joris' allegory. The spiritual point of Joris' clever use of the "Cloven Hoof" may in other words have been lost to the unenlightened. As a result of his conflict with Batenburg in the summer of 1536, Joris had to reduce significantly his use of evocative imagery, although much ambiguity remained.

Far from being mere sophistry, Joris' solution to the issue of vengeance was in critical ways consistent with his hermeneutical principles and indeed with the "Cloven Hoof" analogy inherited from Hoffman himself. Ultimately, however, Joris' solution proved illusory and beyond the comprehension, not to mention the patience, of all but Joris' closest followers.

Polygamy

The subject of marriage did not become an issue of controversy until Jan van Leiden adopted and justified the concept of polygamy in 1534. Rothmann, ideologically agile, prepared a rationale for the new practice in his three tracts of 1534-35. Hoffman and his Strasbourg supporters, on the other hand, clearly rejected both the practice of polygamy and Rothmann's rationalisations for its acceptance.[79] Rothmann based his defense of polygamy on the premise that the purpose of marriage was God's glory and the generation of offspring. The Scriptural proof text came from Genesis 1:27-28, "Be fruitful and multiply and fill the earth." All sexual relations which did not have procreation as their aim were therefore considered sinful and an abomination. Illicit forms included adultery, prostitution and bestiality, "pollution in sleep" and masturbation, as well as sex with a woman in the knowledge that she was unable to conceive.[80] Such acts became for Rothmann punishable crimes in the new kingdom. Curiously, each of these acts had been previously condemned in varying degrees in the Catholic tradition as well. Thus, while the older scholarship tended to ascribe the Münsterite sexual ethic to the promiscuity of its leaders, more recent studies have emphasised an underlying puritan assumption. The Münsterite practice of polygamy, then, was no more or less than an attempt "to put into practice the patriarchal-sexual norms of the Catholic tradition which had its purist expression in monasticism."[81] Hoffman's doctrine of the Celestial Flesh of Christ and the concomitant union of believers (the Bride of Christ) to Christ led in part to a doctrine of "innerworldly asceticism," in which the believer's flesh needed to become *"vergeistlicht und geheiligt."*[82] In this context, sexual relations were honourable only when carried out without lust or passion in *Gelassenheit.* Then, Rothmann affirmed,

> husband and wife both stand in God's fear and pure faith, and aim for nothing more in the marriage duty than that they might increase and multiply. In this state is marriage correct.[83]

Polygamy in Münster was constructed upon the traditional Christ-husband-wife hierarchy with the husband ruling over his wife as Christ ruled the Church. The husband was granted the "glorious freedom" to take more than one wife so as not to waste his seed, especially if his first wife was pregnant or barren.[84] The wife was to submit completely to her husband, "without any grumbling."[85] Male Münsterite leaders therefore had hoped that polygamy would help to control Münsterite women who vastly outnumbered them.[86]

Joris' sexual ethic was somewhat more ambivalent. He too seemed occupied with libidinal sins — "latent sexual feelings of guilt which contaminated the soul."[87] Like Hoffman, Joris was attracted to passages of Scripture which addressed the true believer as the bride of Christ, the chaste bride ready to enter the wedding bed of her lord.[88] He was also familiar with

Rothmann's arguments for polygamy. Deppermann believed that Joris defended Rothmann's position on the subject. However, like other issues discussed above, Joris' concern for unity meant that he sought a *via media*. His attempt at compromise with the Münsterites without necessarily accepting polygamy (a practice with which he was clearly uncomfortable), led to a strange synthesis that lacked nothing in its ascetic rigour. In short, Joris incorporated Rothmann's ascetic proscriptions into a basically monogamistic framework.[89]

Joris agreed with Rothmann that a major cause of societal woe was that women had for various reasons abandoned their role as submissive wifely subjects to the extent that they in some cases ruled over men.[90] In Joris' ideal society, as in the desired state of most male Münsterites, the family unit was nothing if not patriarchal. The contemporary standard was that men were not to allow themselves to be tempted sexually by women as had Sampson. Instead they were to cast away all lusts and become free of female domination.[91]

While Joris agreed with Rothmann's view that sexual relations were strictly for procreation (a commonplace in Catholic thought), he went one step further. Not only was sleeping with menstruating or pregnant wives disallowed, but in the act of procreation both partners were to remove any trace of lust or sexual desire from their relationship. Only in this way could children be conceived without original sin — a condition necessary if they were to become part of the future kingdom and play the role of the apocalyptic pure servants of Christ (the future angels of vengeance). Members of Christ's kingdom were therefore to be biologically created. The secret to fulfilling this requirement lay in the sexual act itself:

> Therefore let each one be admonished by the Spirit of the Lord. In brief, to no longer approach his wife in the lusts of the flesh as is the nature of heathens, nor in sinful desires. For they [children produced by lust] are altogether children of roguishness, children of the devil, impure.... I say the serpent is their father, until the rebirth ... for they were conceived without the Lord in a dishonourable bed, according to the flesh, according to the devil's lust and mind, namely in sins.[92]

That Joris wrote nothing specifically about polygamy in the works examined here may indicate that the issue was not a crucial one for him. There is no doubt, on the other hand, that he and his closest followers were monogamists, and later in the decade he wrote at least one tract promoting monogamy.[93] Bearing this in mind, it seems that his desire for group unity outweighed his personal conviction, so that he was willing to tolerate polygamy among his followers who had come out of the Batenburger movement.[94] It is notable that Joris remarked somewhat later that ''It is a matter of indifference to me if you have one, two, or four wives, just as long as you obey God and the truth.''[95] What was important to Joris was that marriage partners remove lust and its by-product shame from their relationships.

Polygamy was but one contentious issue to which Joris could accommodate himself if necessary. At Bocholt it was agreed that polygamy ought to be avoided.[96] Joris probably realised by this time that the practice of polygamy increased the visibility of Anabaptists and made them more susceptible to capture.

Although Joris shared Rothmann's ascetic assumptions to some degree, it cannot be firmly established that Joris simply continued Rothmann's position regarding polygamy after the fall of Münster. Again, as on other points, it seems best, given the state of evidence, to suggest that Joris attempted to find a mediatory position between the chaste bride imagery of Hoffman and the ascetic-polygamous community of Münster. Joris' solution, however, was formed more by his own background and struggle in ascetic Catholic teaching than by Münsterite ideology itself.

Notes

1. The first two tracts were distributed throughout the Netherlands by Münsterite apostles in December 1534. The last was distributed in February 1535. See Stupperich, *Rothmanns Schriften*. Roland Bainton's contention (in *David Joris*, p. 22) that Joris was influenced only by "Verborgenheit" does not hold water. There is little difference in theme between these three tracts of Rothmann. An earlier abbreviated version of this chapter appeared as "David Joris' Thought in the Context of the Early Anabaptist Movement in the Netherlands, 1534-1536," *MQR*, Vol. LXII, 1988, pp. 296-317.

2. From the report of the incident by Gerardus Nicolai, *DAN*, Vol. I, pp. 111-14. The group dissipated with the arrival of the authorities (Stayer, *Anabaptists and the Sword*, p. 271; Mellink, *De Wederdopers*, pp. 257-58).

3. It may be assumed that Joris had read some of Hoffman's works and several of these were in fact printed in the Netherlands – at least two by Joris' later printer in Deventer, Albert Pafraet. For a list see Deppermann, *Hoffman*, pp. 347-48.

4. Although, as S. Zijlstra (*Blesdijk*, pp. 9-10) has argued, Joris added few new elements to Melchiorite ideology, his synthesis of the traditional elements was unique.

5. While the issue of Hoffman's Heavenly Flesh Christology was an important one, it was shared by most if not all Melchiorites, including Joris, and was one of the agreed-on points at Bocholt.

6. Cited in Deppermann, *Hoffman*, p. 58.

7. Ibid., p. 59. Hoffman wrote "hoe dat hi [St. Paul] niet een diener des wets noch des boeckstauen ofte der scheine / sonder des waren boeckstauen geestes" (*Die eedele hoghe ende troostlike sendebrief / den die heylige Apostel Paulus to den Romeren gescreuen heeft* [n.p., 1533], fol. A4r).

8. Deppermann, *Hoffman*, pp. 212-13. Packull, "A Reinterpretation of Melchior Hoffman's *Exposition* against the Background of Spiritualist Franciscan Eschatology with Special Reference to Peter John Olivi," Horst, *Dutch Dissenters*, p. 32.

9. According to Deppermann (*Hoffman*, p. 214, note 91), Hoffman's "Cloven Hoof" was misapplied by many of his contemporaries such as Jacob van Campen, Dirk Philips and David Joris and misunderstood by recent scholars, especially Roland Bainton, S. Cramer and George Williams.

10. Ibid. Hoffman affirmed "dat he [St. Paul] ooc die ghespouden cleuwe draghe, om te onderscheyden allen teghenloop, want alle woorden Gods tweeuout zijn, een teghen dat ander ... door welcke nv viel dwalende worden, die gheen naersticheit hebben den onderscheyt te soecken, maer waer si een stuck wt der schrift crigen, daer blijven si

hartneck op, ende willen allen tegenloop niet kennen of aen nemen, of die tegen cleuwe bi malcander voeghen" ("Verclaringe van den geuangenen ende vrien wil des menschen," *BRN*, Vol. V, p. 189).

11. Deppermann, *Hoffman*, p. 215.

12. Packull, "The Sign of Thau," pp. 363-74. The "key of David" had been granted to the church of Philadelphia, the sixth church of the Apocalypse, Rev. 3:7.

13. Deppermann, *Hoffman*, p. 214. There is no comparable modern study of Rothmann that is of the same quality as Deppermann's study of Hoffman. For shorter studies, see Martin Brecht, "Die Theologie Bernhard Rothmanns," *Jahrbuch für Westfälische Kirchengeschichte*, Vol. LXXVII, 1985, pp. 49-82; W.J. de Bakker, "De Vroege Theologie van Bernhard Rothmann. De gereformeerde Achtergrond van het Munsterese Doperijk," *Doopsgezinde Bijdragen*, Vol. III (new series), 1977, pp. 9-20; and Stayer, "The Münsterite Rationalization of Bernhard Rothmann," *Journal of the History of Ideas*, Vol. XXVIII, 1967, pp. 179-92.

14. "Restitution Rechter und Gesunder Christlicher Lehre," *Rothmanns Schriften*, p. 221.

15. Ibid., p. 304. Evidently Bainton was mistaken when he argued that "Rothmann talks in this fashion of the throne of David, but never of the Key of David. The omission is significant. This expression was the slogan of the prophets of the Inward Word" (*David Joris*, pp. 23-24). Rothmann does not use the phrase "Key of David," but he certainly had it in mind.

16. "Van Verborgenheit der Schrifft des Rykes Christi vnde van dem Daghe des Heren durch de Gemeinte Christi tho Münster," *Rothmanns Schriften*, p. 306.

17. Ibid., p. 338.

18. "[W]at de letter den vorstande vordregen, dat mit rechten mode, warheit vund seckerheit des herten begrepen, geholden vund vullenbracht wert, dat is de geist der schrifft" (ibid., p. 342).

19. Ibid., p. 353.

20. For the importance of anticlericalism, see Goertz, *Die Täufer*, pp. 23, 40-50.

21. It must also be remembered that Joris was trained as an artist, not as a theologian or writer. See Koegler, "Einiges," pp. 159-60, where he comments: "Den Künstler in Joris haben alle seine Biographen vergessen."

22. "Van die duydelijcke Duytsche Spraecke," *Liedt-Boexcken*, fol. 91v. In several tracts dating to the 1540s, Joris more fully developed his reasons for depreciating the learning of the biblical languages. He also continued to elevate the value of his native Dutch in the mediation of the Word of God. See in particular *Van die Vreemde Tonghen of Talen der Menschen* (n.p., 1545).

23. "Refereyn tot Lof des Nederlandts unde der Duytscher Spraecke," *Liedt-Boexcken*, fol. 85v. The songs probably received their inspiration from Luther's preface to his edition of the *Theologia Deutsch*, where he says "I thank God that I can hear and find my God in the German tongue, the way I do here, in a manner in which I and the German theologians with me so far did not find Him even in Latin, Greek, or Hebrew" (Bengt Hoffman [ed.], *The Theologia Germanica of Martin Luther* [New York: Paulist Press, 1980], p. 54).

24. "Van die duydelijcke Duytsche Spraecke," fol. 92v-r.

25. Joris wrote in 1535: "Behold my counsel in the Lord, for it was brought to me with the power of the Spirit from above, for admonishment, teaching and edification, in order to perfect all things and to restore what has long been lost, corrupted, forgotten or not known. Pay attention, yes take heed just as you would for the word of the Lord our God, and pray for me" (*Van die heerlijcke ende godlijcke Ordeninge der Wonderlijker werckinghen Godes* [n.p., 1535], fol. 86v).

26. Ibid., fols. 82v-83r.
27. Ibid., fol. 80v.
28. In the same passage Joris wrote: "Voorder willen wy gelaten staen in't ghene dat boven onser veeler begrijp is / ende bedden altijt mit betrawen / so sal't wel gelucken" (ibid). The concept was a popular one among Anabaptists. See Steven Ozment, *Mysticism and Dissent* (New Haven: Yale University Press, 1973), pp. 12-13.
29. *Van die heerlijcke*, fol. 61v. The texts which he did set out were indeed the foundational ones for his hermeneutical approach — Jeremiah 30, 31, Malachi 3, 4, Proverbs 1-3. The Jeremiah and Malachi passages were also central to Hoffman (see "Verclaringe van den geuangenen ende vrien wil," *BRN*, Vol. V, pp. 185, 189). They were, in fact, central to any discussion of the Restitution.
30. Anonymous, p. 710.
31. *Van die heerlijcke*, fol. 39r.
32. Ibid., fol. 49v.
33. Joris wrote: "Dies niet te min / of yemant daer-om wilde twisten/ Ick wil al wel daer ongelijck in hebben ende niet om kyven / mogen wy anders over-een dragen in't gene daer onse Salicheyt in verborgen is" (ibid., fol. 84r).
34. *Hoert, hoert, hoert*, fol. 58v.
35. Deppermann, *Hoffman*, p. 60; Packull, "A Reinterpretation," p. 32.
36. Deppermann, *Hoffman*, p. 217. This breakthrough of the Spirit began with Hus, but was suppressed for 140 years, and was now resumed with the Reformation (Packull, "A Reinterpretation," pp. 40ff.). Hoffman's thought is intriguing for it has much in common with the radical Franciscans influenced by the twelfth-century Calabrian monk Joachim of Fiore. See, for a brief introduction, Bernard McGinn (ed.), *Apocalyptic Spirituality* (New York: Paulist Press, 1979), pp. 97-112, 149-58.
37. Packull, "A Reinterpretation," p. 29.
38. Ibid., p. 31.
39. Deppermann, *Hoffman*, p. 67.
40. Deppermann, "Melchior Hoffman and Strasbourg Anabaptism," in Marc Lienhard, *The Origins and Characteristics of Anabaptism* (The Hague: Martinus Nijhoff, 1977), p. 218.
41. "Verborgenheit," p. 333. "Eth ys apenbar vth der schrifft, dat de werlt vernemlicke in dreierley werld offte principael tyde, gelick als ock alle Godes handel, schrifft vnde wercke yn drien verlendiget werden, eren vorloep hefft vnde dat Godt ordentlicke in verschaffinge der vullenkomenheit der tide in Christo alle dinck nu der vorsate sins willens uthrichtet" (ibid., p. 332).
42. "Restitution," p. 271: "wo dan van siner opuarth thoem hemel an, ynwendich overmitz des geistes macht vnd dat vunder den cruce geherschet heft."
43. Ibid., p. 340.
44. "Dat men de schrifft will vorstaen na dem Yongesten dage, dat de dan soll vollenbracht werden, is ein missuerstandt" (ibid., p. 273).
45. Current scholarship denies that this involved a fundamental break between Hoffman and Rothmann (Deppermann, *Hoffman* p. 300; Stayer, *Anabaptists and the Sword*, pp. xxvi-xxvii, against his own earlier view, p. 223). According to Deppermann (*Hoffman*, p. 300), the major difference between the two Anabaptist leaders consisted in that, while Hoffman looked to the legitimate authorities to bring reform, Rothmann rationalized the "revolt of the believing people."
46. "Restitution," p. 282. This change was of course justified by a vision of a man wearing a golden crown and with a sword and rod in his hands (ibid., p. 280).
47. "Bericht van der Wrake," *Rothmanns Schriften*, p. 287.

48. Ibid., p. 295. The saints were now to turn the sword of the godless persecutors against them, "so that it will stab into their own hearts, and they fall into the grave which they themselves have dug" ("Verborgenheit," p. 366). The reference is to Joel 3.
49. Ibid., pp. 296-97.
50. Bainton underestimated the impact of apocalypticism upon Joris. He wrote "For a year or so he shared the crude eschatological hopes of the Melchiorite party" (*David Joris*, p. 36).
51. The following can be considered apocalyptical songs: "Waer sach oyt Mensch dusdanighe bange tyden," 1535 (*Liedt-Boecxken*, fols. 27r-30v); "O Christen Gheesten wilt hier op achten," June 1535 (ibid., fols. 41r-43v); "Die Heer is Coninck in Israel," July 1535 (ibid., fols. 58v-62r). The following are primarily occupied with his pre-Anabaptist themes: "Ick hoorden huyden wayen," 1534 (ibid., fols. 24v-26v); "Alle vleysch is hoy," 1535 (ibid., fols. 30v-32r); "Onse Vader in die Hemelen claer," 1535 (ibid., fols. 32v-36v); "Hoort alle ghy Nacomelinghen," December 1535 (ibid., fols. 37r-40v).
52. "O Christen Gheesten wilt hier op achten (ibid., fols. 41r-43v)," stanzas 4 and 5. Anonymous (p. 708) dates these songs to the last week of June and first week of July, 1535.
53. "Die Heer is Coninck in Israel," *Liedt-Boecxken*, fols. 58v-60r, stanzas 1 and 2.
54. *Van die heerlijcke*, fols. 72v (Title page) and 85r.
55. It was not for another year that he would develop his historical concept of three Davids — King David of Israel; Jesus Christ; and a final present-day servant in whom the Spirit dwelt. See *Hoert, hoert, hoert*, fols. 30v-33v.
56. *Van die heerlijcke*, fol. 83r. This view had been promulgated by the Wassenberg preachers, especially in John Campanus' work on the Restitution (Karl Rembert, *Die Wiedertäufer im Herzogtum Jülich* [Berlin, 1899], p. 210). In a modified form it became the basis for Hoffman's "apostolic community," called out by the apostolic messenger to become the pure bride of Christ.
57. *Van die heerlijcke*, fol. 83r-v. The original reads: "Teen tweeden / hebben oock die van Münster / dien een groot licht ende vreughde omschenen was / die wederbrenginge al meenen te hebben / oock die sy gants wtwendich in voller kracht ende macht meenden te oefenen over die gantsche Aerde / heerschappende over alle Machten ende crachten der Werlt / welck sy onder haer wel meenden te brengen in den Naam Jesu / ende dat geloof aen God ghebenedijt inder Eeuwicheyt / hopende vryheyt / ruymte ende die vercoelinghe of ontfermherticheyt."
58. Ibid., fol. 83r. Again the original is worthy of citation: "Veele sijn daer / die van die Restitution schryven / die wel tot twee Deelen ghekomen sijn / hoe wel yegelijck d'een suyden d'ander nordwaart loopt of teghen den anderen staen / die ick gern te samen voegen ende recht middelen solde / op dat wy tot eenen sin mochten komen ende vrede hadden / ende alsoo Sathan daer buyten hielden / dat waer een lust den Heere." The reference to "one runs south and the other north" may refer to the supporters of Hoffman who were in Strasbourg on the one side and the Münsterite remnant who fled north.
59. Ibid., fol. 83v. "Maer die derde Wederbrenginge of vernieuwinge ... die in't midden moet gestelt sijn / is voor-by heengegaen ende niet op gelet so men solde / ende is van dat eerste tot dat leste of derde ghesprongen / het welck daerom geen volle kracht noch macht / of stand en heeft mogen hebben of beholden: want alle dingen bestaen in Dryen."
60. "Restitution," p. 223.
61. *Van die heerlijcke*, fol. 84r. Joris was willing to concede this point, however, for the sake of unity. He wrote: "Dies niet te min / of yemant daer-om wilde twisten / Ick

wil al wel daer ongelijck in hebben ende niet om kyven / mogen wy anders over-een dragen in't gene daer onse Salicheyt in verborgen is.''

62. Ibid., fol. 84r.
63. Ibid., fol. 84v.
64. Ibid.
65. Ibid., fols. 84v-85r. The complete passage is interesting: ''Siet / dat is dan die Weder-brenginghe / die wy ghewis ende al verzeghelt sijn / door den Gheest des Geloofs in Christo Jesu: hoewel wy't inder kracht noch niet ontfanghen en hebben / ende ons voor ooghen noch niet en schijnt / soo besitten't die Vromen nochtans inder herten al op hope / ende verwachten't door lijdsaemheyt / sonder alle twijffel: Ende also sal alle dingh sijn volkomen Wesen ende levende Gheest kryghen / want het moet also oock ende niet anders sijn / ja die Redenen wysen't wt / dat verstant doet den sin op / die Schriftuyre ghetuyghtet / ende den Geest bevestighet: daerom moeten alle tegen-Gheesten of Wedervechters / die stolte tongen haeren Mont hier op toe-holden / ende en wederstaen die Belofte ende heerlijckheyt Godes / of dat Rijck ones Heeren Jesu Christi inder kracht niet / dat welck alleene die Heylighen of Kleynen sullen wtspreecken.''
66. Ibid., fol. 76v.
67. For a closer examination of Joris' concept of individual perfection, see Appendix VI.
68. Anonymous, p. 710. There were twelve to fourteen participants in the conference.
69. This was probably Damas van Hoorn who had recently taken part in the ''ordination'' of Joris.
70. Anonymous, p. 710.
71. *Liedt-Boexcken*, fols. 29v-30v. The seemingly contradictory reference to the Day of Wrath coming over both Zion and God's enemies is most likely related to the belief that a three-and-a-half-year period of tribulation for the saints would precede the final vengeance on the godless.
72. *Van die heerlijcke*, fol. 75r. Rothmann had written: ''Hyrumme wat sick van Bro-deren her by dat Panier Gades maken kan vnde lust hefft an der gerecticheit Gades, de willen nicht zumen. Want wanner dat feinlyn gerichtet ys vnd de Basune angehet, wilt volle vngelouige gelouich werden vnde hertho treden'' (''Van der Wrake,'' p. 293).
73. Stayer (''David Joris, A Prolegomenon to Further Research,'' *MQR*, Vol. LXI, 1985, p. 356) following Bainton, argued that Joris' ''reanimation of Bernhard Rothmann's prophecies was already lacking the most essential component, a commitment to physi-cal vengeance.''
74. *Van die heerlijcke*, fol. 77r.
75. Ibid., fol. 86r.
76. Ibid., fol. 77v. Even though the world belonged to Christ, he was still killed unjustly. ''Hierom hoewel ons dat selvighe al mit hem ende door hem gegeven is / siet / soo moeten wy daer ghewelt onrecht ende fortse in ghedooghen / bewysende sachtmoedicheyt ende lanckmoedicheyt / tot dat in ons alle dingen van beginsel wedergebracht sijn / ende dat Cleed der heyligher simpelheyt ende onnooselheyt aen-hebben'' (ibid., fol. 76v).
77. Anonymous, p. 724. These angels, however, could be interpreted either as the tradi-tional supernatural beings or as the morally perfect servants of God.
78. *Dat eynde coemt*, fol. 146r.
79. Deppermann (*Hoffman*, p. 317) wrote that ''Diese Rechtfertigung der Polygamie stand in klarem Gegensatz zu allen Lehren Hoffmans.''
80. ''Restitution,'' p. 261.
81. Matthias Hennig, ''Askese und Ausschweifung: Zum Verstandnis der Vielweiberei im

Täuferreich zu Münster 1534/35," *Mennonitische Geschichtsblatter*, Vol. XL, 1983, p. 39.
82. Stayer, "Vielweiberei als 'inner-weltliche Askese,'" *Mennonitische Geschichts-blatter*, Vol. XXXVII, 1980, p. 31. Although Hennig disputes with points of Stayer's thesis, the two views are not diametrically opposed.
83. "Restitution," p. 261. Any other use "ysset doch van Godt geine Ehe dan ein ydel ehebreckerye vnd horerie" (ibid., p. 259).
84. "so ys em fry gelaten, ya van noden, meer fruchtbare frouwen in de Ehe tho nemen" (ibid., p. 263).
85. "[D]e frouwen nicht tho regeren, dan myt stillicheit gehorsam tho syn" (ibid., p. 269). Polygamous relationships in Münster were, however, fraught with such complaints.
86. Hsia ("Münster and the Anabaptists," p. 60) comments that "In spite of the initial excitement and promises of the Evangelical and Anabaptist movements, the Reformation in Münster represented an attempt to subjugate women by restricting their social and religious roles, by transforming them, ultimately, into obedient (and protected) wives and daughters of a polygamous, patriarchal, and sacred tribe."
87. Hennig ("Askese," pp. 36-37) writes "von einem Zusammenhang zwischen Angst, Schuldgefühl und verdrängte Sexualität, das heutigem psychoanalytischen Verständnis erstaunlich nahe kommt, ging David Joris aus."
88. Hoffman, "Ordinance," p. 191.
89. Zijlstra ("David Joris," p. 134) has corrected Deppermann's opinion (*Hoffman*, pp. 316-17) that Joris defended Rothmann's view on polygamy. See Stayer, "David Joris," p. 366 for a summary. See below, chapter 7, for a closer examination of Joris' view of marriage.
90. "[M]oet desgelijcks die Vrouwe onder den Man haren heere / mit grooter gedoogh-saemheyt ende gehoorsaemheyt ootmoedilijcken staen / in allen te wille sijn in den Heere / niet doende noch willende in wercken / woorden noch gedachten / anders dan haren gheloovigen Heere ende Christen-Man wel gelieft" (*Van die heerlijcke*, fol. 77v).
91. "Daerom siet nu toe / het geld v allen / dat ghy uwen baart niet en laet afscheren / behold v macht ende eere / die v God tot sijn lof ghegeven heeft. Aensiet die schoonheyt des Wijfs niet / acht oock op hare treecken ende betooveringe niet / op dat ghy tot haerder begheerlijckheyt niet verweckt en werdet / maer keert alle begeer-lijckheyt des quaden Vleysches ende des buycks verre van v: werdet niet van die Lusten der dolinge ende des byslapens gevangen" (ibid., fol. 79v). Ironically, some of the most influential people in Joris' life were women, especially his mother, wife, and Anneken Jans.
92. *Hoert, hoert, hoert*, fol. 7v-r.
93. See below, chapter 7.
94. In 1539 a group of Davidites were arrested and executed in Delft. Many of these who confessed to polygamy had come from a Batenburg community in Raesfelt, near Bocholt and were under the direct leadership of Heinrich Kaal, a former Batenburg leader. This is the only case where Davidites are known to have practised polygamy (Brandt, *History of the Reformation*, Vol. I, p. 75; Blesdijk, *Christlijke Verantwoor-dinghe*, fols. 29-30).
95. Stayer, "David Joris," p. 357.
96. Zijlstra, "David Joris," pp. 126-29.

Siet datt Lam Gs. welck

der Werelt sonden wechneemt. Joan. i. Apoca. vij.
Hy sal ghelijck een Schaep ter slachbanck swyghende gheleyt
werden: wie datt Lammekin voor synen
beschaerer synen mont
niet opdoen.
Jesa. liij.

Juda du bist, v sullen dyne broederen louen : deyn hant
sal dyne vianden op den halse syn : voor dy sullen v Vaders Kinderen sich burghen.
Juda is een jonghe Leeuw. Ghy sijt opgheclommen/ mijn Zoen /tot den rooff. Jck
wil hem die menichte tot een buete gheuen / ende der stercker rooff sall by deelen:
Daer om datt by syn ziell inden doot vergheten/onder die ouertreders gherelt wert.
Leest. Gene. xlix. Nume. xxiij. xxiiij. Jesaie. liij.
Siet es hadt ouerwonnen die Leuw die daer is vanden gheslachte Juda / die
wortel Dauids. Apoca. v. xi). Esdre. xij.
Went der trooster / die Gheest der waerheyt /coemt /sall by die Werelt straffen.
Johannis. xvj.

Prophette

David Joris, "The Lamb of God and the Lion of Judah" from *Wonder Book*, Part I,
fol. iv°. Courtesy The Mennonite Library, University of Amsterdam.

CHAPTER SIX

Joris and the Post-Münster Radicals, 1536-39

What is David Joris' significance within the broader post-Münster Dutch Anabaptist movement? Recently Samme Zijlstra has suggested that Joris was "the most important Anabaptist leader in the Netherlands from 1536 to 1539."[1] Zijlstra used as evidence Joris' attempts to win over both the Münsterite remnant in Oldenburg and Hoffman's followers in Strasbourg, and his correspondence with a widespread group of supporters. A statistical examination of all known Anabaptist leaders in the Netherlands and a closer study of Joris' dealings with the other radical Anabaptist groups may contribute to the appraisal of Joris' significance.

In attempting to define who were Anabaptist leaders, one is faced immediately with the problem of Melchior Hoffman's suspension of baptism in 1531. Hoffman had intended the suspension as a means to avoid persecution (his own lieutenant, Jan Volkerts Trijpmaker, had been executed in that year) and the widespread adoption of Hoffman's injunction blurs the lines between Melchiorite and other early reform groups. One is left with the possibility that not all who joined Anabaptist conventicles and participated in Anabaptist activities had themselves been baptised.

For reasons similar to Hoffman's, David Joris played down the importance of the visible rite of baptism. Joris' indifference to the practice of baptism was also an attempt to counter the importance placed on it by the radicals who had reinstated the practice. Whether or not one baptised others, therefore, should not be regarded as the sole criterion for defining leaders within the Anabaptist groups. In any case, the available evidence suggests that most or all of the important leaders who joined Joris' side had been baptised before they became Davidites. Joris himself had been baptised and ordained an elder. There appears therefore no valid reason to suggest that Joris' group was not part of the broader stream of Dutch Anabaptism.

It is recognised that after the fall of Münster the Melchiorite movement splintered into several major groups. The Oldenburg Münsterites under Heinrich Krechting and the followers of Jan van Batenburg hoped that the kingdom could be restored either in Münster or in some other city. Some of these radicals attempted to realise this hope in the villages of Hazerswoude and Poeldijk in Holland in the winter and spring of 1535-36. The other groups — Melchiorite (in Strasbourg, the Netherlands and England), Men-

---

Notes to Chapter Six are found on pages 122-26.

nonite and Davidite — were generally non-violent.

Approximately 177 Anabaptist leaders active in the Netherlands from 1533 to 1540 were readily identified from the available sources.[2] Of these, approximately 105, or 60%, were either dead or inactive after the fall of the Anabaptist kingdom at Münster or by late 1535. A list of those still active from 1536 to 1540 therefore indicates the strengths of the various groups during this period.[3] The affiliations of these leaders were identified as shown in Table VI.

Table VI. Anabaptist Leaders

Davidite	22
Melchiorite	12
Münsterite	12
Batenburger	11
Obbenite/Mennonite	4
Unknown	12

Four of the Münsterite leaders were involved in the Hazerswoude and Poeldijk incidents; nine of the "Unknown" category may have been inactive. What can immediately be seen is that the Davidites had the largest number of active leaders of any single group. The Davidite leadership included several who had been prominent before the fall of Münster, including Adriaen van Benscop (Cooman Ariaen); Hans Scheerder (Hans van Leeuwarden); Heinrich Kaal; Andreis Droochscheerder; Meynart van Emden;[4] and Rem van Hoorn.[5]

To shed further light on the importance of Joris' following, it is apparent that the majority of Joris' opponents were working in Friesland, Groningen, the territory of Utrecht, Overijsel, and Westphalia, while only a handful were active to any significant degree in the region of Holland itself.[6] Most importantly, those non-Davidite Anabaptist leaders who were active in the province of Holland tended to be radicals or even terrorists such as the participants in the Poeldijk uprising or the Batenburgers. There is no evidence of any significant peaceful Obbenite or Mennonite leader active in or around Holland during the second half of the 1530s. Joris, therefore, provided the major peaceful leadership in the Netherlands outside of Friesland and Groningen.

A corollary to this proposition is that Joris' following was largely urban-based.[7] Attraction to Joris on the part of Anabaptist city-dwellers can be attributed in part to his willingness to accommodate his teaching to traditional social and religious practices, such as attendance at authorised churches and baptism of infants. While there were some Mennonites active in the cities of Holland by 1543-44, their sectarian, separatist approach, which made them highly visible in an urban milieu, illustrated the rural origins of Menno Simon's group.[8] The Batenburg radicals largely restricted

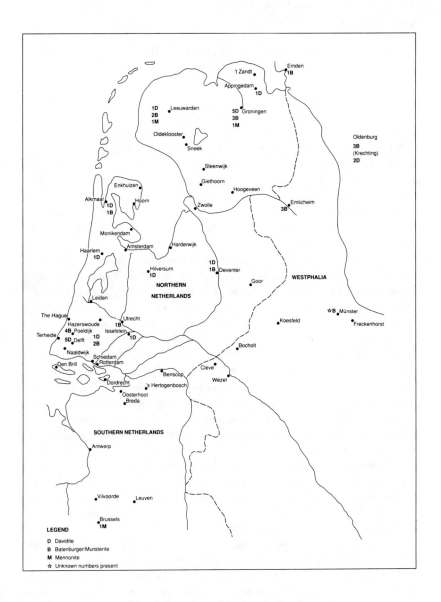

Map 1. Location of Anabaptist Leaders

their residence and activity to the rural setting, although Utrecht, Antwerp and Leiden provided important urban centres for a number of them.[9] Joris' mediating posture between pacifist and revolutionary Anabaptist groups can be seen as a solution evolved within an urban environment.

Joris and the Poeldijk Radicals

Joris certainly saw himself as the major Anabaptist rival to the violent tactics of radical Münsterites and Batenburgers. He believed that his moderating influence "from within" spared the Netherlands from even more damage at the hands of Anabaptist radicals. Joris' belief that he had reduced the level of terrorism might be the target of a healthy skepticism were it not for its confirmation by two sources hostile to the prophet, Nicolaas Meyndertsz van Blesdijk's *Historia vitae*[10] and the terrorist commander himself, Jan van Batenburg, who called David Joris the "head" of the Anabaptist movement.[11] Batenburg's successor, Cornelis Appelman, shared this opinion.[12] A closer examination of Joris' interactions with some of these radical groups will help to clarify the role he played in the adjustment of radicals to post-Münster realities.

Several groups of radicals attempted to replicate the early success of Münster in other towns or villages. Two incidents were of special import to David Joris. The first was the attempt of some sixty armed Anabaptist fugitives to capture the village of Hazerswoude (just a few miles northeast of Delft). These radicals had travelled from Benscop in December of 1535 and were under the leadership of Pieter van den Binchorst, the noble Bailiff of the Gravenzande. In the ensuing mêlée, ten of the Anabaptists were killed and several arrested, while others managed to escape.[13] Joris, as the appointed Anabaptist leader in the area (he was likely in Delft), responded to those who had fled with a letter.[14] The result was that several of the escapees visited Joris one night. Apparently they sought to persuade him of the necessity of direct, violent action. Joris, according to a Davidite source, refused to "follow their life and ways." As a result, the Hazerswoude radicals threatened Joris that "when the vengeance came, he would have to watch out, that it did not come on him as on the others."[15] Obviously then, Joris took his responsibilities as leader seriously enough to confront the remnants of Anabaptist radicalism. This confrontation, only in its nascent stages, was to continue for some time.

In February 1536 Adriaen Adriaens van Hazerswoude, a self-declared prophet, proclaimed himself the King of Israel and set up his reign in Poeldijk, just northwest of Delft. In the following month he collected around himself forty followers, including several of the survivors from the Hazerswoude debacle. The other members were mostly from the nearby villages of Terheide to the west and Naaldwijk to the south. According to the testimony of two of his followers, Adriaens "was to receive out of heaven a horse, crown and a sword in order to punish the unrighteous" and to "smite

all those who were not elected by God."[16] Before Adriaens settled at Poeldijk he had travelled throughout the territory, proclaiming that he had
received the Spirit of power and that he would inflict vengeance against the
persecutors of the Anabaptists, especially the authorities at The Hague. In
March Joris wrote a letter to Adriaens and his group, warning them to
refrain from such activity. He also reprimanded Adriaens' followers for
"setting one up so high and claiming him as a king." Joris desired to meet
with the radicals, but they were captured shortly after the letter reached
them. At any rate, Adriaens' group was in no mood to listen to the Delft
leader, apparently casting his letter into the fire and sending Joris word that
Adriaens was "chosen to be a King and a lord and ruler over the whole
world, in the place of Christ."[17] In spite of this initial reaction, Joris' letter
had some impact, for a number of these men who "had been taken in" by
Adriaens, came to dispute their case with Joris. Apparently their initial
remarks were, to say the least, less than kind. By morning, however, the
radicals had undergone a change of mind, having been convinced of their
error.[18]

While Joris was developing a self-image not radically different from
Adriaens',[19] there appears no valid reason to deny Joris credit for a limited
success in turning some from the suicidal path of revolution. His interaction
with radicals in his home territory may indeed have prepared Joris for the
role he was to play at the Bocholt conference just five months after the failure at Poeldijk.

Joris at the Bocholt Disputation

The event most significantly pushing Joris' leadership beyond the boundaries of Delft was his participation in a conference at Bocholt in Westphalia,
just outside the Netherlands. The meeting was called by a "Heinrich from
England" perhaps Henry Hart, a wealthy English non-conformist.[20]
Presumably concerned with the numerous divisions and disagreements in
the post-Münster movement, Heinrich hoped that a conference of leaders
would reunify the covenanters. Summoned to this meeting were the major
post-Münster leaders of the Melchiorites, including both Obbe Philips and
Jan van Batenburg. An ambitious undertaking, this endeavour was only par-
tially successful. Batenburg did not attend, refusing to risk the dangerous
journey (and perhaps knowing full well that his views would only find con-
demnation). He, however, did send an observer. Obbe Philips was so afraid
of a Batenburg ambush that he did not hazard the trip, and representatives
from Strasbourg turned back due to an unfavourable dream which one of
their number experienced en route.[21] The conference therefore consisted of
around twenty-five participants, including Jan Matthijs van Middelburg
(then residing in England); Jan Maestricht; Jan van Schoonhoven; Joris, and
some others from Holland; Mathijs van Balk and Tjaard van Sneek (two
older leaders), and Seward Klerck, a teacher, all from Friesland; and Jan

Trajectensis, Hans van Jülich and Christoffel and Hendrik van Zutphen from Guelders and Overijsel. Representatives of Heinrich Krechting, the leader of the remaining Münsterites in Oldenburg, and several others also attended.[22] David Joris was apparently reluctant to attend, on account of his fear of Batenburg and the dream which had turned back the Strasbourg Melchiorites.[23] The absence of the other important leaders made the likelihood of true agreement minimal. On the agenda were the questions of the continuing relevance of the Münsterite doctrines of polygamy and the restitution of the material reign of Christ. Joris, despite his reluctance, arrived in Bocholt shortly after the others, late in the month of August.[24] Apparently some of the already gathered representatives (specifically those from England) regarded Joris' participation in the conference as a hindrance to a long-term agreement. At any rate, sides were taken, with defenders of the Münsterite position (mainly the Frisians and Westphalians) opposed to those who saw it as contrary to the teachings of Hoffman (mainly Jan Matthijs and Jan Trajectensis). The debate became so heated that fears of a violent confrontation (with the Münsterites holding the upper hand) nearly turned the conference into a fiasco. According to the two major sources, Joris managed to mediate a peace settlement, promoting his "middle of the road" approach. The accord, apparently written by Joris, affirmed five basic articles on which all participants could agree: (1) Believer's Baptism; (2) The true meaning of the Lord's Supper; (3) The Melchiorite conception of the Incarnation; (4) Free Will; and (5) The doctrine of Perfection.[25] Instead of settling the two controversial questions of vengeance and polygamy, Joris sidestepped them. He proposed that vengeance upon the godless was to be performed only by God and his angels. The identity of the latter remained open. His compromise was seen, on the surface, as a victory by both sides. Joris apparently affirmed that the Münsterite attempt to establish the kingdom of God was not false in principle, only untimely. According to a recent assessment Joris provided

> an explanation within which both parties could find themselves: the opponents of force thought that Joris meant that God and his angels would fulfill the vengeance and the Münsterites believed that they would do it, because they regarded themselves as the angels.[26]

What form these angels took formed the crux of the problem. Joris certainly had intended not to clarify this fundamental matter of interpretation when he drew up the concord.[27] Joris' compromise solution at the Bocholt conference was based on his self-perception as mediator between the various factions of Melchiorites which included a remnant of Münsterites. Although the agreement proved illusory, it served to push Joris into the forefront of the Anabaptist movement, so that for the following few years at least he can justifiably be regarded as the most important Anabaptist leader in the Netherlands.

Joris and the Batenburgers

Probably as a result of his success at Bocholt Joris' stature increased not only in the eyes of other Anabaptists, but in his own as well. Anonymous tells us that his "zeal increased more and more" and in this spirit he wrote some further books and letters on the subject of the Bocholt accord.[28] Unfortunately for Joris these labours backfired, for both sides soon turned against him. Batenburg intensified his attacks on what he saw as Joris' effeteness, while the Obbenites condemned him for being too close to the radicals.

The relationship between David Joris and Jan van Batenburg is most intriguing and perplexing. The illegitimate son of a Dutch nobleman, Batenburg had accepted the mantle of Gideon, the deliverer of God's people, at a meeting of radical Anabaptist leaders at Groningen in April 1535. The group had hoped that Batenburg would become an able replacement for Jan van Leiden, whose campaign to bring in the kingdom was clearly failing.[29] When Joris had first heard of Batenburg's conversion, he wanted to personally welcome him. It soon became apparent, however, that such a meeting might prove hazardous to Joris, for Batenburg was in no mood to tolerate any real or perceived opponents to his tactics. Batenburg, in fact, called Joris a "child of a whore" (an ironic invective for one who was himself a bastard) and "an Absalom," who fought against God and who ultimately desired "to seize the Kingdom from him [i.e., from Batenburg]."[30] Batenburg's hatred of Joris had become so intense that, according to Anonymous, he at one time hired an assassin to stab David to death.[31] Recent scholarship has, however, established that Batenburg and his followers robbed churches and cloisters only as a temporary measure until such time as they believed the new kingdom of Christ was established. Batenburg and Heinrich Krechting planned together to re-establish the kingdom in Münster in 1538, but Batenburg's arrest in 1537 and execution in early 1538 put an end to these designs.[32]

The essence of the dispute between Joris and Batenburg was over leadership. The charismatic style of leadership common among Dutch Anabaptists allowed for only one supreme head. As a result, both Joris and Batenburg demanded exclusive loyalty among their followers. On Joris' part, this was illustrated by a vision he experienced at a time when he was corresponding with Batenburg, in the spring or early summer of 1537. In the vision he saw two bunches of flowers bowing down to a third in the centre.[33] Joris naturally believed the centre pile to signify himself, with the outer two signifying the Batenburgers and perhaps the Strasbourg Melchiorites, with whom he was also corresponding. Joris' obvious sympathy for the Münsterite radicals, in combination with his refusal to actually join in the crusade, could only infuriate the rebel leader.[34]

At the end of 1537 Batenburg was arrested at Artois. This turn of events proved to be a great boon for Joris, for Batenburg had predicted that

God's anointed would be the one who outlived his rival. Batenburg had further prophesied that either he or Joris (whoever was the false prophet) would die by either hail, pestilence or the sword. When the terrorist was put to death some members of the now leaderless movement therefore turned to Joris for direction.

Batenburg, during his confession, implicated Joris in the plans for urban revolt. He then apparently offered to deliver Joris to the authorities if they first released him.[35] The extant versions of Batenburg's confession state merely that in Batenburg's mind Joris was the "head" of the Anabaptists and that the "teaching and ordinances of the Anabaptists was to ruin cities, castles and churches, to reject and despise all ceremonies and sacraments of the church." While it seems that Batenburg meant to implicate his opponents and save his friends, his confession adds to the evidence that in 1537 Joris was considered one of the key Anabaptist leaders. Batenburg's offer to find Joris was of course not taken up, and Batenburg was put to death in April of 1538 at Vilvoorde. With Joris' major rival out of the way, the path to the unification of the Anabaptists under Joris' standard seemed clear of obstacles. Certainly some Batenburgers had joined his ranks, including several important leaders. Could Joris achieve similar success with the Münsterite remnant?

Joris and the Oldenburg Münsterites

Joris' correspondence with the refugees from Münster who had fled to Oldenburg (northern Westphalia) began at least one year before his participation in the conference held there in the spring of 1538.[36] Joris' preoccupation with the abiding influence of Münster is seen from a letter he composed to Anabaptists in England at this time. He had included the line "one will yet bring presents and gifts to you," apparently under the inspiration of the Spirit. He believed this could be interpreted in the Münsterite sense, as "falling upon the goods of people" for the fellowship. He was in a quandary, for when he scratched it out, he feared that he was thereby opposing the Spirit. He therefore restored the sentence.[37] The phrase may indeed have reflected some subconscious radical leanings that Joris found necessary to cover up for the sake of his middle-road approach. His correspondence during this time also won for him a couple of important converts in Westphalia, Christoffel van Zutphen and Anthon Smedes, through whom he came into closer contact with Heinrich Krechting, the former chancellor of Münster and the leader of the Münsterite remnant at Oldenburg.[38]

Possibly at the instigation of some of Joris' Westphalian supporters, a meeting was arranged between Joris and the Münsterite remnant for the spring of 1538.[39] Joris and his companions reached Oldenburg[40] during the time when the Bishop of Münster and the Duke of Oldenburg were at war.[41] Before meeting with the Münsterites, Joris conferred with his own supporters in the region conducting a general discussion of problems which had developed in the post-Münster Melchiorite community, especially regarding marriage.[42]

The account of the meeting with the Münsterites is sketchy, but clearly illustrates the crucial issue in the post-Münster Melchiorite debate regarding religious authority. Among the Münsterites gathered at the meeting were several well-versed in Latin. According to the account, the Münsterites affirmed the veracity of their own dogma, denied any agreement with Davidite doctrine and demanded that Joris prove his ideas. At this point they placed a Bible on the table and exclaimed "Behold, this is our authority." Presumably even these Münsterites had become disillusioned with prophetic leadership which was not solidly based on the Scriptures. While Joris was formulating his response the Bible, seemingly miraculously, fell off the table. The stunned Münsterites adjourned the meeting until the next day where they listened to Joris and were persuaded by him. It seems the Münsterites had not completely given up that reliance on "signs and wonders" which had been so crucial to the development of the Münster enterprise in the first place.[43]

The Münsterites were clearly still oriented to charismatic leadership, but in light of the Münster debacle they had set up a firmer Biblical standard to judge potential leaders. The shock of the fallen Bible only briefly returned them to naive commitment to a prophet/king. In the fall of 1538, after Joris had returned to Delft from Strasbourg, a delegation of Münsterites brought him a list of points on which they wanted further clarification. Unfortunately we must rely on Blesdijk's *Historia vitae* for a summary of the disputed points. According to Blesdijk, the Münsterites objected to the following: (1) That nakedness and the expulsion of shame were useful for obtaining perfection; (2) That one must confess all sins publicly in the fellowship; (3) That the marriage vow was no longer binding for perfection; (4) That there are no evil angels other than the temptation of the spirit by the flesh; and (5) That the present people of God have still to expect and obey another new and universal leader before the coming of Jesus Christ as Judge. Above all the delegation argued that Joris had not sufficiently proven his teachings with the Scriptures.[44]

The question arises whether these points accurately represented Joris' teaching and, even more to the point, whether Blesdijk's report was itself reliable, considering his tendency in his own post-Joris period to interpret Joris negatively. Certainly the points concerning overcoming shame, public confession, and Joris' claims to be a new universal leader seem accurate. The other points are less obvious in Joris' known works. In a later work, written to the Countess Anna of Oldenburg, Joris defended himself, in a rather obtuse fashion, on the controversial points raised by the Münsterites (excluding public nakedness). On the question of marriage Joris argued that it was not against Scripture to leave an unfit wife, as in the case of adultery, but one ought to try forgiveness first.[45] With respect to the question of the non-existence of evil angels, Joris affirmed this point, albeit in a round-about fashion.[46] In other works he was less reticent about denying the physical nature of the devil. In a 1543 letter to the Abbess of Freckenhorst, Agnes von Limburg, Joris argued that the devil was not a physical or creaturely enemy of man or God; instead, one's true enemies were the evil desires of one's heart.[47] It is possible that the issue of public nudity, which appeared in none of Joris' early works, nor in the *Apology*, was one Joris taught only to his devoted followers. According to Blesdijk, Joris taught that the proof that a believer had been reborn was if he could stand in front of or sleep with naked women without becoming sexually aroused.[48] A group of Batenburgers who joined Joris held to a similar practice in Delft in 1538.[49]

Apparently the Münsterite delegation from Oldenburg left Delft unsatisfied.[50] While Joris as a result lost some of his following, he still had a strong group in the area under the direction of Christoffel van Zutphen and Anthon Smedes with whom he was in constant communication. In spite of the supposed defection of the Münsterites Joris achieved a modicum of success in turning radicals from the path of futile revolution.

These data substantiate the thesis that Joris was the most important Anabaptist leader in the Netherlands from 1536 to 1539. He was clearly the most significant leader of the non-violent branch in both South and North Holland from 1536 to 1544. It is also apparent that only the Münsterites and Batenburg radicals provided a significant challenge to his ascendancy over the entire movement in the Low Countries.[51] With a limited success among the radicals, Joris turned his attention to the remnant of Melchiorite leaders, particularly those at Strasbourg.

Notes

1. "David Joris," p. 125.
2. The major sources used were Karel Vos, "Kleine bijdragen," esp. pp. 111-23, who listed 172 from 1531 to 1540, and Mellink, *De Wederdopers*.
3. See Appendix I for a list of active Anabaptist leaders after 1535.
4. *DAN*, Vol. I, p. 174, where he was identified by Dirick Schoemecker, a Davidite converted from the Batenburgers, as a major teacher of Joris. Schoemecker's identification of other Davidite leaders, such as Peter Glassmaker, Andreis Droochscheerder, Seward Klerck, and Andreis Tuchmeister, is confirmed in other sources, such as the confession of Greithe (ibid., p. 176).
5. Mellink, *De Wederdopers*, pp. 174, 414.
6. See Map 1.
7. See below, chapter 8.
8. Menno Simons found it necessary to write a letter to some Anabaptists in Amsterdam in 1545, chastising them for concealing their faith. See Irvin Horst, "Menno Simons," Goertz, *Profiles*, pp. 203-13. Horst speculates that the letter is too conciliatory in tone to have been addressed to Davidites. Clearly survival in the large cities of the Netherlands of the 1540s required a significant degree of accommodation to urban

society and culture and that such Nicodemism was not unique to Joris' followers.

9. Approximately 69% of the 113 Batenburgers identified by place of origin came from the countryside, including villages and small towns. See Gary K. Waite, "From Apocalyptic Crusaders to Anabaptist Terrorists: Anabaptist Radicalism after Münster, 1535-1545," *ARG*, Vol. LXXX, 1989, pp. 173-93.

10. See especially pp. 16-17. Joris believed that were it not for his moderating influence "all of Holland, Friesland, Groningen and Westphalia would have been razed to the ground" (Anonymous, p. 723). See also his comment in the *Onschuldt Davids Jorisz. Gedaen vnde ghepresenteert an die Wolgeborene Vrouw/ Vrouw Anna* (n.p., 1540), fol. 21, translated and edited by Gary K. Waite, in "David Joris' Apology to Countess Anna of Oldenburg," *MQR*, Vol. LXII, 1988, p. 154.

11. Said in his 1538 confession, de Hullu, *Bescheiden*, p. 252.

12. Ibid., p. 291.

13. Stayer, *Anabaptists and the Sword*, p. 287. Jeremy D. Bangs ("Waarom zou je het Nieuwe Jeruzalem zoeken in Hazerswoude, 1535-1536?" *Doopsgezinde Bijdragen*, Vol. VII [New Series], pp. 82-84) relates the uprising in Hazerswoude to dissatisfaction with the local authorities and to disputes between the noble families of this region. See also James D. Tracy, "Heresy Law and Centralization under Mary of Hungary: Conflict between the Council of Holland and the Central Government over the Enforcement of Charles V's Placards," *ARG*, Vol. LXXIII, 1982, pp. 284-307.

14. Zijlstra, *Blesdijk*, p. 7. Later, in 1539, he wrote letters also to the followers of two other self-acclaimed prophets, one in Wesel and the other in Norway. Apparently the Norse prophet, presumably the merchant Hendrik van Hasselt, had said "he would never die, for he would renew the earth, level the mountains in Norway and establish all things according to the Scriptures." According to the source David was able to win over a few of these because his approach during this period focussed on his less ambitious schemes (Anonymous, p. 735). For van Hasselt, see Nippold, "David Joris," p. 524.

15. Anonymous, p. 709. This account mentions that Batenburg himself was one of the 'Haeferson' (as the residents of Hazerswoude were called). According to a confession made by another Batenburger in Amsterdam in 1540, Batenburg had bought weapons for and had intended to participate in the Hazerswoude uprising until he heard that the revolt was not proceeding well. He then divided the weapons among his fellows (*DAN*, Vol. II, pp. 30-31).

16. Mellink (*De Wederdopers*, pp. 218-19) lists those captured. This group practised a form of community of goods.

17. This letter is known only by summary in Anonymous, p. 710.

18. Ibid. As seen in a song from this time (March 1536), the Poeldijk incident had reinvigorated Joris' sense of the apocalyptic, and had heightened the vengeance motif ("Ghy ooren hoort / snel onghestoort," *Liedt-Boecxken*, fols. 69r-70v). One stanza reads:

> Your belly becomes enlarged
> with the red blood of the dead saints,
> which you regard as water,
> Woe to you that you have stirred to drink it,
> You will bring forth [your own] blood with great travail.
> Before the woe presses you
> that has firmly gird you about.

19. Joris' mother had a vision of Joris a few months later (shortly before Joris' visions in December 1536) which closely resembles the image of King Adriaens. She saw her son sitting on a horse, with a hat on his head, a sword at his side and a gun or bow in

his hand, surrounded by a crowd (Anonymous, p. 718). Joris may not have always openly encouraged this veneration, but he did very little to deny it. His woodcut drawings, such as that of the Lamb of God treading upon the "old world" (see p. 95), could also be interpreted to refer to Joris himself.

20. Horst, *The Radical Brethren*, p. 79. Horst mentions that Hart, as a London merchant of some social standing, was quite able to finance the conference (p. 122). Gottwaldt ("Twistreden," *Stadt Strassburg*, 163, note 4) suggests, however, that this "Heinrich from England" was instead the "Hendric in Flanders" who attended the Strasbourg disputation in 1538. Apparently this Henry had at one time been an associate of Joris, and perhaps a native of the Low Countries residing in England would be a more likely candidate to sponsor the meeting. It was not uncommon for Dutch Melchiorites to find refuge in England, something which Jan Matthijs van Middelburg did and Joris attempted in 1535.

21. The dream apparently related that all those gathered at Bocholt — around two dozen in all — would be killed or imprisoned (Anonymous, p. 711).

22. Blesdijk, *Historia vitae*, pp. 13-14; Zijlstra, *Blesdijk*, p. 7; and "David Joris," p. 128, n. 9.

23. The dream had been related to Joris by Jan Matthijs van Middelburg (who had travelled from Strasbourg) (Anonymous, p. 711).

24. Bainton (*David Joris*, p. 25), places the date in September/October. We know that the conference occurred three to four months before Joris' vision in the first or second week in December. Therefore, this author agrees with Zijlstra (*Blesdijk*, pp. 7, 180), in dating the conference in August. See Blesdijk, *Historia vitae*, p. 18; and the "Twistreden," fol. 2r.

25. Blesdijk, *Historia vitae*, pp. 14-15; Anonymous, p. 711; Zijlstra, *Blesdijk*, p. 9; Deppermann, *Hoffman*, p. 374.

26. Zijlstra, *Blesdijk*, p. 9. The original transcript of the conference is presumed lost.

27. According to Deppermann, Joris' compromise provided a "minimal program" for the Melchiorite Anabaptists: "Verzicht auf Rache und Gewalt für eine absehbare Zukunft, Wiederaufnahme der Mission durch Predigt und Taufpraxis, Festhalten an den Hauptdogmen Hoffman" (*Hoffman*, p. 314).

28. Anonymous, p. 711.

29. *DAN*, Vol. I, p. 147; Stayer, *Anabaptists and the Sword*, pp. 284-85.

30. Anonymous, p. 718.

31. Ibid., p. 724.

32. L.G. Jansma, "Revolutionaire Wederdopers na 1535," *Historisch Bewogen*, pp. 54-55. See also Blesdijk, *Historia vitae*, p. 15. Anonymous suggests that the rage of the Batenburgers was due to the harsh measures undertaken by the authorities. He wrote: "For they were made completely despairing, mad, raging and crazy, for each one had seen his wife, friend or maid murdered, and had experienced loss of possessions" (p. 723). This author went so far as to sympathise with the motives of Batenburgers: "Seeing that they were aroused and minded very strongly to vengeance, but certainly not without reason, to speak in a human fashion" (p. 724).

33. Anonymous, p. 725. Joris was hiding in an attic at the time. The event obviously occurred during spring or summer for there to be flowers drying in the attic.

34. Stayer (*Anabaptists and the Sword*, p. 290) says of Joris at this time: "In his aspiration to unite the Melchiorite sects under him David was aided by a sincere enough drive for concord and mutual tolerance. But there was a chameleon-like quality about his spiritualising religion which would accommodate itself to its surroundings almost regardless of where he was or with whom he was speaking." At other times, Joris managed to maintain rather definite views, such as at the earlier Waterland conference

(against armed support for Münster) and at the later Strasbourg conference (see below, chapter 7).

35. Anonymous, p. 725 (if Anonymous can be believed at this point). See also Zijlstra, "David Joris," pp. 130-31. Batenburg's confession is included in *DAN*, Vol. I, p. 144, and de Hullu, *Bescheiden*, p. 252.

36. There is included in the *Hydeckel* a letter by Joris to his supporters in that region. In this letter, Joris tells them to "Siet vorder onder den anderen dat ze iemant onder u die grootste, bequaemste, unde sterckste zi, die stelt tot Dienaers nadie ordeninge van Pauls, vnde bi rade onses Broeders H.C." ("Uprechting der Gemeinten," fol. 335r), most likely a reference to Heinrich Krechting. See also Zijlstra, "David Joris," p. 132.

37. Anonymous, p. 715.

38. Zijlstra, "David Joris," pp. 130-33. Interestingly, Jan van Leeuwarden and Christoffel van Zutphen had both been at Bocholt.

39. Eight to ten days after he had returned from Oldenburg Joris received the summons to meet the Strasbourg Melchiorites, which meeting took place in late June of that year (Anonymous, p. 722). It is not clear if Krechting himself was present. See Zijlstra, "David Joris," p. 132.

40. On the journey, Joris stopped briefly in Raesfelt, where Gossen van Raesfelt, the son-in-law of the Count Barent van Hackfort, one of Duke Karel van Gelder's chief leaders in his wars against the Habsburgs, was living. It is possible, given the unclear wording of the anonymous account, that Joris and van Raesfelt met. Joris later corresponded with van Raesfelt's wife, Jacoba van Hackfort, encouraging her and others of her household in the faith. See his letters in the *Hydeckel*, fols. 406r-v and 458v-60r. It appears that a community of Batenburgers had also made their home here in Raesfelt. Gerdt Eilkeman, an important lieutenant of Batenburg, confessed that after he had accompanied his leader to Strasbourg, he spent three or four years in this region, part of the time residing "with Arndt Bitters of Raesfelt" (de Hullu, *Bescheiden*, p. 267).

41. Anonymous, p. 721. The Bishop and the Duke were in conflict over disputed territory. See Emmius, *Friesische Geschichte*, Vol. VI, p. 901. After settling into an inn, one of Joris' companions was summoned before the Duke. This local ruler, because of his opposition to Bishop Franz von Waldeck, was willing to take Münsterite refugees into his protection. The Münsterites certainly made more than willing allies in the struggle against the prince-bishop. See Karl-Heinz Kirchhoff, "Die Täufer im Münsterland: Verbreitung und Verfolgung des Täufertums im Stift Münster, 1533-1550," *Westfälische Zeitschrift*, Vol. CXIII, 1963, p. 43; and R. Po-chia Hsia, *Society and Religion in Münster, 1535-1618* (New Haven: Yale University Press, 1984), pp. 7-18.

42. Anonymous, p. 721, "Uprechting der Gemeinten," *Hydeckel*, fols. 331r-36r.

43. See Kuratsuka, "Gesamtgilde und Täufer," p. 261.

44. *Historia vitae*, pp. 75-77. See also Nippold, "David Joris," p. 102.

45. *Onschult an Vrouw Anna*, Article XIII, fols. 10v-11r. Regarding the charge that he taught polygamy, Joris replied that he had taught that in the resurrection there will be no marriage, "but not that one may therefore have women in common" (Article XII, fol. 10v [Waite, "Joris' Apology," p. 148]).

46. Ibid., Article V, fols. 6v-7r. He wrote, "I have not said that there are no visible or real devils ... [but they] are nothing or without any ability of their own, outside of man. ... Man is an enemy and devil to himself, he has to guard himself from no one more than himself" (Waite, "Joris' Apology," pp. 145-46).

47. *Hydeckel*, fol. 352r.

48. Zijlstra, *Blesdijk*, p. 32.
49. It is possible that this was no more than a continuation of Batenburg practices.
50. One old man seems to have been the main instigator of the defection (Anonymous, p. 721).
51. Moreover the activities of the radicals were generally concentrated in Westphalia and the northern and eastern provinces of the Netherlands.

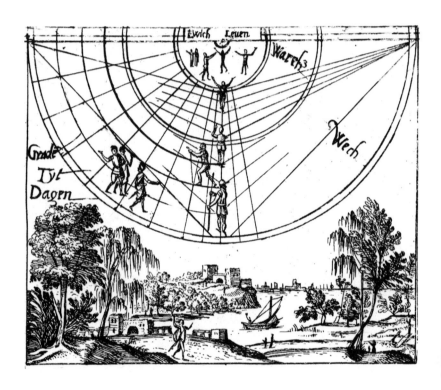

Engraving by Hieronymus Wiericx, after David Joris, "The Steps to the Way, the Truth and the Life" from *Wonder Book*, 1551 edition, Part IV, fol. 20r°. Courtesy The Mennonite Library, University of Amsterdam.

CHAPTER SEVEN

Confrontation with the Elders of Israel: The Strasbourg Debate

The visions Joris experienced at the end of 1536 added confirmation to his belief that he had been chosen to lead the remnant of the Melchiorite movement. In his role as a would-be third David, he took on the burden of leadership for a movement that stretched from Delft throughout the Netherlands to England, Oldenburg and Strasbourg. It was crucial that Joris now convince the small but influential remnant of the Melchiorite group in Strasbourg of his leadership role, for this group was regarded by all Melchiorites, including Joris himself, as the "Elders in Israel."[1] For unless he obtained the approval of the Melchiorites in Strasbourg (where Hoffman himself was still imprisoned) Joris could hardly expect the other Melchiorite groups in the Netherlands, Westphalia and England to transfer their devotion from Hoffman to himself.[2] If he was indeed successful, he would have little major competition for control of the entire movement (excluding of course, Menno Simons, whose activity however at this time was generally restricted to Friesland).

In 1537 Joris first attempted to win over the Strasbourg Melchiorites by sending them several tracts and letters, including a response to a booklet by Johannes Eisenburg on the subject of marriage.[3] A tract published in 1537, entitled *An Instruction or counsel, in order to bridle the thoughts and to make the mouth wise and prudent,*[4] is quite possibly one of those that Joris sent to Strasbourg in 1537. A comparison of the tract's contents with the record of the Strasbourg disputation the following year seems to suggest so. Among other things Joris asserted his prophetic calling and wrote that women ought to keep silent, setting the stage for his confrontation with Barbara Rebstock, who proved a major opponent during the later disputation.[5] An analysis of this tract provides some clues as to how Joris hoped to assert his leadership. He warned the Strasbourg Melchiorites against undue reliance on the letter of Scripture, for "the Word of God is not to be composed or comprehended with ink, letter or pen, but only through the Spirit." Reliance on the letter resulted merely in human, not divine, understanding.[6] Christians are not wise if they can "exercise the letter," for the true training of the mind is situated in the Spirit. Regardless of their beauty, all interpretations of the Scripture not inspired by the Spirit were damned by God.[7]

Notes to Chapter Seven are found on pages 141-44.

Joris further remarked that he had written *An Instruction* through ''a hidden inspiration given to me.'' He continued,

> whoever has received God's Word in his heart through the Holy Spirit
> and proclaims the truth with living understanding, should be heard as
> the LORD himself. But whoever speaks only out of letter understanding
> should not be heard. . . . Furthermore, whoever is truly sent, his words
> are piercing and are worthwhile before God, because they are inspired
> by the Holy Spirit.[8]

These words were, according to Joris, ''inspired by the Spirit, as is Holy
Scripture, and as all other scriptures no less.''[9] The same inspiration which
prompted the writers of Scripture was operative in Joris' time, and particularly in Joris himself. With this belief in mind, the implications of Joris'
warning to his readers can be appreciated:

> Teach not without calling and command. Do no useless work. . . . Nei-
> ther run without his Spirit, but let his angel walk ahead of you, be afraid
> to antagonise his face, and stand always in awe in the things of the
> Lord.[10]

Although Joris did not clearly identify himself as this angel, his comments
in this work leave little room for doubt that at the very least he claimed
divine agency for his writings. He believed that the calling to a spiritual
office must come directly from the Spirit to the heart of the one called, not
from a congregation. The major question to be debated at Strasbourg was in
fact Joris' sense of mission. He warned his readers to ''accept my counsel
which comes from the LORD GOD and remember to humble yourselves.''
These presumptuous warnings appear to have had the wrong effect, however, and could do little to make his peculiar doctrines more palatable to the
Strasbourg Melchiorites.[11]

Even two years after the fall of the Anabaptist Kingdom at Münster,
Joris' writings made veiled allusions to eschatological expectations. The
increasing persecution of his followers served only to show that ''the day
approaches'' when the enemy will rage even more violently. He wrote:

> The dreadful great day of the LORD, the day of weeping and misery, of
> groaning and wailing is near. For that day will flame and burn just like
> an oven before which no flesh, wood, hay, straw nor stubble will remain
> standing. And it is near, in its power and heat. Yes, the great judgement
> hastens, and the unbelieving and the negligent will very quickly and
> hastily fall on their heads.[12]

Only those whose sins are covered and who are therefore forgiven will
endure the fire.[13] Joris' own zeal to propagate his views during the years
1537 and 1538 was due in part to his sense of the nearness of the end of the
age and of the Final Judgement.

At the same time that Joris elevated his own leadership aspirations, he
depreciated the leadership qualities of others, particularly women. He sus-

pected that a major stumbling block to his success at Strasbourg was the respect which the Melchiorites accorded Barbara Rebstock. Joris' view of the role of women in the church was "traditional."[14] Women, he argued, were to be subservient to the spiritual leadership of men. They could not answer questions intended for their husbands, nor should they interrupt his "wise speech." He asked the rhetorical question,

> Is it not proper for her to keep silent? To put her hand over her mouth until her time, or until one questions her? Is it not therefore good, on the other hand, that she be still, prudent and meek, and that she have the maturity and wisdom . . . to speak at the correct time?[15]

Wisdom was to be sought among the elders (male), not among women. Joris credited the poor condition of the church to the fact that women now rule and the "counsel of the brides" went unopposed. This counsel, Joris added, went "against the Lord and resists or opposes the appearance of his majesty."[16] It would appear that, unlike some of his colleagues, Joris left little or no place for women prophets in the movement. Instead, women were expected by their very nature to take care of the home and family.

Apart from the question of leadership, Joris also answered issues raised by Johannes Eisenburg, particularly concerning divorce.[17] Joris' response to Eisenburg's apparent rejection of divorce was based on his separation between flesh and spirit. He agreed with Eisenburg that "what God has brought together, no man can separate," but added that "what Satan, or the fleshly man, or the evil world . . . brings together, God or his Spirit may indeed separate."[18] It was not sufficient for husband and wife to become one flesh, for there must be a unity or agreement of the spirit. If the husband was spiritual, so must his wife be spiritual, else she will drag him down into fleshliness and unchastity.[19] Therefore marriage was more than a physical union. Joris concluded that a marriage based solely on a physical union could be broken, while one based on a union of spirits must not be separated.[20] Joris' ideal for the marriage state was therefore a spiritual union in which sexual relations were condoned solely for the conception of pure, blessed children.[21] Baser sexual passions or the "burning of the flesh" were to be transformed into the "desires of the Spirit," so that a husband could have relations with his wife with a spiritual desire only for the conception of "healthy, blessed children, who are then holy by nature."[22] The physical act of reproduction was not sinful in itself — Joris could find in the Scriptures no more than five or six examples of men who had not been "outwardly defiled by women" — what mattered was purity of heart.[23] Children born of a spiritual union were therefore already regenerate. Joris concluded his reply to Eisenburg with the advice that if one had a pious wife who feared the Lord he should not reject her. Joris therefore advocated monogamy, but monogamy based on a spiritual union for the procreation of holy offspring. Divorce was possible if the union was merely fleshly, or one between a spiritual and a fleshly partner. A spiritual union could not be broken.

The Strasbourg Disputation

It was to present his claims of leadership and to debate the important issues of post-Münster Anabaptism such as marriage that Joris arrived in Strasbourg in June of 1538.[24] The record of the debate, known as the "Twistreden," is one of the more important documents for understanding the development of Joris' thought in the crucial years 1537 and 1538.[25] The vigorous give and take of the discussion reveals more clearly than any other source Joris' conception of himself.

According to Joris, he undertook the journey as a result of visions that revealed to him that "the day of the Lord is very near." He came only to instruct the Melchiorites so that they would not be able to claim innocence at the Final Judgement. In truth Joris sought the stamp of approval from the Strasbourg Melchiorites, assuming that their approval would provide him with the authority of Melchior Hoffman himself. He remarked that he had come to the conference to discover if the Strasbourg Melchiorites "still stood upon Mel[chior] and desired to do nothing apart from him."[26]

Participants in the debate itself included on one side the educated Melchiorites such as Peter Tasch (von Geyen) and Johannes Eisenburg (Pont), and the prophets Leonard Jost and Barbara Rebstock. On the other side were Joris and his travelling companions, among them Leonard van Dam and Jorien Ketel. Peter Glassmaker and Jan Matthijs van Middelburg (leader of the Dutch Melchiorite refugees in England), who had earlier attempted to mediate an agreement, were also present. While the main issue concerned the narcissistic claims of Joris, the discussions that followed — the debate itself lasted three days — touched also on the questions concerning perfection and confession of sins.

The disputation opened with Joris' presentation of what he considered the essential issue, whether or not the Strasbourg Melchiorites were willing to accept his teachings as correct. He asked, "Have you, brothers, considered well and thought over my words . . . whether they are of the Spirit of God or from the Devil? For I am not disposed . . . to dispute with you, but to admonish you and set what I have written before you as correct."[27] Obviously such an attitude left little room for open discussion. The Strasbourg participants complained that it was unfair for Joris to expect them to adopt his leadership without a thorough examination of his teaching. They were not prepared to be browbeaten into submission by allusions to "true wisdom, chastity and the fear of God." Eisenburg demanded that Joris provide rational and Scriptural proofs for his claims:

> prove your pretensions, then we will believe. Faith without reason merely falls to the ground. We have previously accepted M[elchior] H[offman] and others as a result of examination. If we are to believe you, you must instruct us more reasonably and with truth.[28]

Eisenburg's demand for Scriptural and rational proof was supported by

Peter Tasch, who asked why they should believe Joris over all the other supposed Elijahs, such as Heinric Schoemaker[29] or the now slain Jan van Batenburg? "Should we have believed all of those who have claimed to have spoken in the Spirit? . . . If I stood in your place, would you believe me?"[30] However, Joris was either unwilling or unable to engage in rational dialogue on this issue. Instead he appealed to the Spirit and encouraged the participants to engage in self-examination. Several times he advised his hearers to remove all human wisdom from their minds in order to clear the slate for his more enlightened spiritual teachings. When Eisenburg asked, "So tell us, must we let go all words and understanding which we have learned from M[elchior] H[offman], the apostles and the whole Scriptures?" Joris replied, "I do not mean that you should regard good doctrine as evil. I desire simply that you should fulfill it . . . for although you have heard the word from M[elchior] H[offman], you have not yet understood it all, and if you have understood it, you have not acted upon it."[31] It is clear, therefore, that Joris considered himself as the interpreter and perfecter of Hoffman's original doctrine, as his successor in a tradition of progressive revelation.

However, the educated leaders of the Strasbourg group had become leery of the implied subjectivism in Joris' position. Eisenburg reiterated that he wanted to be convinced by Scripture or reason:

> For we have accepted Le[onard] Jost's and M[elchior] H[offman]'s . . . teachings on the testimony of Scripture. M[elchior] H[offman] introduced nothing new which was not proven with the clear testimony of Scripture. . . . He commanded us also "do not let yourselves be driven from the Scriptures."[32]

Thus the lines were drawn between Hoffman and Joris; it was assumed (from his massive commentaries) that the former rested his teaching on the basis of Scriptures, while the latter appealed to authentication on the basis of visions and inner spiritual enlightenment. This is not to imply that Joris rejected the Scriptures. He simply held that to understand their true meaning the reader required the same inspiration that had animated the original writers. The focus of authority had therefore shifted from paper and ink to the heart, where the living Spirit wrote and revealed the true meaning. Joris had progressed from an epistemology based on the visual media of his Catholic period (pictures, statues, the Mass), through the literary medium of the early Reformation (printed Scriptures) and back by means of an enhanced visual epistemology now based on immediate visions, formulated from the Scriptures. This he called the "living word."[33]

It was his claim to inspiration that formed the major stumbling block for the Strasbourg leaders. It seemed to them that Joris exhibited none of the humility he advocated for them. He had told them point-blank:

I speak as the Lord impels me to speak, and desire indeed, that all my words would be written down just as they come forth. For I know that I will stand before the Lord . . . not I, but the Lord who works in me has spoken. I regard myself like the black earth through which [the word] runs like a clear fountain.[34]

When asked "do you think you have all the truth?" he responded, "Behold, I speak from the Spirit and testify it to be from God. . . . Therefore you have heard God's voice."[35] Clearly Joris accepted no challenge to his authority or revision of his teachings. He left the participants little room for genuine dialogue. They could either reject his word as inspired by the devil or accept it as the message of God. Such a view could only spawn a relationship in which the prophet held almost cultic sway over his followers.

Joris could counter the Strasbourg Melchiorites' insistent demands that he prove his contentions with Scripture by depreciating the usefulness of proof-texts. As for the other issues discussed, Joris himself admitted that his unique doctrines (which included the public confession of sins; the complete purification of the believer, particularly from sexual lusts; and his concept of marriage free of sexual passion) were not obtained through the study of the Scriptures, "either the Old or New," but through direct revelation. Only afterwards did Joris add Scriptural texts suggested to him by the Lord. These were not necessary for the "simple, godfearing believers," but only for the "disbelievers and scribes."[36] Proof-texts were therefore necessary only for the skeptic. As he explained,

> Though I will confirm it with Scriptures, which I have noted down by God's grace in the booklet concerning confession . . . for the benefit of the opponents. To [cite Scripture] is not necessary, however, for its own sake, it was done out of mercy through divine grace.[37]

Joris' attitude was, however, not as arbitrary as it may seem to the modern reader. Behind his depreciation of the authority of the letter lay the heightened anti-materialist piety inherited from his involvement in the early Dutch Reformation. Joris preferred to follow this spiritual meaning, obtained directly from God, rather than the "dissimilar books of Scripture, for they erred and contradict each other at many places, especially in the words, as I believe."[38]

Related to this rationale was Joris' argument that the texts of Scripture were not authoritative in and of themselves, but received their authority from their inspired authors. To Johannes Eisenburg's insistence that he prove his contentions with the Scriptures, Joris replied:

> When the prophecies were first spoken, where were they confirmed with Scripture? All that was written and spoken by the fathers, patriarchs, apostles and saints, is that also confirmed by Scripture? Brothers, examine that what is being said to you now at this time is also not found so

written down, nevertheless you are compelled or admonished [by the Spirit] to believe it, whether you agree with its meaning or not.[39]

There were in fact, according to Joris, many "written, spoken and taught Scriptures which we do not have now in the letters." Furthermore, the Scriptures (both Old and New Testaments), when interpreted literally, were limited in their relevance to the "past condition of men." Finally, Joris put forth a concept of progressive revelation, arguing that even more "Scriptures" will be revealed at the time of the apocalyptical seventh trumpet, "when the hiddenness of God will be completed in which all things that conceal will be removed through that most clear sevenfold light."[40]

Joris also undercut the Melchiorites' demands for a rational discussion of authority by insisting that they must become like children in understanding, "for the Word of God is given to the little ones, understanding to the innocent and to no one else."[41] Joris could claim a Melchiorite consensus for his position that spiritual discernment was necessary to understand the Scriptures. Eisenburg agreed that to understand the Scriptures one "must have a special gift of discernment of Scripture, that one must be endowed with special gifts of the Spirit as only the Spirit can distribute."[42] He also agreed with Joris that wisdom gained from formal education, "which has been taught from the a.b.c.'s," and that gained from mere human understanding "without the fear of God," was to be rejected. However, he rebutted Joris' argument by stating that "not all learning of the letter is to be rejected in this way, for Christ himself spoke of letter-learning in the kingdom of Heaven."[43] Eisenburg added that the Jews had been condemned by Jesus not because they were committed to and had used written Scriptures, but because they misused and falsified them. Joris, on the other hand, emphasised the need to become like the "little ones." This meant putting to death one's own intelligence. Humble believers who relied on the Spirit instead of their own wisdom would "know much more truly in their ignorance and would be able to rightly divide the Scriptures." Those who remained in their own intelligence were no better that the "scribes and Pharisees, for they have more regard for the writing than for the rule of truth."[44]

It is clear that Joris had come to place the source of religious authority in the divinely inspired prophet and not in the texts of Scripture *per se*, nor in the hands of those especially trained or skilled to expound them. The Melchiorites on the other hand had obviously moved to a more formal position on authority, based on a consensus reading of the Scriptures. The meaning of such a tendency becomes clear from the position now held by Leonard Jost in the group. He had formerly been one of the most influential prophets of the Strasbourg Melchiorites and his and his wife's visions, along with Barbara Rebstock's, were widely read and published. They had helped to confirm Hoffman's own opinions.[45] During the disputation, however, Eisenburg and Tasch had relegated Jost to the sidelines. Apparently he accepted their leadership in the discussions. Joris felt a kindred spirit in Jost and attempted to draw him into the discussions on his side. When he turned to Jost with the words, "The Lord gives wisdom to the little ones," Jost replied,

> This is true. The Lord has given much to me, of which I understood little at the time. But through the help of the brothers it has been opened to me, and the Lord adds more daily.

It seems that Joris attempted now to drive a wedge between Jost and his comrades. He made himself a champion of Jost's right to participate in the discussions as an equal partner, claiming that Eisenburg and Tasch had disparaged Jost's ability to contribute because he lacked learning in the Scriptures.[46] Later he approached Jost directly with:

> My spirit and your spirit gloried at the first witness. Therefore I had desired to speak with you. For I know that you had the fear of the Lord, also wisdom and understanding. . . . I suspected that you could understand me better than all of them, because [your knowledge] was not in the letter. For I too have given up the letter, I have felt the Spirit of truth in my hands now that I have found God's grace.

Since Joris' overture threatened to split the solidarity of the Elders of Israel, Eisenburg was forced to explain to Jost,

> we have shown that you have the divine gift of prophecy and the fear of God and love (more than all of us), but you do not have the gift of speech, nor of interpreting the differences or contradictions in the Scriptures. . . . We said this about you yesterday, not to despise you, but in appreciation of your spirit of *gelassenheit*.[47]

Joris also attempted to drive a wedge between the other major prophet, Barbara Rebstock, and the educated leadership of the Strasbourg Melchiorites. Joris had suspected beforehand that he might have problems convincing Rebstock of his authority. Therefore, instead of attempting to win her confidence, Joris denied her participation in the conference altogether. His suspicion of Rebstock's intransigence was not without reason. When Joris asked the Strasbourg Melchiorites whether or not they knew what the fear of the Lord was (implying of course they did not), Barbara asked permission of Eisenburg to reply. Eisenburg affirmed "Yes, since the Spirit inspires you, why should you not speak?" So, under the inspiration of the Spirit, Barbara then advised her colleagues not to respond at all to Joris' question, for their words would be judged ultimately by the Lord.[48] Joris doubted that she spoke from the Lord, for she hindered the response to his "inspired" question. Eisenburg defended Rebstock's right to participate in the debate, for "she has been of the fear of the Lord for many years."[49] Joris, hoping to divide his opponents, then drove in his wedge: "Men, keep your [authority] above the woman, so you will not be deceived."[50] He refused, in fact, to continue the debate but was persuaded to proceed after informal discussions with Eisenburg and Tasch. Rebstock, however, made no further interjections during the course of the debate.

It seems that Joris' attempt to divide Jost from the other Melchiorites had failed. On the surface Joris may appear to have defended a more democratic approach (at least for male leaders) to deciding religious issues. Eisenburg and Tasch seemed to assert a certain tutelage over the less educated Jost. But in effect, as seen from his censorious remarks to Barbara, Joris' interest appears to have been primarily to find support for his leadership claims. The discussion that followed made this point particularly clear. When Eisenburg consulted with the others to give Joris a consensus response to the question whether or not they were willing to accept his writings as divinely inspired, Joris accused him of lacking leadership qualities:

> I have spoken by the leading of the Lord against your consulting with each other before giving me an answer. For we teachers are responsible for the brothers, therefore we should receive our wisdom from the voice of the Spirit, which speaks to our inner being. . . . You should answer first, then let all the brothers judge.[51]

The exchange suggests that the Strasbourg Melchiorites had opted for a less charismatic form of religious leadership. Scripture and "reason" were to be court of final appeal. Joris appealed instead to a more illusive but for him a self-evident "spiritual" authority.

Some ramifications of Joris' charismatic prophetic approach were seen in the discussion of the Scriptural texts which Joris had cited in his booklet on confession.[52] Joris agreed to read these passages aloud and each was then discussed. A case in point concerned passages from Ezekiel 36 and 37. Joris applied them to his doctrine of the confession of sins, while the Melchiorites applied them more traditionally to the final restoration of all things. After Joris read them aloud, Eisenburg remarked that "as far as we can see these passages do not serve at all to confession." Joris replied, "I would not be able to understand the passages either if I did not have the revelation of the Spirit." Again Eisenburg disagreed: "We understand these to be about the Restitution, not about confession." The fact that these passages at first reading had little to do with the doctrine at hand did not particularly concern Joris, for he tended to internalise the meaning of passages and appropriate them spiritually or psychologically. He could then use Old Testament passages which originally referred to the Israelite kingdom and apply them to the individual believer. Hence the restoration of the kingdom, in Joris' scheme, was fulfilled in the individual Christian through the public confession of sins which restored him to a state of spiritual health. The passage which Joris read from Ezekiel 36:31-34 was particularly relevant:

> Then you will remember your evil ways and your past which was not good, and then you will mourn for your sin and idolatry. Such will I do, but not for your sake, says the Lord God, let it be known to you. You must shame yourselves, O you of the house of Israel, because of your ways.[53]

Joris' doctrine of public confession as he presented it at the conference was little changed from its earlier form, although he clarified several of its aspects and purposes. First, he reiterated that one of the purposes of confession was to alleviate the guilt and shame resulting from unconfessed sins. Joris also remarked that "we must not be ashamed to spit out our sins, nor be restrained from confession of our guilt and transgressions, or I say to you, you still remain with sins and the old man."[54] Thus the Davidite form of confession was intended to bring psychological relief to overburdened consciences.

Second, Joris fitted his doctrine of confession into the traditional Melchiorite apocalyptical picture. Another of Joris' proof-texts was Luke 18:9-14, where, he argued, believers were told by Christ to confess their sins "like the public sinners of the world," for in that way they will best humble and abase themselves. Joris continued,

> Are we not required to profess and confess our sins . . . ? For what [evil] deeds we have done from our youth were previously concealed from men, but they are not concealed before God and they remain known to his angels, and they will be revealed indeed when we [stand] with our faithful church before the Lord and his angels. This is what we ought to do, in order to come to humility, meekness and lowliness.[55]

At the last day all sins will be revealed. It was best therefore to deal openly with them now, so that they would not be seen by "all the unrighteous heathen," who "will all stand as incriminators in that day."[56] No doubt this insistence on public confession within the brotherhood served to enhance group solidarity. Confession and absolution had been taken from the hands of the priests and vested in the brotherhood. It is possible to see the function of confession also as a tool to exercise discipline and control.[57]

The role of confession in the creation and maintenance of group solidarity can be seen in other statements by Joris, such as: "If we are to become one body . . . then the individual will not be afraid, ashamed or shy to confess his sins before the others as one body."[58] By confessing his sins before the others in the fellowship the confessee enabled not only the leader but also other members to keep tabs on his spiritual health, activities, and conformity. By sharing one's intimate secrets, one was bound even more closely to the group. Furthermore, this heightened group identity gave a sense of distinctiveness to the adherents over against outsiders. Again in contrast to other branches of Anabaptism, the Davidite concept of community involved the internalisation of differences with the outside world. Something acted out in secret (group confession), not a separatist ethic, gave meaning and identity. Such a practice must have served a therapeutic function as well. This factor may help to explain the intense devotion shown by Davidites to their leader and to each other.

Another issue was the question of perfectionism. Hoffman had taught that conscious sins committed after baptism could not be forgiven. The

Anabaptists were often accused of perfectionist tendencies by their opponents. The doctrine of perfection was in fact one of the agreed-upon points
at Bocholt.[59] Joris himself had written on the subject. This aspect of Joris'
teaching was not as controversial as the others, for even Eisenburg remarked
that he and his colleagues had learned of progressive stages to perfection
from the Scriptures. Even with this broad agreement between Melchiorite
groups, there was some suspicion on the part of Eisenburg that Joris' conception was somewhat different. He asked Joris to explain his understanding of striving for perfection.[60]

On the surface Joris' concept of the Christian progression to a final state of
spiritual perfection did not appear unusual. For example Joris remarked:

> You must perceive your years and birth, see where you stand and under-
> stand how far you have gone and have yet to go. This you must
> know . . . that a person is not born first as a man, but as a child . . . but
> the child must grow and leave behind his childish understanding. . . .
> Therefore he must let himself be taught by his elders to forget his child-
> ish nature, or he will not please the Lord. For it must die, even if it were
> a hundred years old . . . so that they might come to perfection, ascending
> from the one virtue to the next, from the one clarity to the next, unto the
> perfect manliness of the maturity of Christ.[61]

Several times during the disputation Joris admonished his hearers to examine where they stood in terms of advancing in the divine understanding of
the "heavenly man."[62] As seen above, one first had to become like a child
in order to enter the route to perfection. Then by listening to Joris one could
progress from "grade to grade in life."[63]

What were these stages of progression? According to Joris, the first
stage was the removal of the old man and his replacement with the mind of
Christ. Essentially this involved letting go of all of one's own wisdom and
entering again into the first schooling under the tutelage of the Holy Spirit as
mediated by Joris himself. Was Joris himself perfect, Eisenburg inquired?
Joris replied: "I may speak as Paul did, although he was not yet perfect,
nevertheless he had received the spirit of perfection out of grace, in order to
lead the people to perfection. I am also in this fashion."[64] What was
required was to remove the accumulated layers of learning and to become
totally receptive to the Spirit's teaching, as presented of course by Joris. He
could then direct the believer on the true path to growth and perfection.[65]
The Strasbourg Melchiorites refused to take this first step, and therefore
Joris declined to present to them any instructions concerning the next stages.
Joris summarised his position:

> But if you have not felt or done the same, then you do not yet have the
> Spirit or gifts. The first [natural man] must perish, in order that you
> might come to the perfection. . . . See, how else can we then ask or judge
> about much deeper matters? Even if there was just one man on the earth
> who came to me to be taught to the perfection I would be happy indeed.

The route to perfection, Joris continued, could only be found by means of
many prayers, fasts and watching, although the latter two practices were not
to be regarded as "outward."[66] Joris appears to have adopted traditional
ascetic ideas (the death to self and new life in Christ) but again gave them a
strongly internalised application.

Because of what he regarded as the obstinacy of the Strasbourg Melchiorites, Joris did not clarify the precise character of the perfect heavenly
man. However, from his earlier writings it is possible to conclude that a
major part of perfection was the eradication of sexual lusts.[67] The topic of
nudity before fellow believers did not come up at this disputation, possibly
because the practice was one of the later stages of perfection which Joris
revealed only to the believing. This could account for its inclusion among
the questions brought to Joris by the Oldenburg Münsterites — who initially
had believed Joris — and its exclusion here.

The Process of Disillusionment

According to the Strasbourg participants, Joris had failed to prove his special call to leadership with either Scripture or reason. Joris' goal of gaining
their adherence was ultimately thwarted. This failure was a serious blow to
his leadership aspirations, and it was to be compounded by the defection of
the Münsterites shortly after the Strasbourg disputation. While he still
maintained a sizeable group of followers and was still an important leader of
the Dutch Anabaptists, from the time of the Strasbourg meeting Joris' desire
to see all of northern, post-Melchiorite Anabaptism united under his control
was dashed. His disillusionment with the Strasbourg Melchiorites and with
Hoffman himself is readily apparent from works written shortly after the
conference. In one tract, Joris remarked:

> Think about what kind of people and teachers they are [i.e., those who
> rely on the literal text] . . . they are still children in their understanding.
> They held Melchior Hofman [*sic*] above everyone, as a servant of the
> Lord, filled with the Holy Spirit and with all riches of the truth and
> knowledge of God. Namely, as the true Elijah, Michael, the promised
> David, the mighty angel of heaven, whom one must hear and follow.
> Indeed, the one who was joined with him, namely Enoch, stood far
> behind him, and will not come nearly as far into the glory as he. But
> they nevertheless presumed and pretended that they administered the
> letter to him (Melchior Hofman) [*sic*] but he ministered the Spirit to
> them. Is that not an abomination and shame? Yes, a terrible defamation
> by the saints in Israel. . . . And although I have said, written and pointed
> out to them their foolishness more than enough, yet they still will not
> believe me.[68]

The Strasbourg Melchiorites had abandoned rule by charismatic prophet for
the safer haven of direction by a group of teachers well versed in Scriptural
interpretation. Joris' concern to maintain the early Melchiorite stress on

charismatic leadership, while a sincere attempt at continuity, did not accord well with the Elders of Israel's current state of disillusionment. The Strasbourg Melchiorites were in the process of removing themselves ideologically from the context where charismatic or prophetic leadership was decisive. They found themselves in a city where a number of Reformers and an active city council directed religious life. The Strasbourg Melchiorites were, already in 1538, well on the way to the Reformed position.[69] The uprooted Joris, on the other hand, preferred to pursue the notion that prophetic leadership was still possible and that charismatic appeal and personal inspiration would continue to attract a naively obedient following.

Notes

1. "Twistreden," fol. 20v.
2. See Deppermann, *Hoffman*, p. 317. Another important Anabaptist leader, Jan van Batenburg, had also attempted to gain the support of the Strasbourg Melchiorites. Batenburg, with the aid of a Münsterite companion, Gert Reyninck, circulated his writings there (*DAN*, Vol. I, p. 163).
3. Blesdijk (*Historia vitae*, p. 26) entitled Joris' reply as "Responsum Davidis Georgii ad libellum Joannem Eisenburch." The original is in the *Hydeckel*, fols. 305v-321r: "Den wisen zi dit gescreven, den onwetenden en latens niet al weten. Wilt dat heilichdom niet den honden geven, noch u peerlen unde rosen voor die vercken stroyen. Och letter up. Antwoort up Hans Eisenburgs voorreden." See Zijlstra, "David Joris," pp. 133-34. It is followed immediately in the *Hydeckel* by a work entitled "Eeen ellenden Roep," in which Joris comments "Ghi Mannen Lieue Broeders wiltgi bestaende bliuen, zo hoort den kleinen vnde simpelen. Hoe goet ist tespreken toten ooren der Ouden, vnde verburgen reden wttespreken vordie herten der wisen." It is conceivable that this work too was intended for the Elders in Israel.
4. *Eene onderwysinge*.
5. Joris said to the Strasbourg Melchiorites, "Vnd ziet: Het is geschiet, dat ic, D(auid), haer tot Straetsburch twee brieuen int eerste vant seuendertichste jaer sant, daer zy weinich af verscrict vnde gebetert geweest zyn, mer hildense, zo zy haren verstant vnde Barbaren tegen was, valsch und ooc duyuels. Dwelc ooc was duert seggen een vrouwen Berbera, die zy in haren drovmen, gesichten vnde woorden hooren vnde geloouen als God. Mer hieraff wist ic doen tertyt niet, want zy en deden my gheen antwoort" ("Twistreden," fol. 2v).
6. *Eene onderwysinge*, fol. 84v.
7. Ibid., fol. 85v.
8. Ibid., fol. 81r. He also wrote "Daer omme nemet mijne raet op / dye voert compt van den HEREN" (fol. 86v).
9. Ibid., fol. 85r.
10. Ibid., fol. 85v.
11. Ibid., fol. 86v.
12. Ibid., fol. 82r.
13. Although obscure here, Joris' reference to the covering of sins may have been to his doctrine of public confession, especially as presented later to the Strasbourg Melchiorites.
14. He warned his male readers that as long as they continued to be like women or chil-

dren in their understanding, Jerusalem would not be restored (ibid., fol. 84r).

15. Ibid., fol. 82v.

16. Ibid., fol. 83r. "[A]llderley voerraet des broets ontagen werden / Angesyen dat ere tonge end doen / tegen den HEREN is / ende dat aenschyn synder maiesteyten verstellen off wedderstaan." See the "Twistreden," fol. 26r, where Joris added this marginal comment concerning Barbara's remarks at the Strasbourg disputation: "zoud ic haer mont met swigen doen vullen, haer hant tegen mÿ: inde waerheit op haer mont hieten leggen hebben."

17. Eisenburg had earlier sent his tract to Joris. Zijlstra identifies Eisenburg's work as probably "Ein kurze erclerung von der waren gotlichen Ordnung des eelichen Standes." The tract has been lost, but Zijlstra ("David Joris," p. 134) rediscovered Joris' reply and has corrected Blesdijk's claim (*Historia vitae*, p. 26) that Joris advocated polygamy in this work.

18. "Antwoort vp Hans Eysenburchs," fol. 306r.

19. Ibid., fol. 310r. "Soe dan die man is, euen zalt wyff moeten zein. Is he Geest, namelyc met Christo ingelyft, zo zal zi ooc moeten geestlyc gesint zy, als he is, of zie en is geen een lichaem mettie Man. . . . Desgelyc die Man, alwaer he een Christen, hanget he eenen onkuischen wiue, of hoer an, zo is he een Lichaem met haer, vnde niet met Christo." Joris added that husbands who allow themselves to be led about by their wives become effeminate. In sixteenth century society, husbands who allowed themselves to be "cuckolded" by their wives were frequently objects of ridicule. See Natalie Z. Davis, *Society and Culture in Early Modern France* (Stanford: Stanford University Press, 1975), pp. 124-51.

20. "Vorder ghi meent om datter staet. Twee zullen een vleis zein, daerom zalmense een vleis laten; sonder twee zullen een Geest zein, zo mochtmense wel scheiden" ("Antwoort up Hans Eysenburchs," fol. 314v).

21. Ibid., fol. 316r.

22. "Merket datghy nu wel verstaet . . . niet wttie begeerlicht of brant des Vleis, dan alleen wt L. des waren Geestes met Lusten inden Geest, unde met eenen vlammenden Geest tot haer Huisvrouwe ingaen om der telinge wille der gesonder, gesegender kinderen, die heilich van nature zein: als Simpson, Samuel, Joannes die Dooper" (ibid., fol. 319r). How one was to perceive the difference between the burning of the flesh and the desires of the Spirit during sexual relations is not explained.

23. "Meendi dattet sein die ghene huisvrouwen hebben? Waer woudi die hondertunduierundueertichduisent vinden? Daer ghi nauwelyc meer dan vyf of ses, ia niet zo vele sekerey en soud indie gansche Scrift vinden, die onbesmit van vrouwen wtwendich geweest zein?" (ibid., fol. 319v).

24. The conference, held around Pentecost (June 1538), coincided with a major Strasbourg market, thus making it easier to avoid detection from the authorities. For similar examples of detection avoidance, see chapter 4 above.

25. The "Twistreden" was recorded and edited by Peter Tasch, with help from Leonard [van Dam] on the side of the Davidites and Paulus Goldsmith on the side of the Strasbourg Melchiorites. Some parts were added afterwards from memory by Peter Tasch. While not completely happy, Joris added his signature to those of the other participants. The document is generally regarded as reliable ("Twistreden," fol. 99r-v).

26. Ibid., fol. 4v.

27. Ibid., fol. 15v.

28. Ibid., fol. 23v.

29. The identity of this prophet is unknown. Perhaps he was Harmen Schoenmaker who had proclaimed himself "God the Father" and entranced with his preaching hundreds of Ana-

baptists who had originally gathered at 't Zandt to march in relief of Münster in 1534.
30. Ibid., fols. 48v-49r.
31. Ibid., fols. 41v-43v.
32. Ibid., fol. 34v.
33. "But this I say to you, that God's word, the fountain of wisdom, does not lie in the literal or the letter, but in the deed and power, this word is fiery, eternal and living. It is not to be understood by anyone except he who has cast away his own wisdom and is poor of spirit, for the Word of God is given to the little ones, understanding to the innocent, and to no one else" (ibid., fol. 17v).
34. Ibid., fol. 14r.
35. Ibid., fol. 16r-v. Joris said at another point, "If you will believe me on this, so will I then speak to you, of what the Lord, not any man or letter, has taught me, and they will not nor shall not be confirmed with external things" (ibid., fol. 23r).
36. Ibid., fol. 31v. Even a quick overview of any of Joris' tracts will show that he was not averse to using a profusion of proof-texts himself.
37. Ibid., fol. 84r.
38. Ibid., fol. 71v.
39. Ibid., fol. 33r.
40. Ibid., fol. 91r-v.
41. Ibid., fol. 17v.
42. Ibid., fol. 85v.
43. Following Matthew 13:52.
44. "Twistreden," fols. 41v-43r.
45. Deppermann, *Hoffman*, pp. 179-85. See also Deppermann, "Melchior Hoffman and Strasbourg Anabaptism," p. 217. Hoffman had some of the visions of the Josts published in 1530 as *Prophetische Gesichte und Offenbarungen vom Werken Gottes in dieser Zeit*, selections of which are in Heinold Fast (ed.), *Der linke Flügel der Reformation* (Bremen: Carl Schunemann Verlag, 1962).
46. "Twistreden," fols. 17v-18r. This earlier discussion was not recorded, but its contents can be inferred from Joris' and Eisenburg's present remarks.
47. Ibid., fol. 18r-v.
48. "For I think that there are some here who desire to pluck the fruits of our tree before they are ripe" (ibid., fols. 25v-26r).
49. Ibid., fol. 26v.
50. Ibid., fol. 27v.
51. Ibid., fol. 39r-v. The reference is to Gal.1:16, where the Apostle Paul remarked that after his "conversion" he did not immediately confer with flesh and blood. This was regarded as proof that the Apostle had not received his knowledge of Christ from other men.
52. "Twistreden," fol. 66v. A closer examination of Joris' practice of confession is found in Appendix V.
53. Ibid., fol. 67v. As translated from the ``Twistreden."
54. Ibid., fol. 33r. He later remarked: "See, I have not only once or twice confessed my iniquities, but indeed six or eight times, and furthermore, it will not harm me to do so even more" (ibid., fol. 36v).
55. Ibid., fol. 53r-v.
56. Ibid., fol. 70v.
57. See Tentler, *Sin and Confession*, p. 220. See also Appendix V for a more detailed discussion of the social control aspect of confession.
58. Ibid., fols. 81v-82r.

59. Zijlstra, *Blesdijk*, p. 9.
60. "Twistreden," fol. 20r.
61. Ibid., fols. 19v-20r.
62. Ibid., fol. 46r. See above, p. 88.
63. Ibid., fol. 47r. For Joris' visual rendition of the steps to spiritual progression, see above p. 127. This picture depicts a pilgrim on the road to the earthly Jerusalem who points upward to the spiritual route to the heavenly Jerusalem.
64. Ibid., fol. 44r.
65. Peter Tasch had commented to Joris that "we sit here to hear and learn." Joris replied, "Oh brothers, if you knew what you said. . . . For I say to you as a word from the Lord, that all brothers must bow themselves under the Spirit, whoever desires to come to the perfection in the Kingdom of God" (ibid., fols. 47v-48r).
66. Ibid., fols. 57v-58r. Later Joris argued, "Soe ghi dat minste voorgeuen van my niet en verstaet noch voer goet op en nemet, namelyc die belidinge, zo en kan ic wider van dat meerder oft hemelscheliker met v niet spreken" (ibid., fols. 98v-99r).
67. See Appendix VI.
68. *Een salighe Leeringe voor die hongherighe bekommerde Zielen* (n.p., n.d.), fols. 123v-124r. While undated, *Een salighe Leeringe* was clearly written shortly after the disputation. This tract, not listed in any of the bibliographies of Joris' works, is available in the Manuscript department, Universiteit Amsterdam (#2497 B19). It contrasts the true, elect Bride of Christ, forced to drink of the cup of bitterness and suffering, with the proud scribes who trust merely in the letter, but not the spirit of the Scriptures (fol. 111v).
69. Deppermann ("Melchior Hoffman," Goertz, *Profiles*, p. 188) noted that in this same year "Johannes Eisenburg and Peter Tasch deceived Hoffman. They spread the false report that the master had totally recanted in their presence, thus inducing the majority of Melchiorites in Strassburg to fall away."

CHAPTER EIGHT

Joris' Followers and Supporters: A Social Analysis

Joris in his time was surrounded by a group of deeply devoted supporters who contributed immeasurably to his success as an Anabaptist leader. What was the social background of Joris' following, and the dialectical relationship between Joris and his devotees? A social analysis of Joris' supporters, and a closer scrutiny of several key Davidite[1] leaders follows.

Joris' Followers

Although concentrated in a triangular area bounded by Alkmaar in North Holland, Deventer and Goor in Overijsel and Antwerp on the south, Joris' movement was spread throughout the Netherlands and Westphalia, with major pockets in other cities such as Groningen.[2] Likewise, the leaders of Joris' various local groups were most active in Holland itself. Interestingly enough, there also were six working in the province of Groningen and one is reported to have been located in Friesland.[3] The urban character of the Davidite circle may be illustrated by a list of localities (Table VII) where a number of followers were identified, imprisoned or executed. It may be assumed that each city contained conventicles although in most cases their strength can no longer be determined.

Of the 219 Davidites identified, about 70% were located in the major cities of the Netherlands. This reinforces the finding that Joris' followers were drawn primarily from the urban setting. Here again the proportions are predictable — approximately 66% (137) were located in the Holland triangle, 10% (20) in or around Groningen, and 5% (10) in Friesland. Very few members from groups other than Joris' or Jan van Batenburg's appear in documents from this triangle during the half-decade after the fall of Münster, so that it appears that Joris had very little competition from other non-violent Anabaptist leaders in his home territory.

Not surprisingly, the social background of Davidites from 1536 to 1544 is comparable to that of Dutch Anabaptists in general before the fall of Münster. In the circle of 219 known supporters, 81 were women (37%), a slightly higher percentage than that gleaned from the sources for the earlier Anabaptist movement in Amsterdam.[4] In terms of occupation, generally speaking both segments were made up and led by those of the artisanal stratum of society. While the occupations of 73 of the men are unknown, the

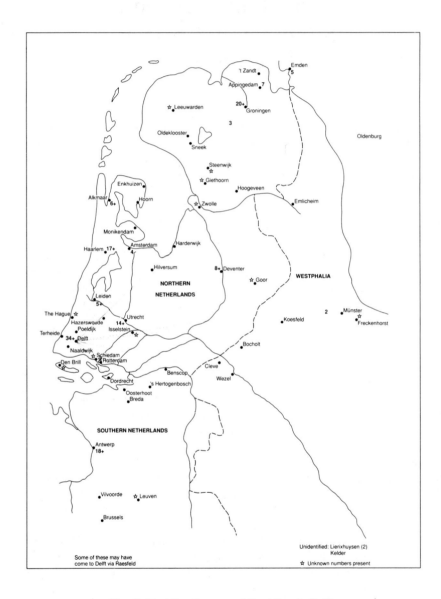

't Zandt
Emden
5
Appingedam 7
☆ Leeuwarden
20+
Groningen
3
Oldeklooster
Oldenburg
Sneek
Steenwijk
☆
Enkhuizen
☆ Giethoorn
Hoogeveen
Alkmaar
Hoorn
6+
☆ Zwolle
Emlicheim
Monikendam
Amsterdam
Harderwijk
Haarlem 17+
4
Hilversum
8+ Deventer
WESTPHALIA
☆ Goor
NORTHERN
NETHERLANDS
Leiden
5+
The Hague ☆
Münster
2
Utrecht
Hazerswoude
14+
Koesfeld
☆
Poeldijk
Freckenhorst
Isselstein
Terheide
☆
34+ Delft
Naaldwijk
Bocholt
Schiedam
Den Brill
Rotterdam
Cleve
Benscop
Wezel
Dordrecht
's Hertogenbosch
Oosterhoot
Breda

SOUTHERN NETHERLANDS

Antwerp
18+

Vilvoorde
☆ Leuven

Brussels

Unidentified: Lierixhuysen (2)
Kelder

Some of these may have
come to Delft via Raesfeld

☆ Unknown numbers present

Map 2. Davidite Groups and Davidites in Delft

Table VII. Localities of Davidites

34	Delft (27 executed in 1539), 5 leaders
20	Groningen
18	Antwerp (most after 1539)
17	Haarlem
14	Utrecht
9	Westphalia
8	Deventer
7	Appingedam
6	Alkmaar
5	Leiden
5	Emden
4 each	Amsterdam and Friesland
2 or more	Rotterdam, Isselstein, Goor (several), Leeuwarden, Scilde, Hilversum, The Hague, Giethoorn (several), East Frisia and Sloten (several)

remaining 65 included four merchants and 47 artisans, twelve of whom were involved in the cloth industry, which at this time was undergoing a period of stagnation.[5] A notable distinction between Joris' movement and its precursor is the slightly higher proportion of the educated elite in Joris' group. Joris also gained supporters from the nobility. Seventeen members of his group had achieved a higher education or had come from noble ranks, including four teachers and four clerics.[6] This elite therefore made up a strong 26% — one quarter of the total known occupations. Several of these more learned or wealthy supporters joined after 1539, and they were largely won by the efforts of Jorien Ketel. Perhaps Joris' own upper-class background attracted support from the higher social circles.

The question of the relationship between Joris' internalised spirituality and its attraction to urbanites and members of the upper strata of society is an interesting one. Joris' return to the Sacramentarian position (where the external observations of religious ceremonies were regarded as less significant compared with their internal meaning) was complete by the early 1540s. He and his urban followers may have adopted this position for very practical reasons. It was dangerous to be an obvious non-conformist or separatist in an urban environment. Therefore assuming a hidden or less visible form of radicalism significantly reduced the danger of discovery and arrest. Internalising beliefs and practices was one reason why Joris' teaching was found more palatable to urban Anabaptists than the more separatist or sectarian attitudes of Menno Simons.

A further correlation between the social composition of the Davidites and that of the Anabaptists prior to 1535 is that many members of both shared the common element of uprootedness. Of the 27 Davidites executed in Delft in 1539, only two, Katryn Huggen and Joris' own mother, are known to have been natives of the city. The remainder came from such diverse places as the province of North Brabant (4); Westphalia (4); Groningen (3); the city of Leiden (3); and elsewhere.[7] Employment opportunities may have accounted for their presence in Delft. Five of the fifteen men executed were carpenters (three from North Brabant, one each from Utrecht and Groningen) who most likely had come to Delft to participate in the rebuilding of that city after the great fire of 1536.

A similar situation to this can be seen in Haarlem and Utrecht. Of fifteen Haarlem Davidites in 1539 (thirteen executed), at least seven were not native to the city, with a minimum of four of these coming from the territory of Münster. Of the fourteen Utrecht Davidites, four were from the territory of Münster, four from the Southern Netherlands and two were from Overijsel. It appears, therefore, that many of Joris' followers were uprooted artisans who, having been caught up in the revolutionary excitement of the early Melchiorite movement, now found it safer to be away from home.

Did these people gravitate to the cities for economic or for religious reasons? The evidence suggests both. Carpenters, for example, who moved into Delft did so for obvious economic reasons. Others may have moved to this city to flee persecution or to be closer to Joris. The last factor provided strong motivation for Heinrich Kaal and several women who came to Delft in 1537-38. Joris' anonymous biographer remarked that these women came to Delft seeking "salvation and to meet the needs of the soul. They desired to remain with the man David because of the kingdom of God."[8] Some of these female sympathisers actually joined Joris' group in order to escape Batenburger polygamous relationships. One in particular, Merieke Steinmetzer, had been forced to marry Gerdt van Zwolle, a Batenburger, after her first husband was murdered by the Batenburger Gerdt Eilkeman. When this husband was himself killed, she was given to his brother, Hensselin. At this time she escaped to Joris.[9]

While one can surmise a broad general picture, detailed background information on the rank and file of David's movement is unfortunately lacking. Evidence suggests that many Davidites had been rebaptised prior to the fall of Münster.[10] A large number of those executed in Delft in 1539 appear to have been in fact former Batenburgers who joined Joris' Delft fellowship under the influence of Kaal. Three of these ex-Batenburgers had confessed that they had never actually seen Joris in person and that they had certainly not learned their polygamy from him. One confessed that he had heard about Joris from a young girl named Ael;[11] another, Cornelis Wolfartsz, learned of Joris' doctrine from his books; and a third, Dammas Jacobsz, seems to have been informed by Kaal. They affirmed, however, that they regarded Joris as their prophet. Most in this group had been baptised. Jacobsz also confessed that he regarded Rothmann's *On Vengeance* as the Word of God. They had travelled to Delft via Rotterdam and most likely had come from the territory of Münster, perhaps Raesfelt. In late 1538 the Delft authorities made an unsuccessful search for Kaal and his associates, having heard rumours that they plotted insurrection. From this, then, it seems that Joris attracted former Batenburgers. This group retained the practice of polygamy and interpreted Joris' doctrines in a rather idiosyncratic fashion. Geertgen Cornelis, one of three wives of Fransz Philipsz, confessed to the Delft authorities on January 23, 1539, that this group of Davidites "had entirely mortified the flesh, that they could appear naked before each other with no more concern than Adam and Eve while in the state of innocence."[12]

Former Batenburgers tended to interpret Joris' thought in continuity with their earlier radical beliefs, although they normally laid down their swords, if only to wait for the divinely appointed time of vengeance. Dirick Schoemecker confessed in 1546 that:

> David Joris' opinion and teaching is that he is the Promised David, and that all who believe on him shall reign with him here on earth, and that he shall root out, exterminate and kill all princes, lords and kings.[13]

Although Schoemecker's remarks cannot be said to reflect Joris' teaching accurately, nor can one imagine Schoemecker as a typical follower, his comments illustrate how Joris' doctrine could be reshaped in a Batenburger context. The above examples also serve to illustrate that Joris' movement was largely decentralised and unstructured.[14] The variety that existed among "Davidites" is evidence that Joris' authoritative claims did not always extend to the grassroots level in terms of direct control over the beliefs and actions of his followers. This loose organisational structure may have permitted a few isolated incidents of polygamy or other practices not condoned by Joris. There is, however, no evidence that polygamy was practised by Davidite groups which had not come out of a Batenburger background. Certainly nothing resembling polygamous behaviour appears from the groups in Haarlem or Utrecht. That Batenburgers could associate with Joris and yet maintain their polygamous or even violent activities reflects both the ambivalence inherent in Joris' esoteric teaching and the important role of individual lieutenants such as Kaal.

Joris' Lieutenants

In order to put the historical role of David Joris into context, it is necessary to examine the key associates who gathered around him as his messengers and advisors. The relation appears to have been reciprocal, for Joris was also influenced by them. Joris in fact became, through the course of the late 1530s, dependent upon his associates for his own survival.[15] Indeed, the relationship between Joris and his lieutenants was a dialectical one. A brief social analysis of twenty-two Davidite leaders will set the background for a closer examination of this dialectical relationship between Joris and a few key supporters.

Records between 1536 and 1544 identify 25 Davidite teachers or leaders.[16] At least five were fairly well educated, including two teachers,

Andreis Tuchmeister and Seward Klerck, both of Groningen. Two others, Nicolaas Meyndertsz van Blesdijk and Hans de Wael, were skilled in Latin or other languages.[17] Four others were merchants, including Jorien Ketel, who also appears to have had a good education. The rest of those whose occupations were identified were artisans like Joris himself, as is demonstrated in Table VIII.

Table VIII. Occupations of
Davidite Leaders

Formally Educated	4
Teachers (2)	
Artillery Master	
Blesdijk	
Cloth Trade	5
Silk Merchant	
Cloth Cutter (2)	
Weaver	
Tailor	
Merchants (excluding the above)	3
Other Artisans	6
Miller	
Cooper	
Rakemaker	
Furrier	
Glassmaker	
Reelmaker	

It is therefore apparent that Joris had at least half a dozen co-workers whose education matched or surpassed his own. This also suggests that in much the same way as in the rest of society, on the whole those with a better education and the more prestigious and lucrative professions assumed leadership roles, despite Joris' emphasis on spiritual qualities for prospective teachers.

The affiliation of these leaders prior to their joining Joris' group is instructive. As noted above, most of those who became important in Joris' movement after 1536 had been active Anabaptist leaders before that year. Several began their Anabaptist career as radical Melchiorites who looked to Münster with keen interest. Many joined the search for a new King David when it became apparent that Jan van Leiden's course of action would fail. Some joined Batenburg's movement.[18] With Batenburg's execution in April 1538, several of these radical Anabaptists, in search of charismatic leadership, turned their devotion to Joris. Menno Simons, noting Joris' success in winning radicals to his side, remarked sarcastically:

> Is it not a grievous error that you suffer yourselves to be so woefully seduced by such worthless persons, and so sadly misled from one unclean sect to another: first to that of Münster, next to Batenburg, now Davidian; then from Beelzebub to Lucifer, and from Belial to Behemoth?[19]

With this negative attitude on the part of Menno, it is no wonder that radical Anabaptists were more prone to join Joris rather than the Mennonites. A brief description of four prominent Anabaptists who made the transition from Melchiorite to Batenburger to Davidite will suffice as examples.

Andreis Droochscheerder was perhaps one of the most prominent and intelligent Münsterites to survive the fall of the kingdom.[20] In 1534-35, he had preached throughout Groningen and Friesland as one of the Münsterite emissaries. In January 1535 he was a participant in the attempt to gather forces to relieve Münster at 't Zandt. When the gathering was taken over by the ecstatic and totally unrealistic Harmen Schoenmaker, Andreis managed to capture the prophet and bind him with ropes until associates of Schoenmaker freed him.[21] In the spring of that year Droochscheerder was at the meeting which selected Batenburg, and it was his sermon, taken from both the Old and New Testaments, which finally convinced Batenburg that he was to be the third David and avenger of God.[22] Although the known details of Andreis' activities after this meeting are few, it is evident that he became a prominent preacher of Davidite doctrine in Groningen, probably before 1538.[23]

A second example is provided by Hans Scheerder. Ordained an Anabaptist bishop in 1533 with Obbe Philips, he, Obbe and Jacob van Campen debated the following year in Amsterdam. In 1535 he was again in Groningen, assisting in the capture of the Oldeklooster monastery.[24] He was probably at the spring 1535 meeting with Batenburg and was a participant at the Bocholt conference in August, 1536. He seems to have joined Batenburg's movement for a brief time, apparently participating in the robbing of churches near Cleves and Wesel. In 1537 he was contacted by Joris and became one of his supporters. He may have worked with Jorien Ketel in Deventer in 1539, helping to correct and distribute Joris' published works. He seems to have then moved back north to proselytise in Appingedam.[25]

Adriaen van Benscop had likewise worked in both Groningen and Amsterdam, playing a major role in the attempted take-over of the latter city in 1535.[26] He joined Batenburg's radicals after the failure of the Münster kingdom, and then sided with Joris after the execution of Batenburg. As a Davidite he acted as a messenger, and in one of Joris' letters from 1539 there is a reference to a "brother Ari." Since Adriaen was known also as Cooman Ariaen, this is probably a reference to him. This brother had gone on a mission to Goch, apparently supported financially by the Davidites with whom Joris was corresponding.[27]

Finally, Heinrich Kaal provides the clearest glimpse into the attitudes of radicals who joined Joris. A soldier who had become a grain merchant, Kaal (his full name was Heynderich Pietersz Koel van Gelre) had also been at the spring 1535 meeting in Groningen. It was he who had informed Batenburg of the forthcoming attempt on Amsterdam in May of 1535.[28] After this time he seems to have joined the terrorists and was among the Westphalian Batenburgers at Raesfelt in the summer of 1537. The following autumn, he, with several of his associates, joined Joris' fellowship in Delft. The account of his meeting with Joris is instructive. One evening Kaal came into Joris' house (apparently the two had never met before):

> David took him by the hand, and desired, according to the usual custom, to give him a brotherly kiss, but the man [Kaal] stepped back and bowed down, and falling prostrate he said, "O my Lord David, forgive me the evil, which I have done against you," and told him [Joris] of his evil disparate activities. . . . The next day he [Kaal] was more smitten in his heart, so that David could not go before H[einrich] K[aal] without him [Kaal] bowing down on his knees before him even as many as twenty times a day. David wanted to stop him, but he begged, that he might not deprive him, it must be in this way.[29]

When Kaal was arrested in December 1538, the authorities discovered on his person a book containing descriptions of his own apocalyptic dreams. Apparently Kaal confessed to his captors that:

> the Holy Ghost rested upon David Joris, and that his Writings were of divine inspiration. He added, that he did not believe that the said David ever intended to plunder Towns and Villages, or to promote his affairs by violence.[30]

The reverence paid to Joris by these former Batenburgers is reminiscent of the adulation formerly accorded to Jan van Leiden and Jan van Batenburg. Each of these three leaders was regarded by their followers as the third David who would bring in the kingdom of God.[31] It is clear that Joris was influenced by this adulation, and it could only help to strengthen his belief that he was indeed the apocalyptical David. This belief Joris began to develop at the end of 1536[32] and was firmly in place by the early 1540s.

These former Münsterites or Batenburgers who became supporters of Joris then stood out as important figures in the spread of Joris' thought outside of southern Holland. Former radicals helped to establish Davidite conventicles in the province of Groningen (Andreis Droochscheerder, Hans Scheerder, Andreis Tuchmeister and Jacob up de Kelder); in the cities of Alkmaar (Rem van Hoorn),[33] Hilversum and Naarden of North Holland (Bauke Molenaer);[34] in Westphalia (Christoffel van Zutphen, Anthon Smedes, Peter von der Lippe, Henrick Reekers and later Blesdijk); and Sloten in Friesland (Henrich Herckemaicker).[35] These were areas where Batenburgers were also quite active and it appears that David's ex-radical supporters proselytised among the radicals whenever possible. There seem to have been rather extensive contacts between Davidites and Batenburgers, as seen in several confessions of the latter.[36]

After Batenburg's death, a remnant group of guerrillas was led by Cornelis Appelman. According to a recent study of the Batenburgers, Appelman's group was noted for its "ideological poverty."[37] Appelman's associates therefore may have sought ideological help from Joris' writings. Appelman himself sent two of his associates to Jorien Ketel to obtain a copy of Joris' *Wonder Book*. Ketel, after correspondence with his leader, turned down Appelman's request for the book.[38] Several other active Batenburgers identified themselves with "David's doctrine." Johan Morveldinck is a good example. Baptised into Anabaptism by two later Davidites, Peter Glassmaker and Christoffel van Zutphen, he was an active terrorist in Overijsel. He also claimed to be of the "party and doctrine of David Joris' folk," who

> believe not in the worthy holy sacrament but only in the Son of God sitting at the right hand of his heavenly father, and that our teaching is that men may damage churches and keep all church goods in common.[39]

Whether Morveldinck and his associates can be regarded as anything more than nominal Davidites is a moot point, although they may have found Joris' teaching (as they understood it) to be more congenial than that of Menno Simons.

Hans de Wael is another Davidite with close connections with the Batenburgers. Hans was the *Busmeester* (paymaster or artillery master) of Deventer and a skilled linguist (Latin, French, High German, and Italian).[40] Appelman and three other Batenburgers accused him of "wavering in his sect because he has joined the sect of David Joris."[41] No evidence exists that de Wael had participated in violent activities. Nevertheless, he was accused of counterfeiting church keys so that the Batenburgers could enter the churches at Utrecht and Appeldoorn. An intriguing clue to de Wael's affiliation was provided by Appelman. According to the terrorist commander, de Wael had requested of the Duke of Bueren that de Wael be installed as the *Busmeester* of Isselstein. This request appears perplexing, until one examines the situation more closely. The bailiff of Isselstein, Gijsbrecht von Baeck, was a supporter of Anabaptists and had housed Heinrich Rol in 1534. Ten years later his wife, Elsa von Sostardt, was jailed for four years on suspicion of being a Davidite.[42] De Wael may have sought a home more tolerant of Davidites.[43]

Jorien Ketel

Joris had at his side two extremely important supporters, Jorien Ketel and Nicolaas Meyndertsz van Blesdijk. Blesdijk has recently received excellent scholarly attention.[44] Ketel, on the other hand, has received little study to date, although he must be regarded as Joris' top lieutenant until Ketel's own execution in 1544.[45]

Ketel was born into the gentry around 1511 and received therefore a good education. He apparently spent some time as a personal attendant to the Lady of Bueren, consort to Floris van Egmond and mother of the then stadholder of Overijsel.[46] Apparently he was economically well off since he joined the silk merchants. Baptised in 1533-34, his early Anabaptist activities or affiliations remain unknown. It was previously thought that he had been a Batenburger, but the evidence for this contention lacks credibility. It consists primarily of Appelman's confession that Ketel had been party to his own terrorist activity. However, it seems that Appelman, like his former leader Batenburg, deliberately sought to implicate Joris and his friends who represented the major rival.[47] We know that Ketel had turned down Appelman's request for a copy of the *Wonder Book*, suggesting that they were on less than friendly terms. N. van der Zijp's identification of Ketel with the Batenburger Jorien van Goor (Henrickson) is the result of a less than careful reading of the sources.[48] Van der Zijp also used Blesdijk's statement that Ketel had been "converted from a profligate life" to Joris as evidence that Ketel had been a Batenburger. Blesdijk's statement, however, is a reference to Ketel's "vain" life in the court of nobles, and probably refers to his first adoption of Anabaptism.[49] The fact that Ketel may have joined David's movement at about the same time as some Batenburgers could imply that he too had been a revolutionary, but the evidence is lacking. It must also be remembered that the lines between the various groups were fluid and not clearly drawn in the early period. During the disputation at Strasbourg in 1538, Ketel joined in the discussion concerning the validity of Joris' concept of public confession of sins. He remarked:

> See, I had also opposed this position, as you [Strasbourg Melchiorites] do. At the first I had opposed Batenburg's position or teaching, which in part also immodestly opposed [Joris'] position. But it was revealed to me afterwards while I was in great turmoil from the fire of unchastity: "behold, this is the thing which you oppose," and I was forced to confess and to hold it as correct.[50]

It appears from this obscure passage that Ketel had at one time opposed both Joris and Batenburg, but finally joined the former because of Joris' teaching concerning sexual temptation.

Late in 1537 Ketel was apparently in Haarlem, and he may have had contact with Davidites there.[51] Upon joining the Davidites Ketel moved very quickly into Joris' confidence, becoming in fact his right-hand man. In June of 1538 Ketel accompanied Joris to the Strasbourg conference, presumably functioning as a kind of bodyguard. When not with Joris, Ketel was busy assisting the Davidites in Utrecht and establishing contacts in his home province of Overijsel and the Southern Netherlands. Many of these contacts were from the upper classes or nobility, and when Joris was forced to seek refuge outside of Delft, Ketel sought to find shelter for him with several of these upper-class sympathisers.[52]

In July of 1539 Ketel's first wife, Elsken, was executed with other Davidites in Utrecht. While presumably still grieving, Ketel went the following month on his mission to deliver Joris' letter to Landgrave Philip.[53] That year Ketel, now based in his home city of Deventer, also arranged for the publication of at least three of Joris' works with the prominent Deventer printer Albert Pafraet, and again two more in 1542. Ketel and an associate (Hans, possibly Hans Scheerder), had done the editing.[54] Also in 1543 Ketel arranged for the publication of Joris' *magnum opus*, the *Wonder Book* (along with some smaller works), with another Deventer printer, Dirk van Borne.[55] Later, both printers faced disciplinary action for their activity.[56] Ketel spent his time also winning sympathisers to David's cause and raising funds for the publication of the *Wonder Book*. He appears to have travelled extensively, for he worked with Blesdijk in Regensburg in 1541.[57] His recruiting a wealthy family from Antwerp, the van Berchems, was crucial both for the publication of Joris' works and for his acceptance into the city of Basel in 1544.

Ketel also attempted to win over Karel van Gelder, bastard son of Duke Karel van Gelder and the former Stadholder of Groningen. Van Gelder, in fact, had spent a night at Ketel's house in Deventer and had received a copy of the *Wonder Book*. Ketel confessed that van Gelder had agreed to help finance Joris' publications, a claim not directly denied by van Gelder. While van Gelder admitted he had spent some time with Ketel, he disavowed Ketel's charge that he had joined the Anabaptist movement.[58] Overall, van Gelder appears to have been rather sympathetic to the movement, although it is not likely that he had actually joined it. Ketel also made the acquaintance of a former monk and the supposed spiritual mentor of van Gelder, Gerrit Goldt.[59] Furthermore, Ketel had some contact with members of the Loisten sect of Antwerp, in particular Christopher Herroult.[60] While in the city Joris himself became embroiled in a dispute with them.[61]

Fortunately Ketel produced some writings of his own which permit insight into his ideas. They date from the time of his three-month imprisonment preceding his execution on August 9, 1544. Ketel had been compromised in the confession of Appelman (captured in Leiden) and was ordered arrested by the Stadholder of Overijsel.[62] Ketel's writings include: "A Testament which I, Jorien Ketel, have written to my dear children at the end of my life"; "A New Song," attached to the "Testament" and published together as *Wholesome Teaching*;[63] "Confession, a letter written to his wife"; and "A pure, beautiful teaching."[64] All but *Wholesome Teaching* are available only in late seventeenth-century handwritten manuscript. There is also a second-hand account of his martyrdom, written by a sympathetic eye-witness.

Ketel's "Testament" and letters read like those of other Anabaptist martyrs and there is nothing in them that would automatically exclude him from membership in the Mennonite martyrology, *Het Offer des Heern*. He exhorts his children to fear the Lord, to be quick to forgive, to avoid liars, to honour their mother and to take care of one another. He requested the older children (N. and N.) to care for the younger ones, and to "let them go to school."[65] They were to take heart that the "day of grief for God's right-eous and the day of rejoicing in vanity for the unrighteous will both con-clude soon."[66] Ketel asked his second wife to care for the children of his first marriage and for his mother, "who has suffered so much sorrow on my account." He concluded with "I have died so many deaths before I die [a reference to the several bouts of torture he was forced to endure], that I can-not write it all to you. Written in my last hour."[67]

The account of Ketel's martyrdom is the most interesting document. Here Ketel's devotion to Joris is clearly seen, and he admitted that Joris had

> taught me nothing but good, namely God's Word, and all his doctrine was proven and confirmed to me with divine Scriptures; how that I should put to death and tread under the old man with all his evil lusts and should put on or become a new man. He counselled and taught all this to me, such a dunce [*ezelscop*]. For this reason should I not listen to him, believe him and follow after him?[68]

When offered a crucifix by a monk, Ketel replied, "No, I will not take your cross, I bear Jesus Christ and his cross in my heart, that is enough for me."[69] After being led to the executioner's block, Ketel turned to the crowd and proclaimed:

> I suffer death not as a rogue, thief, murderer, or other evildoer, but I die for the sake of eternal righteousness and the truth of God. Moreover, that I am in agreement with D[avid] J[oris], this I confess and is well known. I believe in God the Almighty Father and in his Son Jesus Christ, the true anointed of God, which D.J. also does, and my founda-tion and ground stands upon the teaching of the apostles and prophets, where D.J.'s foundation also rests.[70]

According to the eyewitness, Ketel died joyfully and as a pious martyr. He also died as a warning to those who

> sleep, namely you who are lusting and are impure in sins. For the day of the Lord, the terrifying judgement of God, is at the door, when all those who do not better their lives out of wisdom, who have despised the counsel of the Holy Spirit, her chastisement, love and trust, will per-ish.[71]

The admonition was so typically Jorist that it was most likely written by the prophet himself. Considering the fact that Joris had acted earlier as editor for another martyr's testament and song, it is quite likely that he played a key role in collecting, editing and publishing Ketel's works.[72] They were cer-tainly published together with several of Joris' own works.

It is clear that Joris' most important assistant until 1544 was Jorien Ketel, and it was chiefly as a result of his activities that Joris gained so many wealthy supporters. Ketel was also largely responsible for the publication of most of Joris' early works, including the *Wonder Book*. He was a key member of the support group that kept Joris alive during his fugitive existence, and it was to Ketel's credit that Joris was able to find a permanent refuge in Basel. No doubt Joris felt Ketel's death to be a serious blow, but the slack was quickly taken up by Blesdijk, an even more capable second-in-command.

Leonard van Dam

Unfortunately, almost nothing is known concerning the other important figure in Joris' movement, Leonard van Dam, who travelled frequently with his leader, including to the Strasbourg conference. His vision of a divine-human figure, experienced in 1539 and relating clearly to Joris, illustrates the intense devotion which Joris received from his closest followers. In the vision van Dam first saw a human figure, floating naked between heaven and earth, not having a place to rest. Then he saw the image growing out of the ground as a flower, and when the image had fully appeared out of the ground, van Dam was not allowed to touch him, for "he is still dead and not yet living."[73] Van Dam looked, and the man's face shone like a sun, with a beautiful red beard. He appeared so mighty and frightening that he need fear no one, for even the "kings and emperors of this world were before his eyes as the worms upon and in the earth are regarded by men." When the image disappeared, a voice said to him, "this is God, the Messiah, the new creature, the first true human God from heaven."[74] Joris was esteemed very highly indeed among his supporters and it is almost certain that this adulation had a not inconsiderable impact on Joris' self-conception as a prophet in the lineage of Jesus Christ himself.

Notes

1. I follow Stayer ("Davidite vs. Mennonite," p. 460) in using the term Davidite instead of David Jorite or Davidian for the followers of Joris. Identification of an Anabaptist as a Davidite was usually indicated by his or her belief that Joris was the prophet for the Anabaptist movement as a whole.
2. See Map 2.
3. See footnote 35 below.
4. The actual percentile may be higher in both cases, given the lower visibility of women within Anabaptism — few bore leadership roles which would have made them more susceptible to identification and arrest.
5. Posthumus, *Inquiry*, Vol. II.
6. One of these was the Abbess of Freckenhorst, Countess Agnes von Limburg, who, according to Dirick Schoemecker, "only took Jorists into her service." Apparently the convent's cook and fishermen were Davidites, and Joris' followers in this region met together within the convent walls (Kirchhoff, "Die Tufer im Münsterland," p. 87). Several letters from Joris to Agnes are found in the *Hydeckel*. For the difficulties being experienced by the

Dutch nobility in the sixteenth century, see H.F.K. van Nierop, *Van ridders tot regenten: De Hollandse adel in de zestiende en de eerste helft van de zeventiende eeuw* (Amsterdam: Stichting Hollandse Historische Reeks, 1984).

7. The authorities of Leiden took very stringent measures to dislodge Anabaptists from their city. This included the doubling of guards on the gates from December 1538 to June 1539. Joris showed considerable reluctance even to pass through the city. See Anonymous, p. 736, and Mellink, *De Wederdopers*, p. 195. See also Map 2.

8. Anonymous, p. 721.

9. Merieke was brought to Joris from Raesfelt by Heinrich Kaal at the time of the Oldenburg meeting (ibid., pp. 721-22; *DAN*, Vol. I, p. 175). Batenburg husbands were known to punish disobedient wives with death.

10. Included were Anneken Jans (baptised 1534); Claes Claes (banned from Leiden in 1535); Cornelisz Evertsz (baptised 1534).

11. Art Jansz van Osche. This girl was perhaps Ael Schellen, one of three wives of Cornelis Wolfartsz and one of the Delft martyrs. Some of these wives may have been those who had earlier fled Raesfelt.

12. Brandt, *History of the Reformation*, I, p. 75; Nippold, "David Joris," pp. 88-92. All the evidence points to a former Batenburger affiliation for this group. Kaal, in the spring of 1535, had told Batenburg of the planned attempt on Amsterdam. See de Hullu, *Bescheiden*, p. 251. Gerdt Eilkeman, an important Batenburg leader, had stayed for a time in or near Raesfelt during the late 1530s; from 1535 to 1539 he was based in Havixbeck, fifty kilometres northeast of Raesfelt (ibid., p. 267).

13. According to Stayer (*Anabaptists and the Sword*, p. 298), Jaspar Smedes confessed in 1538 that "David was against murder and arson, but not against plundering catholic churches, provided the booty was given to the poor."

14. Evidence suggests, however, that a form of organisation did exist on a local scale. In a letter to some followers in Westphalia, Joris told them to choose their elders with care and to hold them in high esteem. However, Joris seems to have used the terms "Ouders," "Dieners," and "Priesters" rather indiscriminantly ("Uprechting der Gemeinten," *Hydeckel*, fols. 332v-333r).

15. See above, Chapter 4. The role of women in Joris' movement is worthy of a study on its own. See Packull, "Anna Jansz," for an example.

16. Davidite leaders were those who led local Davidite cells or who were recognised as key messengers of Joris. For example, Dirick Shoemecker identified Henrick Reekers and Peter von der Lippe (a merchant) as two "apostles" of Joris who converted him to the movement. Apparently Reekers was prosperous, for he purchased a house in Warendorf (east of Münster) for 500 gulden (Kirchhoff, "Die Tufer im Münsterland," p. 87).

17. Blesdijk seems to have made his role as Joris' lieutenant his career. He was only nineteen when he joined. After he left the Davidites, Blesdijk became a pastor in the Reformed Church. De Wael was the Deventer artillery (or pay) master. See de Hullu, *Bescheiden*, p. 292.

18. Bauke Molenaer, Andreis Droochscheerder, Heinrich Kaal and probably Hans Scheerder were at the spring 1535 meeting in Groningen which saw Jan van Batenburg chosen as the new David.

19. "Is 't niet een bedroefde dwalinge ... dat gy van alsulcken onnutten menschen so deerlijk betooveren ende soo jammerlijck van de eene onreijne secte in de andere laet voeren, eerstmael Münstersch, daerna Batenborghs, nu Davitis, ende alsoo van Beelzebul tot Lucifer ende van Belial tot Behemoth" (J.C. Wenger [ed.], *The Complete Writings of Menno Simons* [Scottdale: Herald Press, 1956], p. 215). The Dutch original is also in de Hullu, *Bescheiden*, p. 274, taken from Menno's *Fundament in klare Aenwijsing* of 1539.

20. Batenburg had remarked that Andreis thought that he was "wiser than the others" (de Hullu, *Bescheiden*, p. 248).
21. *DAN*, Vol. I, p. 118.
22. De Hullu, *Bescheiden*, p. 249. Droochscheerder, according to Batenburg, had concluded that "God had chosen him [Batenburg] as David, who as a leader and captain ... of the people of God, should help him punish with the sword Babel and the whore of Babylon."
23. He was identified as such by another Batenburger turned Davidite, Peter Shoemaker, in 1546 (*DAN*, Vol. I, pp. 173-74). The fact that Batenburg mentions Andreis in his confession implies that Andreis had already left the radical movement. Batenburg did not implicate any of his current followers.
24. The capture of this Frisian monastery near Bolswart, on the part of some three hundred Anabaptists on March 30, 1535 was led by the emissaries from Münster, most importantly Jan van Geelen. Van Geelen escaped from this fiasco to lead the attempt on Amsterdam six weeks later. See Stayer, "Oldeklooster and Menno," p. 52.
25. See Zijlstra, *Blesdijk*, p. 12; Mellink, *De Wederdopers*, pp. 262-63; *ME*, Vol. II, p. 651.
26. Mellink, *De Wederdopers*, p. 264, notes that he travelled to Groningen to win support on behalf of the Amsterdam take-over bid. See also Zijlstra, *Blesdijk*, p. 14.
27. Joris, *Het derde Boeck der Christelijcker Sendbrieven* (n.p., 1611), Vol. III, Part 1, fol. 29v.
28. De Hullu, *Bescheiden*, pp. 248-53, Zijlstra, *Blesdijk*, p. 16.
29. Anonymous, p. 726. Another Davidite who had travelled with Joris to Strasbourg had a dream in which he saw a beautiful woman transformed into a whore, then into an ugly dog. Initially he thought the woman to be Joris (this follower seems to have fallen away) but eventually he changed his mind, finally interpreting the woman to be Batenburg. He then fell down with uncovered head before Joris, and called him Lord. Joris, according to the account, asked the man not to prostrate himself or to call Joris Lord ("who am but a man") but finally relented in the light of the man's persistence.
30. Brandt, *History of the Reformation*, Vol. I, p. 75; Nippold, "David Joris," p. 95.
31. Concerning the Groningen meeting which chose Batenburg, Jansma ("Revolutionaire Wederdopers," p. 50) remarked that Jan van Leiden was no longer regarded as the David who could deliver the people of God, therefore the mantle passed to Batenburg.
32. See *Hoert, hoert, hoert*, fols. 30r-33v.
33. One Alkmaar Davidite confessed in 1544 that "Rem van Hoorn gedaen werde dexpositie nae de leeringen van den voorsz David opte figure van een menschen ende alle zijn leden" (Mellink, *De Wederdopers*, pp. 174, 414). Joris included a picture of a naked man — "The New Heavenly Man" — in his *Twonder-Boeck*. See above, p. 88.
34. Before 1540 he was living in Hilversum, after that year in Naarden (*DAN*, Vol. II, p. 35).
35. As a Batenburger, he had helped to rob the church of Oldelemmer in 1536-37. He joined Joris' movement before 1539 in Giethorn, where there was a circle of Davidites (de Hullu, *Bescheiden*, p. 294, and Zijlstra, *Blesdijk*, p. 15). Later in 1539 Henrich was living in Sloten where he told Jan Willems (Hansken), a Batenburger, that "David voors van God geseynt was omme de werldt inne te neemen." Willems also confessed that his sister was converted to the Davidites by Peter van Schiedam, but he himself resisted. He also remarked that "David Jorysz. veel anhangers heeft ende in Oostland ende ellders aloome zijn verstroyt ..." (*DAN*, Vol. II, p. 29).
36. Cornelis de Kuiper (from Delft) converted a Batenburger, Johan Peters, to Joris' position (Mellink, *De Wederdopers*, p. 174). The propensity of Batenburgers to falsely implicate Davidites in terrorist activities makes the sifting of evidence from these confessions difficult. See also the confessions of Hanskin (*DAN*, Vol. II, p. 29); Gheryt Jacobs (ibid., p. 35); Johan Peters (Mellink, *De Wederdopers*, p. 174, and Stayer, *Ana-*

baptists and the Sword, p. 295); and Johan Morveldinck (de Hullu, *Bescheiden*, pp. 263-64). Fransz Jans, a Batenburger, helped to break out several Davidites from the Leiden prison in 1539 (Mellink, *De Wederdopers*, p. 238).

37. Jansma, "Revolutionaire Wederdopers," p. 60.
38. De Hullu, *Bescheiden*, p. 293. This refusal on Ketel's part may have been a contributing cause to Appelman's implication of Ketel in terrorist activity.
39. Ibid., p. 264. Joris himself admitted that some claimed to be of his doctrine who still practised violence against his wishes (Stayer, *Anabaptists and the Sword*, p. 299).
40. *Busmeester* can refer to either artillery master or to the guardian of the money chest or offering box. De Wael's linguistic abilities and possession of church keys may suggest the latter meaning in his case.
41. De Hullu, *Bescheiden*, p. 292; Mellink, *De Wederdopers*, p. 239.
42. Rembert, *Die Wiedertäufer*, pp. 316-19. She was released in 1548.
43. It may also be possible that de Wael was the "gifted, intelligent man" who had sought to support Joris against the Strasbourg Melchiorites in 1538, but who was left behind at Cologne because of illness (Anonymous, p. 722).
44. Zijlstra, *Blesdijk*; Stayer, "Davidite vs. Mennonite," pp. 459-76.
45. Zijlstra (*Blesdijk*, p. 1) noted that Blesdijk joined Joris in 1539 and became one of his most important supporters, becoming most active in the mid-1540s.
46. Blesdijk, *Historia vitae*, p. 101; de Hullu, *Bescheiden*, p. 291; Mellink, *De Wederdopers*, p. 280.
47. De Hullu (*Bescheiden*, p. 278) considers the charge as a mistake in the document.
48. "Jorien Ketel," *ME*, Vol. III, p. 122. In May 1544, the Deventer authorities had requested information from the Haarlem authorities concerning Ketel or other Anabaptists. The Haarlem secretary responded with the report that there was a Batenburger, Jorien Henricksen van Goor, who had stayed outside the walls a few years earlier. Van der Zijp identified this Jorien van Goor with Ketel, but in 1544 Appelman sent Jorien van Goor to Jorien Ketel to obtain a copy of the *Twonder-Boeck* (de Hullu, *Bescheiden*, p. 293).
49. "Ad eundem modum Georgius [Jorien Ketel] a teneris in principum aulis verlatus, & horum novorum prophetarum opera a crassiorbem vitiis & meliorem vitam conversus, hujus perceptae mutationis sensa & seducia sola fretus confidenter testatur in hujus sui prophetae doctrina nullum esse errorem" (*Historia vitae*, p. 124). I am indebted to Werner O. Packull for his help in the translation of this passage.
50. "Twistreden," fols. 69r-v.
51. In his confession of February 1538, Batenburg named him as an Anabaptist in that city. Batenburg was arrested in Artois (South Netherlands) in late 1537, thus his confession must have been a summary of his knowledge before his arrest (de Hullu, *Bescheiden*, p. 255; Mellink, *De Wederdopers*, p. 183). The identification of Haarlem comes from the Amsterdam version of Batenburg's confession. This version added that Ketel was housed with Bauke and Oelffaert Molenaers, the latter a known Davidite.
52. In 1539 Ketel took Joris to the home of a nobleman outside of Deventer, but the sympathiser had since changed his mind (Anonymous, pp. 736-37). Leonard van Dam took Joris to potential benefactors in Breda (South Netherlands) and Guelders, and these may have been arranged by Ketel as well.
53. See below, chapter 9. See Blesdijk, *Historia vitae*, p. 101, and Zijlstra, *Blesdijk*, p. 19.
54. De Hullu, *Bescheiden*, pp. 321-24. There were three to four hundred copies made of each, for which Pafraet was paid ten to twelve gulden. The books printed in 1539 included: *Een seer schoen tractaet off onderwijs van menigerley art der menschen vianden; Een zer zuverlijck tractaet van de lyeffde* (two to three hundred copies); and

in 1542: *Troest, raedt, leer ende onderwisenge* and *Ach des dages die so treffelijck is.* The first tract listed contains chapter summaries written in the third person, presumably by an editor seeking to explain Joris' writing in a more lucid and concise fashion. This editor was most likely Ketel. For example, before chapter 9, the editor wrote: "Here he says how that the law must appear first / if the gospel is to be revealed ..." (*Een seer schoen tractaet*, fol. 101v).

55. De Hullu, *Bescheiden*, pp. 317-19.
56. While Pafraet maintained his innocence, saying he had been told that the books were not against the Church and denying he was an Anabaptist, he had, contrary to his usual custom, not printed his name on these works. In July 1544 he was ordered to march in a procession with a lit candle as punishment. Van Borne was, however, imprisoned for half a year from July 1544 to January 1545. See de Hullu, *Bescheiden*, p. 319, and Blesdijk, *Billijcke Verantwoordinge ende eenvoldighe wederlegginghe Nicolaes Meynertsz van Blesdijk op eenen scheltlasterighen brief door doctorem Hieronimum Wilhelmi ... int jaer 1544* (n.p., 1544), fol. 95.
57. Zijlstra, *Blesdijk*, p. 20.
58. Van Gelder does appear to have been familiar with the *Twonder Boeck* (de Hullu, *Bescheiden*, pp. 296-99; Blesdijk, *Billijcke Verantwoordinge*, fols. 17v-20v; Mellink, *De Wederdopers*, pp. 263-64, 279).
59. De Hullu, *Bescheiden*, p. 299; Mellink, *De Wederdopers*, p. 289.
60. De Hullu, *Bescheiden*, p. 308. Herroult was a French jeweller. Ketel observed that Herroult and many of his co-religionists in Antwerp were "Sadducees, not believing in the resurrection of the dead." The Loists were followers of Loy de Schaliedecker (Eligius Pruystinck), a prominent Antwerp religious radical.
61. Zijlstra, *Blesdijk*, p. 62.
62. Brandt, *History of the Reformation*, Vol. I, p. 81; de Hullu, *Bescheiden*, pp. 277-79.
63. Published in 1544-45 with a number of Joris' tracts. It had previously been thought that this work existed only in an early seventeenth-century copy. It was reprinted by Blesdijk in his *Billijcke Verantwoordinge* of 1547 (published 1610) with only insignificant alterations.
64. Hillerbrand, *Bibliography*, #2964, dates the publication of this work as 1545. It was not available to me.
65. *Wholesome Teaching*, no pagination [fol. Bi(v)].
66. Ibid., fol. [Bi(r)].
67. "A letter written to his wife," de Hullu, *Bescheiden*, p. 317. See Appendix III for an English translation. Apparently the torture was so severe that he was made "no longer fit to live in this world" (ibid., p. 311).
68. Ibid., p. 313. See Appendix II for a translation of this account.
69. Ibid., p. 314.
70. Ibid., p. 315.
71. Ibid., p. 316.
72. See Packull, "Anna Jansz," pp. 22-23. De Hullu remarked that the account was not written by a native of Overijsel. Blesdijk could have been the eyewitness, although Joris cannot be excluded from consideration. The eyewitness and editor were not necessarily the same person.
73. Anonymous, p. 730. The similarity of this with the resurrection account of Christ telling Mary "do not touch me, for I have not yet ascended to my father," is perhaps due to the time period — just after Easter — when this incident occurred. The vision was apparently published, probably by Ketel or Joris. For a translation, see Appendix IV.
74. Ibid., p. 731.

Title page: *Wonder Book* (Deventer: Dirk van Borne, *c.* 1543). Courtesy
The Mennonite Library, University of Amsterdam.

Joris' Asylum in Antwerp, 1539-44

After several futile attempts to find lodging in Breda, Rotterdam and Gueld-ers, Joris and his company finally found refuge in Antwerp in the late sum-mer of 1539.[1] It was in Antwerp under relatively secure living conditions that Joris returned to a form of neo-Sacramentarian Nicodemism. Joris remained in or near this city with his family for four years, during which time he both corresponded with his followers and pondered the finer points of his theology and his future. A letter written shortly after his arrival in the fall of 1539 is especially enlightening. Addressed to Landgrave Philip of Hesse, this telling missive requested asylum of the Landgrave. In heart-rending prose Joris described to Philip how Christ's true followers were being persecuted by the bloodthirsty authorities in the Netherlands.[2] Philip, mistaking Joris for an Evangelical, responded favourably to this letter, remarking to its courier, Jorien Ketel,

> that his master in Holland appears to be persecuted on behalf of the Faith, so he could find, just as any other, dwelling and protection in Hesse, if he agrees to the Augsburg Confession, unless he can show any errors in it from the Scriptures.[3]

Judging from the complex matrix of his thinking and circumstances at this juncture, it is most likely that the Augsburg Confession would not have greatly interfered with Joris' theological stance, but for reasons which are as yet unclear Joris did not accept Philip's offer.[4]

In the meantime Joris had become preoccupied and even enamoured of two wealthy noble families of Antwerp, the van Liers and the van Berchems. The fugitives had apparently found sanctuary around 1542 in the manor at Schilde, where resided the Lady of Schilde, Anna van Etten, widow of Jan van Berchem, with four of her offspring: Joachim, the eldest son at 22 years, Anna, Reinier and Willem. The elder daughter, Wybrecht, had mar-ried Cornelis van Lier, Lord of Berchem in 1532 and hence she had become Lady of Berchem. Furthermore, Cornelis' sister, Anna van Lier, was a regu-lar visitor to the Schilde *hof*. Infatuated with Joris' daughter Clara (she could not have been older than eighteen years), Joachim ignored the vast distinction in social status and married her, although presumably not in a church.[5] It appears, then, that Joris' first noble patrons in and around

---

Notes to Chapter Nine are found on pages 172-74.

Antwerp were Anna van Etten and Anna van Lier, respectively mother-in-law and sister to the Lord of Berchem. It may have been as a result of their personal sway that Cornelis van Lier was won to Joris' side. Taken with Joris and his ideals, these supporters were willing to underwrite Joris' later move to Basel. It is also apparent that there was a considerable change in the attitude of the fugitive prophet toward the nobility. Like his fellow Anabaptists, Joris, prior to his acquaintance with the van Berchems, had mixed feelings about the nobility and other authorities. He had warned in a 1537 missive:

> Judges and commanders stand in great peril. If they are [too] kind, so they will perish as a result. Understand this. . . . See, it is free to them [i.e., to hold office], as long as they do all things correctly in the faith and do not hinder Christians nor the gospel, but instead further it. If this is not [the case], then it is better to abandon [the office] with Moses and to suffer trouble with the people of God.[6]

In the *Wonder Book*, which appeared sometime in 1543, Joris' caution has turned to praise. He now suggested that the honour given to kings and lords, who protect their lands from rebellion, was a symbol of the even greater honour that one should give to the Lord God.

> All kings, lords and princes, all princes, judges and fathers have their own total will, authority and command in their realm, humbling all they possess and bringing rebels under them. Yes, they rule everything that lives, everyone born to women. The world presents its sons and daughters to them and they glory in each other. Each is a head, the one over the other; the mightiest and highest are given the greatest honour and esteem. What should be done then to the Lord of all these? Does none of this honour nor fear belong also to him?[7]

Joris furthermore declared: "O you noble persons, wake up and write wisdom in the time of idleness, print the words of truth in the innermost part of your hearts and learn to know that wisdom, knowledge and understanding in the truth."[8] In spite of his lowly birth, Joris could now strengthen his identity as a member of God's royal household, as the third in the lineage of king Davids.[9] He could therefore comfortably fraternise with and even chastise members of the worldly nobility.[10]

Joris therefore stayed in Antwerp while his lieutenants, Nicolaas Meyndertsz van Blesdijk and Jorien Ketel, spread his teaching throughout the Netherlands and Germany. Both Blesdijk and Ketel for example appeared at the Regensburg disputation in 1541, where Ketel attempted to convince the Strasbourg reformer Martin Bucer of the truth of Joris' doctrine. Whether or not these discussions included attempts to work out a compromise between Joris and Bucer is not altogether clear.[11]

In the year 1542 Joris began a literary dispute with Menno Simons. After having read a copy of Menno's *magnum opus*, the *Fundamentboeck*,

Joris was prompted to write a letter to its author, initiating a feud which was to last for several years. The debate between the two leaders had to do with Joris' Nicodemite lifestyle and spiritualising motif, and climaxed in several meetings between Blesdijk and the Mennonites from 1546 to 1547 in the North German city of Lübeck. This debate has received adequate scholarly attention and falls outside of the chronological limits of this study.[12] Another Mennonite leader, probably Adam Pastor, also countered Joris' charismatic leadership claims and unique doctrines in a 1542 tract, eliciting a written defence from Joris.[13] The dispute with the Mennonites marked a new stage in Joris' Anabaptist career, for despite his success in winning some Mennonites to his side, Joris' status within the Anabaptist movement declined considerably as a result of Menno's vociferous opposition to Davidite practices.

It is therefore clear that after moving to Antwerp, Joris ceased to propagate his views in person, opting instead to rely on lieutenants such as Blesdijk and Ketel and on his writings to transmit his thoughts.[14] The importance of Blesdijk and Ketel is also apparent in the debate between Joris and the Reformed Superintendent of Frisia, Johannes à Lasco, a conflict expressed initially by letter which culminated in a meeting between Blesdijk and à Lasco in 1544.[15]

Joris' Developing Spiritualism

During the Antwerp exile, then, Joris seems to have moved gradually to a more Spiritualist position than one that can be seen as Anabaptist. Spiritualism, as the name implies, stresses the supremacy of the spirit over matter; the Spirit of God works directly in the heart of man and is not bound to any external means, such as the Scriptures or sacraments.[16] At the heart of the Spiritualist approach is a fundamental dualism; the contrast between letter and spirit, inner word and outer, old man and new, visible church and invisible, received sharp definition.[17] An undercurrent of this dualism was long present in Joris' works. In a 1537 tract, he had asked

> Beloved, how are these reconciled? Flesh and spirit, the earthly and the heavenly, the perishable and the imperishable, the chaff and the kernel . . . are not [God's] thoughts and ways as different from our thoughts and ways as heaven and earth are from each other?[18]

The contrast between flesh and spirit, however, was also a commonplace in Anabaptist thought, especially among the Melchiorites.[19]

From a position of relative security in Antwerp Joris was free to reflect on recent events and as a result made several revisions in his program. Tendencies toward internalisation (present from the beginning in Joris' thought) became more and more obvious. Joris' movement towards a Spiritualist position was moreover accelerated by his failure to win the permanent allegiance of the Oldenburg Münsterites and the breakdown of dialogue with the Strasbourg Melchiorites. During the following five years Joris moved

slowly and tentatively to the full Spiritualist position which he later lived
out at Basel from 1544 to 1556. This development is also evident in Joris'
writing style. While the works Joris had written before moving to Antwerp
are relatively straightforward and easy to comprehend, in the early 1540s he
developed the concept of a "spiritual language," understood only by a spiritually enlightened elite. He spelled out this idea in his *Clear Report on how
Man has fallen from God*, which was completed in 1543:

> Because many read so quickly that the meaning passes them by, I will,
> dear reader, warn you not to hold to such a practice or idea, especially in
> divine matters, in things brought forth by the Spirit with true godly
> understanding, in a spiritual or heavenly language. For only the spiritual
> ones will understand the new heavenly language by means of the heav-
> enly birth of God.[20]

His writings, always difficult to understand, became even more turgid,
inspiring one well-educated contemporary to remark: "It was difficult for
me to understand the meaning of the thoughts because of the terribly
obscure and confused style of the writing."[21] In the Antwerp works Joris'
ideas are therefore increasingly spiritualised and shrouded by his use of an
elitist "spiritual" language.

By 1539 Joris had already arrived at a significant degree of theological
spiritualisation. He went so far as to remark, in *A Very Good Examination
of Wisdom*, that

> Sin, death, the devil, hell and damnation, you must understand, are
> inside man and not outside of him. Therefore all of these must be killed,
> defeated, brought to nothing and completely be taken out of sight inside
> man, in the power of the name of our Lord Jesus Christ.[22]

What Joris was driving at was that the worst enemies of the soul of the believer were not the authorities, nor were they any external agent of evil.
Instead these devils were evil desires and inclinations within the individual
heart. Joris went on to say that

> man must first begin the fight against himself and take up enmity against
> his own devil or his own sinful flesh, as it belongs to do for a new crea-
> ture in the light of the knowledge of Christ. . . . There can be no other
> way into eternity.[23]

This spiritualisation was extended to Joris' thoughts on the return of Christ.
In 1539 Joris was able to write of a visible return of Christ, but this idea of
revisitation could only take place, he cautioned, in the souls of believers.
According to Joris

> Christ . . . who was taken out of sight in the clouds into heaven, so again
> will he come forth gloriously, in order to appear visibly and with might,
> honour and force. Namely in his saints, heaven, stool, throne and dwell-
> ing or column of clouds. . . . But before this great glorious day, Christ

must suffer much suffering in all his members, and be rejected by this nature or evil generation . . . until the third day.[24]

Until that "third day," Joris maintained, Christ would suffer with his disciples and the kingdom of God would remain hidden in the hearts of believers. In Joris' opinion, certain spiritual preconditions had to exist before the Lord would physically return. He therefore compared the necessary spiritual conditions for deliverance to

"three measures of flour" [that] must be completely cleansed, the kernel of wheat must die, the fruit must be in the mouth, the love become revealed, the Spirit of understanding come forth in power, before the King of glory in his beauty, his Son from eternity, Christ upon his throne of the Kingdom and the end of all old things, can appear.[25]

In short, Joris believed that the time for the humiliation of Jerusalem had been extended.[26] The rebuilding of the city of God was in fact to be performed by the anointed servant and shepherd, the third David. This promised third David was the apocalyptical figure upon whom the Spirit of God rested and who would complete the work begun by Jesus Christ, the second David. The third David (or "Christ David") would finally

sit and rule upon the LORD'S throne (or stool) like a king and the priest shall also sit upon his throne, for it will be one body, with peace and unity between both. Namely between God and man, with Christ and the church, as husband and wife.[27]

In spite of Joris' emphasis on the "spiritual restitution" fulfilled in the minds and hearts of individual believers, as late as 1539 he still maintained Melchiorite expectations of a concrete fulfillment of the kingdom of God on earth.

Echoes of the earlier apocalyptic excitement were still noticeable in the *Wonder Book*, but Joris had by 1543 nearly eradicated all expectations of a tangible fulfillment of the eschatological kingdom or of the return of Christ. Concerning this, Joris wrote:

I say to you, inside, in your innermost heart will it [the day of the Lord] come upon you. Your conscience will be examined, your words, works and thoughts be weighed and measured, where you are accused by yourself. . . . For in this way exists his coming. . . . For when he comes, he comes without delay to terrify the earth and judge the nations, to rule the peoples and to make even and straight all things. However, such a coming is unknown and believed or examined by few.[28]

The last judgement would for Joris take place not visibly, with the standard trumpet-blast form, but secretly within men.[29] The trumpet proclamation of judgement became in Joris' framework a rather noiseless affair, for the trumpets of the Apocalypse would resound externally only through the mouths of believers as the "teaching of wisdom and the voice of eternal truth."[30] During the few years when Joris hid securely in Antwerp, he took full advantage of the leisure of intellectual reflection, which allowed for the development of a more internalising tendency. This, at a time when Joris had to conform outwardly to urban society, served to drive his Melchiorite theology more completely to the back recesses of his thought. What resulted can in some respects be regarded as a return to the anti-materialism of Joris' reform past.

In this development, Joris may have been influenced by the works of Spiritualists such as Sebastian Franck or Caspar Schwenckfeld. The Spiritualists' stress on the inner word, the spiritual meaning of the sacraments, and religious toleration reinforced Joris' own tendency toward Spiritualism.[31] Sebastian Franck's "Letter to Campanus" was in Dutch translation by 1541 and would have provided Joris with a good summary of Spiritualist thought on which to base his own ideological reconstruction. For example, Franck asserted that the Holy Spirit, anticipating the misuse of the outward ceremonies shortly after the death of Christ, "gladly yielded these tokens to Satan and fed, gave to drink, baptised, and gathered the faithful with the Spirit and the truth" in a purely spiritual fashion.[32] Furthermore, Joris' reliance on visions and the inner word was similar to Franck's assertion that

> Scripture and [another] person can only give to a person and a believing brother some testimony, but cannot teach what is divine. . . . Faith is not learned out of books nor from a person, however saintly he may be, but rather it is learned and poured in by God in the School of the Lord, that is, under the cross.[33]

Joris' developing position on the external rites of the church appears remarkably parallel to Franck's.

There are, on the other hand, significant differences between the two. Franck claimed that "at the present time not a single true and natural word of the Lord Jesus Christ, the Son of God, is acknowledged on earth, yea, that no one has begun to recognise the righteousness of faith,"[34] a view hardly to be reconciled with Joris' still firmly held belief in the third David and his role as the sole authoritative spokesman for God.[35] Joris' development towards Spiritualism clearly owed much to the literary works of Franck and other Spiritualists, but he blended it with a still pronounced apocalyptical-Anabaptist framework. It was not until he moved to Basel in 1544 and befriended the Basel Spiritualists such as Sebastian Castellio that he would dismantle the Anabaptist framework and become a more consistent Spiritualist.[36]

The New Birth

Along with the increased spiritualisation of the Melchiorite apocalyptic message, Joris began to emphasise more clearly the concept of "new birth."[37] From the beginning of his Antwerp residence, Joris made repeated references in his tracts to "the rebirth of the Spirit" and to a "second more holy and greater birth.''[38] With the attainment of this "new creature or heavenly birth of the Spirit," the believer in Joris' eyes also obtained a "perfect maturity in understanding," seeing for the first time the "unveiled face of Jesus Christ." Joris' concept of rebirth, however, must not be confused with similar evangelical notions, however much these ideas may have played a similar social function in group identification. In his unique way, Joris perceived "rebirth" as merely part of the gradual, step-by-step attainment of perfection, described in the following citation:

> So then, we are called out of faith to hope, from hope to love. That is, from a child to a youth, from a youth to a man, to come to perfect maturity in Christ. Then is seen and known the true understanding of God, like the sunshine and the perfect knowledge of love in the Spirit.[39]

Joris used a framework of progression similar to that of Bernhard Rothmann, but without Rothmann's concrete communal *Sitz im Leben*. Because he led an underground existence Joris applied this framework to the spiritual state of individual believers. It is instructive to notice that Rothmann had taken the divisions in the Israelite tabernacle to be the forecourt, the holy place, and the holy of holies, constructing a scheme for the progression of Christ and the body of believers. Rothmann's scheme can be represented (see Table IX).

Table IX. Anabaptist Progression

FORECOURT	HOLY	MOST HOLY
The Way	The Truth	The Life
Death	Resurrection	Ascension
Faith	Hope	Love
Child	Youth	Adult
Joris added:		
Flesh	Soul	Spirit

The first level of Rothmann's scheme involved death or mortification of sins as well as the first elements of Christian doctrine. The second level was the enlightenment of the truth. The third consisted of true life or resignation in Christ and following his example.[40] What were for Rothmann stages in the achievement of Christlike behaviour with direct application in a socio-political context, became in Joris' framework steps in a mystical ontological (metaphysical) transformation of the believer's psyche from imperfection to perfection, indeed from humanity to divinity. Perfection meant possessing the "mind of the Spirit," with which one could obtain true power and might.[41] According to Joris, one had to proceed through each stage, however, before achieving the final goal. In these writings from Antwerp Joris clearly felt more comfortable in spelling out the steps of progression than he had at the Strasbourg disputation.

Spiritualising the crusade actually increased Joris' sense of calling, particularly with respect to his self-understanding as the third David. In Joris' view at this time one's spiritual identity came from internal beliefs, not conformity to mere external standards. It was therefore possible to conform outwardly but remain inwardly separate. With this principle in mind it was possible to see that the function of the apocalyptical David now more closely approximated that of Joris himself — divinely enlightened teacher of spiritual truths. Coming as Joris believed from the mouth of God, the "voice" of the promised David would transform all things. Joris encouraged his readers therefore to listen earnestly "to this voice."[42] Clearly Joris regarded himself, like the Biblical prophets, as the mouthpiece of God.

> Listen to the voice of the Archangel, know the trumpet's sound, the war cry which is heard from heaven over all. I say to you, behold, I am truly (believe me if you will) awakened to this by the LORD GOD, and am driven to warn you all.[43]

Elsewhere Joris commented, "See, I, DAVID, have been awakened in faith by God's grace at this last time, to place before you the eternal truth."[44] No external confirmation or signs were therefore required to authenticate Joris' leadership. He identified himself, albeit obliquely, with the "promised, elect David," whom "you should hear as Moses, namely as God or Jesus Christ himself, for he himself is the one who speaks to you. Mark it well, it shall be found in this fashion."[45] Joris further believed that this apocalyptical David would obtain the victory, and thus perfect what God had begun with the first.[46] Christ (for Joris, the second David) did not himself build the temple of the Lord, but instead "has broken, with Sampson, the house of sin, through his body [i.e. sacrifice] and has destroyed the enemy. He has, with David, the son of Jesse, in his resurrection prepared everything according to the Spirit," presumably for the third David.[47] The promised David of Joris' day would instead fulfill all things and in him would be found:

> the seals of the King's signet or authority, the seven eyes, the level [*waterpas*], the true point or eye of sight. There also is the true art of all understanding of grammar, dialectic, rhetoric, music, geometry, arithmetic, astronomy, inwardly according to the Spirit. All perfect beauty in the end shall be found [in him]. The basis of the principal style or stations, rulers and guardians of the whole earth.[48]

Naturally this view elevated Joris' self-esteem vis-à-vis his more learned opponents.

There is no doubt that Joris, as the third David and vessel of the Holy Spirit, claimed more for himself than the "exalted prerogatives which will be enjoyed in the new age by all Christians."[49] What is obvious from a reading of the material he wrote in Antwerp is that Joris' thought was moving in two directions; one, toward a purely spiritual-internal application of former Melchiorite teachings; and second, toward an even greater emphasis on his own authority. Both of these directions were in part responses to the failures and successes which he experienced in the late 1530s. He failed to gain the support of the Münsterites and the Strasbourg Melchiorites, accelerating Joris' spiritualisation of Melchiorite beliefs. He succeeded in gaining the allegiance of several other radicals, some of whom tended to venerate him with absolute loyalty, understandably increasing the assurance of his calling as the third David.

Joris' Apology, 1543

By 1543, Joris found himself increasingly on the defensive against the more rigorously ethical followers of Menno Simons who had evolved in a different direction, and the debates between Davidites and Mennonites had begun.[50] Joris' *Apology* to the Countess Anna may be considered a response to Mennonite accusations. It is clear that the probable author of these accusations, Adam Pastor, misunderstood much of Joris' teachings. At several points Pastor attributed Batenburg's teachings to Joris, claiming that Joris taught his believers to murder and steal, to confiscate the property of the godless and to practise polygamy.[51] Pastor also misunderstood Joris' spiritualist meaning when he charged Joris with teaching that Christ would not return for judgement (article six) or that the resurrection of the dead had already taken place (article fourteen).[52] In light of Joris' evasive writing style, Pastor's confusion seems understandable. A few of Pastor's points were affirmed by Joris without much argument: especially article three, public confession; article thirteen, a believer could leave unfit wives — Joris added that they were to be treated mercifully; article fifteen, that the kingdom of God would appear visibly on earth — Joris added that it was primarily spiritual and internal; article nineteen, that infant baptism was permissible; and article twenty, that believers were free to attend any church. Most of the other charges by Pastor were similarly accurate representations of Joris' teaching, but Joris chose to deny or conceal them in his evasive replies. A case in point was identification of Joris himself as the apocalyptical third David. Joris' modest denial seems unconvincing. True, his understanding of the role of the third David may have differed from that of Jan van Leiden; nevertheless, it seems clear that he accepted an equally authoritative mantle of leadership for himself.[53] While he denied having identified himself as the third David, he observed that the anointed David was present in the form of the one in whom the Spirit dwelt.[54] Since he had claimed a special portion of the Spirit for himself, Joris' denial that he called "literalists" all those who defended themselves with Scripture is also farfetched. One need only recall his comments at the Strasbourg disputation to sense a certain underhandedness in this particular defence. Overall, however, the *Apology* is a relatively reliable treatment of Joris' doctrine, if read in the light of his other works from the time. Aside from the question regarding the third David, Joris is relatively truthful, if often obscure.

When in the summer of 1544, Joris and his companions moved to Basel in the Swiss Cantons, Joris removed himself from the geographic centre of Anabaptist growth. Leadership of the Dutch Anabaptists could therefore shift more easily to Menno Simons and his associates. Nevertheless Joris seems to have enjoyed influential contacts by way of his voluminous correspondence and publications. He did not give up directing his scattered following, but adjusted his leadership style in the changing circumstances. Joris, in short, had reached the pinnacle of his authority as an Anabaptist leader before his move to Antwerp. His move to Basel may therefore simply have confirmed the inevitable, that his years as a charismatic leader were numbered.

Notes

1. The evidence for Antwerp as Joris' residence is overwhelming; see Zijlstra, *Blesdijk*, p. 61.
2. See Blesdijk, *Historia vitae*, p. 87, and Nippold, "David Joris," p. 118. Joris also complained to the Landgrave that women ruled over some provinces, which was for him a sign of the Babylonian Whore (Nippold, p. 119). This is ironic in the light of an Apology (the *Onschult an Vrouw Anna*) he wrote to one of these female rulers, Countess Anna of Oldenburg, a few years later.
3. Nippold, "David Joris," p. 123.
4. That Joris was in this respect open-minded can be seen in his orthodox commentary of the Apostle's Creed, *Onschult an Vrouw Anna*, fol. 22v (Waite, "Joris' Apology," p. 155).
5. This is the conclusion of Floris Prims, whose work *Geschiedenis van Berchem* (Berchem: Gemeentebestuur van Berchem, 1949, esp. pp. 94-98) provides the basis for this discussion of the van Berchems and van Liers. Secret marriages contracted between upper class husbands and lower class brides were not uncommon. For an example, see Gene Brucker, *Giovanni and Lusanna. Love and Marriage in Renaissance Florence* (Berkeley: University of California Press, 1986).
6. *Hydeckel*, fol. 294r.
7. *Twonder-Boeck*, fol. 12r [actually 7r]. Joris entitled this chapter (part 1, chapter 12) "Wat ontsich die Werltlicke Ouericheyt heefft" and chapter 11, "Een vermaeninghe aen Vorsten ende Wysen."
8. Ibid. Joris also had some words for the sin of pride to which members of the nobility were presumably prone: "Daerom kent by tijts uwe geborte / Geest / werck end bedrijf / v lant / stadt / iaren / maeden / daghen / vren end tyden. Roemet niet bouen uwe macht / want het is v selfs schande ende schade. . . . Daer ouer treedt niet / gaet niet wyder / tastet niet hoogher dan ghy verreycken off ouerspannen moecht / vlyeghet niet hogher dan ghi vlogelen hebt" (ibid., 7r [actually 8r]).
9. As will be shown below, the 1543 *Wonder-Boeck* provides the strongest explication of Joris' role as the third David, although it had first appeared in 1536.
10. For more on Joris and the nobility, see Gary K. Waite, "The Dutch Nobility and Anabaptism, 1535-1545," to be published in the *SCJ*, 1991.
11. Zijlstra, *Blesdijk*, pp. 20-21. Most of the rest of the participants in the Regensburg Colloquy had left by the time the Davidites arrived.
12. These disputes have been summarised well by both Zijlstra and Stayer. See Stayer, "Davidite vs. Mennonite," pp. 459-76; Zijlstra, *Blesdijk*, pp. 26-60; and "Menno

Simons and David Joris,'' pp. 249-56.

13. This resulted in the *Onschult an Vrouw Anna*. See Zijlstra, *Blesdijk*, pp. 40-42. The *Onschult* will be analysed below.

14. Twelve other messengers during the period of his Antwerp residency can be identified from Joris' code in the *Hydeckel*.

15. Zijlstra, *Blesdijk*, pp. 64-75. À Lasco was Superintendent under Countess Anna. Several of Joris' letters to à Lasco are extant, including *Cort Bericht vn schriftlyck Antwoort D.J. op den Brief des Eerwaardichen Heeren J.A.L.* (n.p., 1544). This debate too has received scholarly attention: C.W.A. Willemse, "De briefwisseling tussen David Joris en Johannes a Lasco," *Doopsgezinde Bijdragen*, Vol. IV (New Series), 1978, pp. 9-22; Bainton, *David Joris*, p. 53.

16. Wiebe Bergsma, *Aggaeus van Albada (c.1525-1587), schwenckfeldiaan, staatsman en strijder voor verdraagzaamheid*, pub. doctoral diss., University of Groningen, 1983, p. 44.

17. Ibid., p. 52.

18. *Eene onderwijsinge*, fol. 83v. He further stated that "God's Word is not to be composed with ink, letter or pen, nor is it to be proclaimed nor comprehended in letters, but only through the understanding of the Spirit in truth" (ibid., fol. 84v).

19. See Deppermann, "Melchior Hoffman," in Goertz, *Profiles*, p. 185.

20. *Clare Berichtinge, Hoe die Mensch van Godt ghevallen ende jn wat manieren hy weder tot Godt gebrocht wert een claere ende leuendige opsluytinge* (n.p., 1543), fol. 97v.

21. The Evangelical Rentmeester of Groningen, Hieronymus Wilhelmi, writing to Junker Karel van Gelder after the latter had sent him a copy of Joris' *Twonder-Boeck*. The letter is found in Blesdijk, *Billijcke Verantwoordinge*, fol. 102v.

22. *Seer goet onderwysinghe der wysheyt / leeringhe der waerheyt/ Beyde voor Ouden vnde Jonghen* (n.p., 1539), fol. 69v.

23. Ibid., fols. 71v-72r.

24. *Een zeer zuuerlyck traectaet*, fols. 98v-99r.

25. Ibid., fols. 120v-121r.

26. Ibid., fols. 128v-129r. "Hierusalem / de stadt des HEREN gantz eenlick en woest gelegen heft / ende mitten vooten der heydenen vertreden geweest is ... tot haere dagen en iaeren de bestemt stonden / een eynde hadden / ... Also moet Zyons verneringe ijrst vervult sijn ..."

27. Ibid., fol. 128r.

28. *Twonder-Boeck*, fol. vii(v). See Bainton, *David Joris*, p. 43.

29. "In this way will the day of the Lord come secretly and quietly in all respects break through, as is written" (*Twonder-Boeck*, fol. lxxxvi[r]).

30. Joris did acknowledge that an external sound may be necessary at first, "on account of our weakness," but it is to be essentially a "spiritual sound" (ibid., fol. cviij[r]).

31. The only surviving Dutch version of Franck's "Letter to John Campanus" is dated to 1541 (Williams, *S.A.W.*, p. 147), and only his *Paradoxa* is known to have been published in the Netherlands prior to 1540 (Nijhoff & Kronenberg, *Nederlandsche Bibliographie*, no. 948). The 1531 edition of Franck's *Chronica* received wide circulation throughout Europe, and appears to have been used by Menno shortly after its publication (Bergsma and Voolstra, *Uyt Babel ghevloden*, p. 26). For Franck, see H. Weigelt, *Sebastian Franck und die lutherische Reformation* (Gütersloh: Gerd Mohn, 1972); for Schwenckfeld, see R. Emmet McLaughlin, *Caspar Schwenckfeld: Reluctant Radical, His Life to 1540* (New Haven: Yale University Press, 1986). Useful introductions to both Spiritualists are provided in Goertz, *Profiles*.

32. "Letter to Campanus," p. 150.
33. Ibid., p. 157.
34. Ibid., p. 158.
35. This difference must not be depreciated. Bergsma (*Albada*, p. 57) points out that "Schwenckfeld kunnen we ook niet op een lijn stellen met de 'vergodete' profeten David Joris en Hendrik Niclaes. Hij beschouwde zichzelf niet als een messias, of een profeet. Zijn individualism ging uiteindelijk zover dat hij zijn volgelingen aanspoorde de juistheid van zijn denkbeelden in twijfel te trekken." One cannot imagine Joris doing the same for his followers.
36. Bergsma (ibid., pp. 61-62) discusses the influence of Schwenckfeld on Joris' thought. The primary aim of this chapter is to describe the social and psychological reasons behind Joris' spiritualising of Anabaptist tenets, not to fully discuss his Spiritualist phase.
37. Zijlstra (*Blesdijk*, pp. 28-29) has argued that the emphasis on "rebirth" was a major element in Joris' thought. However, it was not until 1539 that Joris' writings began to emphasise the concept of "rebirth." It may have been implicit in his view that the old man must be crucified and the new man put on, but he did not extensively use the phrase itself until 1539. This leads one to inquire if perhaps Blesdijk, who became an important worker for Joris in this year, was the source for this new emphasis. Schwenckfeld's influence might also be visible here. This Spiritualist was known as the "theologian of the rebirth." See Bergsma, *Albada*, p. 52.
38. See *Een seer suuerlick tractaet*, fols. 107r-108r.
39. Ibid., fol. 110v.
40. Stupperich, *Rothmanns Schriften*, pp. 309-26.
41. *Een seer suuerlick tractaet*, fol. 99v. See also p. 127 above.
42. *Twonder-Boeck*, fol. iiij(r).
43. Ibid., fol. xii(v).
44. Ibid., fol. xiii(r).
45. Ibid., fols. li(v)-lii(r).
46. Ibid., fol. lii(v). "Die derde (Dauidt) int alderheylchste van dien comen die Coninghen / die hoofden en mannen in Juda / die regierders in Israhel / doer die perfect te voleyeynden / dat G. in deerste begonnen heeft; Wiens rijck int rechte ware wesen een eewich rijck is."
47. Ibid., fol. lviiij(v).
48. Ibid., fol. xxix(v).
49. Contra Bainton, *David Joris*, p. 34.
50. Zijlstra, *Blesdijk*, p. 42.
51. *Onschuldt an Vrouw Anna*, articles eleven, eighteen, and twelve respectively. Article ten, that those outside of David Joris' fellowship are regarded as cats and dogs, also sounds more like Batenburg. The *Onschuldt* was published with the date 1540, but Zijlstra (*Blesdijk*, pp. 40-42) has convincingly shown that it was more likely written some time in 1543 as a reply to Adam Pastor's summary of Joris' doctrine.
52. Others which Pastor may have misunderstood are article four, that there are no angels; article five, that there are no devils — Joris argued that the devil had no power outside of man; and article nine, that Christ equalled David Joris.
53. Ibid., articles one and nine.
54. Ibid., article eight.

Joris' château in Binningen, near Basel. Author's photograph.

CHAPTER TEN

Joris in Basel, 1544-56

The relationship between David Joris and Dutch Anabaptism had more or less come apart by 1544. It would not be fitting, however, if we did not review the last years of the Dutch prophet's life. While he resided in the Swiss city of Basel between the execution of Jorien Ketel in 1544 and his own death in 1556, Joris' ideas underwent significant changes; his production of books, tracts and letters increased dramatically; and his lifestyle shifted from that of a hunted fugitive to one more appropriate for a leisured gentleman. He was also now geographically removed from the Dutch Anabaptist movement, although he kept up an extensive correspondence with a remarkable number of his supporters in the Low Countries and elsewhere.

Basel and Religious Toleration

Much of the improvement in Joris' living conditions had to do with his place of refuge. The Imperial Free City of Basel had joined the Swiss Confederacy in 1501, and twenty years later its guild-dominated council cast off all remnants of episcopal authority.[1] At the same time, humanists such as Wolfgang Capito, Conrad Pellican and Johannes Oecolampadius were attracted to the city by its vigorous printing establishments, and Basel became the educational centre of the Swiss Confederacy, indeed, one of the major cultural centres in the empire.[2] During his frequent residences in the city between 1514 and 1529 the most famous humanist of the sixteenth century, Erasmus of Rotterdam, was the central figure of this humanist *"Sodalitas Basiliensis."* According to Hans R. Guggisberg, Erasmus' and his fellow humanists' aversion to controversy was paralleled by the city council's repudiation of extremist political positions.[3] Basel had become one of the most tolerant cities in the empire. The dramatic events surrounding the success of the Reformation in the late 1520s, however, put an end — albeit temporarily — to this idyllic situation.

While Luther's works were already being printed by Basel printers such as Johannes Froben in 1518, the Reformation took a relatively long time to take root in the city. The major Reformer was the preacher and university teacher Oecolampadius, who had arrived as a refugee in 1522.[4] As in most other Imperial Free Cities, the religious reform movement went hand in hand with the political and social demands of the lower orders. The fears

Notes to Chapter Ten are found on pages 187-92.

of social revolution inspired by the Peasants' Revolt of 1525, the demands of the guilds for a democratic form of government, and the iconoclastic revolts of 1528 inspired the political elite to accept Oecolampadius' Reform program in 1529. By this year the Reformation had become firmly established.[5] The consequence, however, was a return to conservatism in both politics and religion. The ruling elite retained its hold over the powerful Little Council and the Council in turn compelled all its citizens to attend the now Reformed church and to swear allegiance to the Basel confession of faith. As a result, the persecution of Anabaptists was renewed in 1530-31 and most of them were rooted out from the *Landschaft*. In spite of these repressive measures, the city council could show surprising leniency, especially when dealing with prominent citizens or visitors. In fact, persecution does not seem to have been the normal means Basel magistrates used to deal with religious dissenters. After the severe persecution against the Anabaptists had ended in the early 1530s, religious radicals found it possible to move to Basel and live undisturbed, as long as they did not unsettle the social and political tranquillity of the city.[6] Guggisberg affirms that ''from the early 1530s until the early 1580s the intellectual atmosphere of Basel was relatively open-minded.''[7] By 1540 Basel had become a major destination for religious refugees, particularly those from France, Italy and the Netherlands.[8] David Joris and his entourage were therefore part of a larger wave of immigrants seeking religious toleration when they arrived in Basel in 1544.

Joris' Move to Basel

In Antwerp the situation for Joris and his followers had been insecure at best. Antwerp magistrates had taken frequent and severe actions against religious dissent, and during the early 1540s several more suspected heretics were publicly executed.[9] While the patronage of an important nobleman offered some protection, Joris and his fellows could not take the chance of exposure. Interestingly, in 1558 a noted printer of Basel, Peter van Mechelen, testified to the Basel magistracy that sometime between 1542 and 1543 a stranger had come from the Netherlands and had asked him how Anabaptists were treated in Basel. Van Mechelen had responded that

> they were not tolerated, but if they kept quiet, did not disturb the peace nor disseminate strange doctrines, if they went to church and conducted themselves in a Christian manner, they need have nothing to fear, etc. Then he told me that there was a great persecution at Antwerp, and that a number had been driven out because of the Gospel, who would like to settle here. They would bring much money, he added. His own master was rich and learned and published many books.[10]

Van Mechelen undoubtedly was referring to a messenger (perhaps Jorien Ketel) sent on behalf of Joris. Under the circumstances Antwerp could only remain a place of temporary refuge for the seer from Delft.[11] Basel appeared the ideal location for the New Jerusalem, although the concept of the godly city no longer contained the socio-political ramifications that it had in Münster. Instead, the city would provide Joris and his followers with the peace to establish the kingdom of God in their own hearts.

In spring 1544 the mission of the messenger to Basel was followed by the arrival of Joris and his patrons Cornelis van Lier, Joachim and Reinier van Berchem, and Anna van Etten, along with Jorien Ketel, Joris' secretary Heinrich van Schor,[12] and several others.[13] The group had set out from Antwerp on the second Monday in Lent (March 17) but had stopped first in Speyer, where Cornelis made an arrangement with his brother, Jan van Lier, allowing the latter to take over as Lord of Berchem in the absence of Cornelis.[14] In early April Joris introduced himself to the Basel magistrates as Johann van Brugge, a merchant and refugee for the Gospel [i.e., an Evangelical], seeking a place of safety for his family and fortune.[15] Impressed by the dignified bearing of this obviously noble company the city council gave their leader a favourable hearing.[16] The fugitives therefore returned to Antwerp in good spirits, where they soon discovered that their decision to move had been a prudent one. When Ketel was arrested in Deventer some time before mid-May,[17] he gave to the authorities all the details of the refugees' plans to settle in Basel (including Joris' pseudonym). Haste was therefore critical. In July, the imperial authorities commanded that all the property of Cornelis van Lier and his cohorts be confiscated, and other Antwerpers named in Ketel's confession were condemned and burned, most notably the leader of the "Loists," Loy de Schaliedecker. Joris and his noble supporters left quickly, escaping with considerable wealth and arriving back in Basel in August, this time with their families.[18] For reasons that are no longer clear, Cornelis van Lier did not remain long with the colonists in Basel, but after a year or so moved to Strasbourg where he was to spend the rest of his life.[19] Remarkably, Joris was granted Basel citizenship almost immediately (on August 25) and he became a highly respected and admired member of the community.[20] Four years after the arrival of the refugees from Antwerp, Blesdijk joined the colony and married one of Joris' daughters.[21] Neither Joris nor any of his companions experienced any qualms in giving the oath of allegiance or in providing their assent to the city's statement of faith.[22] Joris' Nicodemism was now fully formed.

Joris as Patriarch

The wealth of his noble patrons and the continuing financial support of his numerous adherents allowed Joris to live an embarrassingly (considering his earlier ascetic tendencies) luxurious life as the "old gentleman of Binningen."[23] Even before the move, Joris' lifestyle in the Schilde manor near Antwerp had necessitated some explanation. In a letter to another noble sympathiser he had written:

So know, my beloved, that such outward things do not gladden me. I
would much prefer to live in the poorest habit [*habijt*], house and manor
[*hof*]. But I cannot render advice to anyone except to live in godly attention according to my encouragement or to the opportunity of the Holy
Spirit. For I do not find nor feel my kingdom [here], for it is not of this
world. Therefore do not take joyful pride in these things, but use them
like I do, with thanks to God who has willed it.[24]

Portraits of Joris and his companions in Basel painted by an unknown
artist(s) show that Joris had adopted an aristocratic lifestyle. All the trap-
pings of a noble household are found: velvet robe, sword, even a black servant boy.[25] It is known that Joris designed for himself a coat of arms, a symbol of social status normally reserved for aristocrats.[26] An inventory of the
Joris estate after the prophet's death confirms the wealth of the refugees.
Included were bonds worth thousands of gulden on the city of Nuremberg
and several properties in and around Basel, including the Spieshof (which
was built for Joris) in the heart of the city, a country manor in nearby Binningen, and a small convent church for the Netherlanders' worship.[27] Daily
life for Joris had also changed considerably since his days as a hunted heretic. Rising late, Joris spent his days in writing, reading, gardening, visiting
the neighbours, riding around Binningen, or playing with the children. He
apparently also returned to his artistic endeavours, including glasspainting,
although he warned his household never to mention this activity.[28] If his
later reflections can be trusted, Blesdijk was disgusted by his father-in-law's
unbecoming behaviour and his apparent repudiation of his prophetic
office.[29] Perhaps most telling of all in this regard were Joris' sexual
improprieties. It appears from several sources, not all dubious, that Joris
had a concubine, Anna van Berchem, the sister of Joachim, by whom he
fathered two children.[30] Evidence for this contention is found in the arrange-
ments made by Jan Boelsen, Anna's later husband, for the inheritance of his
stepchildren.[31] This incident has been used to prove the contention that Joris
had openly continued the Münsterite practice of polygamy. It is, however,
highly unlikely that he would have dared such a public flaunting of social
mores in Basel.[32] Instead, it is more likely that Joris' relationship with Anna
was akin to the concubinage and bastardy which were common features of
noble households. This would once again confirm that Joris now saw himself as a member of the aristocracy, no longer as a mere craftsman. Interestingly, bastardy had been repudiated most vociferously by guildsmen who
saw it as "a distinctive feature of the amorous life of the nobility and the
urban aristocracy."[33] Joris' relationship with Anna van Berchem, however
rationalised, could easily be winked at by the noble van Liers and van Berchems, and perhaps also by Basel's patrician elite.

      Relations between Joris and his fellow Basel citizens were cordial and
the Netherlanders were recognised as among the most generous of city-
dwellers. They spent considerable sums on construction and made

significant donations to charity.[34] Even his later detractors were forced to admit that Joris had lived a blameless life, giving alms to the poor and helping the sick. He had furthermore forbidden his household to mention either his true identity or to discuss his teachings in the city itself, and hence the civil authorities could have had no idea that he was a fugitive from the law.[35]

One incident illustrates the level to which the Netherland emigrants participated in the cultural life of Basel. In 1553 a playwright by the name of Thomas Platter reported that

> I put on a comedy which was attended by a number of the magistrates. There would have been a larger crowd had it been commonly known that the play would be in German. The chief of the Netherlanders was there with the whole clan. They gave a gold gulden. So did the University, but nobody else.[36]

Considering Joris' presumed interest in the Chamber of Rhetoric performances in his homeland, it is no wonder that he patronised dramatic performances here. To cement their allegiance to their new place of residence, the former refugees married several of their offspring, including two of Joris' own, into Basel families.

Joris also made important friends in the city. One of these was the French doctor Jean Bauhin, who had arrived in Basel in 1541 and who became Joris' physician.[37] According to Paul Burckhardt, Bauhin had been significantly influenced by Erasmus' ideas, and is best described as a humanist-Spiritualist.[38] Bauhin became close friends with the Savoyard humanist scholar Sebastian Castellio, who had moved to Basel just a few months after the Netherlanders.[39] Castellio, formerly an associate of the Genevan Reformer John Calvin, had become dissatisfied with Calvin's stress on church discipline, and by the time of his trip to Basel had already developed an emphasis on individual conscience.[40] It appears that Bauhin introduced Castellio to Joris. Considering the language difficulties – Joris knew no Latin and Castellio no Dutch – it is unlikely that the two became intimate friends. Their acquaintanceship, however, is indicated by a letter written by Joris to the Savoyard in October of 1550. In this missive, Joris mentions that he had received and examined Castellio's letter and was delighted with Castellio's "resigned (*ghelaten*) heart." It was apparent to Joris that his scholarly friend was of like mind, desiring to fulfil the counsel of God, something which very few others seemed willing to do.[41] Joris encouraged Castellio to "be like a child in the simplicity of Christ" and to keep his inner heart, the "ground of the soul," free from all darkness.[42] Castellio was to "follow only God's Word" and to be "like a dove which does not hear and a dumb man who cannot speak" until he had come into the "revelation of the light of truth" which would help him discern good from evil.[43] Responsibility for imparting this revelation was in the hands of Joris, who affirmed that he had been given the "gift of the Spirit . . . to distinguish truth from lies," a burden forced on him by the needs of his friends and brethren for advice and teaching.[44] Clearly the relationship between Joris and Castellio was seen by the former as one between teacher and pupil, with Joris instructing the university professor in matters of spiritual enlightenment. But, as the following quotation from Joris' letter shows, Castellio performed valuable services for the Dutch prophet as well:

> Thus far I have written to you with friendly greetings, thinking that if it pleases your soul and you regard it as good and right, that it should not be left here but that you may continue to handle it. I encourage your desire to translate, so that our concern might be regarded as good in it. For I have not been sent to the Latinists, and give myself no concern for them. I am willing to leave the task to others if it be done without peril. I have examined the preface to your Bible and it pleases me well. God grant that it may be accepted. I have made a few suggestions, and have toned down a word here and there or a name, where it seemed to me too harsh. I hope you will take it well. I thus place it in your dear hands. I could not do otherwise. . . . Written from below as a result of the war and delivered by a faithful messenger, through whom you can have a response delivered, if you like. . . . I send this penny as a greeting.[45]

Several things are apparent from the missive. Castellio seems to have been translating some of Joris' tracts into Latin, and there is evidence that he also translated at least one into French.[46] Perhaps Joris gave this work to Castellio, for several years in severe financial straits, as an act of charity.[47] Castellio, on his part, had asked Joris to review a copy of the preface to his Latin translation of the Bible.[48] Unless Joris' interest and ability in Latin had improved considerably, it is likely that someone, perhaps Blesdijk, had provided him with a translation of the work. In any case, Castellio appears to have valued Joris' opinion.

Joris' Basel Writings

Several authors, in particular Bainton, have made much of the friendship between Joris and Castellio for their respective intellectual developments. In this scheme, the relationship between the two helped develop Joris' increasing interest in and Castellio's increasing criticism of humanistic scholarship.[49] Zijlstra has rightly pointed out that there is far too little evidence to prove any formative influences on the part of each towards the other.[50] What is more likely is that Bauhin and Blesdijk, fellow Latinists, developed closer relationships with Castellio than did Joris, and perhaps had convinced Joris to have some of his tracts translated by the Basel professor.[51] In any event, there is no doubt that Joris' ideas underwent significant changes during the last dozen years of his life.

His residence in Basel finally providing the opportunity for quiet reflection, Joris' literary output increased enormously. The three large volumes of his published correspondence are dominated by letters from Basel, and reveal a remarkable range of acquaintances. Joris communicated with admirers in places ranging from Paris to Denmark.[52] A survey of Joris' literary *corpus* also illustrates this development. Of the over 240 printed works that still survive, 182 can be dated. Of these, fourteen were composed during Joris' fugitive years in the Netherlands (1535-39), no more than 48 during his Antwerp residency (1540-44), and a daunting 120 from his years in Basel (1545-56).[53] While works produced in the fugitive years were relatively straightforward, in Basel Joris continued to obscure and spiritualise his ideas by writing in his "spiritual language."

One way to come to terms with the changes in Joris' thought during his Basel residence would be to compare the second edition of the *Wonder Book*, which appeared in 1551, with the first from 1542-43. While such a massive project is beyond the scope of this chapter, we might examine Joris' narcissistic attitude concerning the third David.[54] The first edition had brought to a climax his self-conception as the apocalyptic agent of God. If by the time of the second edition in 1551 Joris had toned down this belief, then it would be possible to argue that Joris had moved to a theological position closer to that of Spiritualists such as Castellio or Sebastian Franck, even if the specific causes for the transition are not very clear.[55]

At first glance, the chapters of the *Wonder Book* concerned with the subject of the third David appear remarkably similar. On closer examination, however, it becomes clear that Joris had made some quite subtle revisions by 1551. For example, when in the first edition he announced: "This is the promised, elect David, the authoritative prince," in the second edition he proclaimed: "This is the principal spirit of power, the promised, elect David...."[56] The difference was enough to bring into question whether the promised David was to be identified with a person (i.e., Joris) or with the Holy Spirit. Furthermore, Joris in the later version added a section explaining his current view of the promised David and the kingdom. Here the third David was closely identified with the Spirit, and the kingdom of the promised David was spiritualised to mean little more than the community of those who had experienced the rebirth of Christ. He wrote

> concerning this promised Spirit of truth, or David. This one was not proclaimed in this name [i.e., David], but in the true, zealous Spirit, which should begin and end in the truth. For it is certain that the eternally enduring kingdom was not established in the birth of our Lord Jesus, seeing that (as one speaks of a kingdom) it was disturbed by the Antichrist, the scarlet whore.... And the eternally enduring kingdom must remain rigid [and] undisturbed, completely crushing and bringing to nought all previous kingdoms. We clearly see that this has still not happened in our time. For this reason my profession here is that when the true Christ in the eternity is born in us according to the Spirit and truth, this shall be another David according to the Spirit and truth (as was professed and as Peter has testified). Then this eternally enduring

kingdom (of which Daniel has spoken) will be established and remain
standing firm and undisturbed, as the Scriptures affirm.[57]

While Joris in his later career maintained a doctrine of the third David, he
had lessened the implication that he and the third David were the same, and
had instead strengthened the connection between that apocalyptical figure
and the Holy Spirit. Further developments have been noted. Joris' criticism
of the learned are less strident than before, and he even cites Erasmus.[58] Just
as his suspicion of the nobility lessened as he gained their patronage in
Antwerp, so it appears that his attitude toward humanists or scholars became
more positive as he made the acquaintance of a few of them in Basel.

One of the most well-known and enduring of Joris' writings was his letter
pleading for the release of the Spanish anti-Trinitarian Michael Servetus, who
had been arrested on charges of heresy in Geneva. The letter, if it was delivered,
had no effect, and Servetus was burned at the stake on October 27, 1553.[59] Naturally Joris had long been an opponent of capital punishment for the crime of
heresy, although in all of his other missives chastising the authorities for their
harsh treatment of religious dissenters, those for whom he was pleading were his
own followers. In this case Joris, like a good number of fellow religious refugees in exile in the Protestant Swiss Cantons, must have felt his own survival
threatened by the treatment of the infamous Rationalist.[60] Servetus' execution
therefore provoked a storm of controversy that was highlighted by the publication in the following year of Castellio's most famous work, *De haereticis
an sint persequendi.* Castellio, using the pseudonym of Martinus Bellius,
had collected a wide range of texts in favour of religious toleration and
against capital punishment for heresy.[61] Aside from Castellio himself, prominent authors included Martin Luther, the Württemberg Reformer Johannes
Brenz, Sebastian Franck, and Erasmus. Also contributing was a certain
Georgius Kleinbergius. Zijlstra has recently and in convincing fashion
revived the view that this Kleinbergius was none other than David Joris.[62]
Joris in the 1550s was becoming an eloquent promoter of religious toleration in an exceedingly intolerant age.[63]

Divisions in the Basel Colony

Beneath the outwardly serene life of the Netherlander exiles in Basel
seethed some very real conflicts. Finances were a constant source of consternation. Some of the van Berchems complained about the unequal dis-
bursement of funds.[64] Even more troublesome were the religious divisions
centred around Joris' most important living disciple. Blesdijk had for a long
time harboured doubts about some of Joris' teaching. In particular, he had
misgivings about Joris' messianic pretensions and the practice of nudity
associated with public confession.[65] Current scholarship affirms that Blesdijk was always more of a "conventional New Testament" Christian than
his father-in-law.[66] Blesdijk's doubts did not seem to be serious enough to
hinder his activities in Germany and the Low Countries, where he was busy

proselytising and debating on behalf of the Dutch prophet. With his arrival in Basel in 1548, he saw first-hand that "the austere prophet had become the genial patriarch, cultivating his garden, painting pictures and romping with the children beyond the decorum befitting his age."[67] Here again Blesdijk's association with Castellio may also have hastened the disenchantment with Joris' mystical approach. By 1553 Bauhin too appears to have been distancing himself from the Netherlanders. In any event, an internal division developed between Blesdijk and Bauhin and the faction supporting Joris led by Joachim van Berchem. Formal discussions were held between Joris and Blesdijk in 1554 and 1555 and, while Joris apparently agreed that his earlier narcissistic claims had been exaggerated, his son-in-law was unsatisfied.[68] Joachim and his party called Blesdijk an apostate. With the increasing invective came renewed fears of public disclosure of the Netherlanders' true identities. According to Bainton, a report from a traveller from the Low Countries announcing that Joris was not a noble but a heretic helped speed the death of the ill Frau Joris.[69] Joris, sick, distraught by his wife's death, and saddened by the deepening divisions within his movement, died shortly thereafter on August 25, 1556. The Netherlander was buried with full honours in St. Leonhard's Church as Johann van Brugge.

The death of Joris brought into the open the internal conflicts among the Dutch exiles. The question of leadership was critical. Joachim took over control of the Basel fellowship, castigating Blesdijk for seeking to usurp his position and both Blesdijk and Bauhin for their rationalism. With the master dead, Blesdijk's doubts about Joris' teaching and criticism of Davidite practices were set in writing. He returned to the Low Countries and eventually became Joris' staunchest critic.[70]

Within three years of his death the fact that Johann van Brugge had been the notorious heretic was public knowledge.[71] Basel's preachers were faced with the disclosures first of van Schor and then of Peter van Mechelen. In 1558 van Mechelen apparently had approached one of the city's ministers who reported that van Mechelen had asked him

> Did I know anything about the Davidists. Yes, but I did not know what they taught. He answered that their founder was the old gentleman from Binningen and his teaching was perfectly horrible. I told him that I had heard nothing but good reports of the Netherlanders and could not credit unconfirmed rumours, especially against people held in such esteem and of whom one would not lightly believe anything of the sort.[72]

Examination of van Schor confirmed van Mechelen's testimony. Joachim van Berchem fled to Strasbourg, but because neither Bauhin nor Blesdijk would testify, no further action could be taken. It was not until November of 1558 that the jurist Bonifacius Amerbach, normally a protector of the city's distrusted foreigners,[73] finally forced the city's magistrates to investigate the matter.

During the winter months the suspects were all examined, but they confessed nothing and several of the magistrates wanted to let the matter drop. The faculties of law and theology of the university were consulted, and their report argued on behalf of the burning of heretics, either alive or dead.[74] Finally in the spring of 1559 several of the suspected heretics (including Blesdijk) were arrested and their premises were searched. The inquisitors discovered a large number of Joris' works and portraits of the deceased master. Under examination (without torture) the accused eventually confessed and abjured. Castellio himself was forced to repudiate Joris' ideas.[75] Sentence was passed against Joris at the end of April. His body was to be disinterred and burned at the stake along with his books and portraits. On May 11 the recanted Davidites were released with relatively light punishment.[76] Two days later Joris' corpse and writings were publicly burned to ash. The *auto da fé* was observed by a great crowd of spectators. During the public recantation of their errors in the Basel cathedral in June, the prophet's disciples were reminded of the magnanimity of the Basel magistrates and then released. Perhaps in no other city of the empire would Joris and his followers have experienced such toleration. Their choice of residence had indeed been an astute one.

Joris' Abiding Influence

With the Joris trial, the Davidite movement seemed to have come to an end. But had it? Even as late as the 1620s there were still many followers of Joris' teaching in the Netherlands, for a Reformed Synod of 1623 found it necessary to denounce the Jorists in the Reformed Church.[77] Through the second half of the sixteenth century disciples of Joris took it upon themselves to respond to what they regarded as the slander of those who accused him of heresy.[78] Many of Joris' devotees in the Low Countries, moreover, continued to read and publish his writings. Their devotion to Joris had not been tempered by disillusionment with his Basel lifestyle. Shortly after the death of the leader, Davidites in the Low Countries and France wrote letters castigating the disputers in Basel for neglecting Joris' teaching on love and forbearance.[79] In the 1580s several works, including the second edition of the *Wonder Book*, were reissued in the printing establishments of Dirk Mullem of Rotterdam and Jan Canin of Dordrecht.[80] Of all cities, Emden, the birthplace of the Melchiorite movement, offered a particularly lucrative market for Joris' writings in this period.[81] Another of those accused with sponsoring the post-mortem reproduction of Joris' works was the Reformed pastor Herman Herberts of Dordrecht and Gouda.[82] Apparently Herberts was an enthusiastic devotee of Joris' teachings, thirty years after the prophet's death.[83] It appears that Joris' Nicodemism had come full circle. Instead of religious dissenters using the cover of Reformed orthodoxy to hide their true mystical beliefs, a Reformed pastor was now having the works of an Anabaptist/Spiritualist printed and disseminated, presumably to heighten the spiritual fervour of his fellow Reformed. In the several decades following the death of their formulator, the writings of David Joris continued to appeal to those dissatisfied with official religion, in this case those unhappy with the Reformed faith. Undoubtedly Joris' works gave to Catholics and other opponents of strict Calvinism in the 1580s the same option which they had earlier provided to Anabaptists and other religious dissenters during the age of Catholic orthodoxy. This option was the combination of Spiritualism and Nicodemism which the Dutch prophet had developed over the course of his eventful and controversial life.[84]

Notes

1. Basel had been ruled by a prince-bishop. These remarks on Basel are based on Hans R. Guggisberg, *Basel in the Sixteenth Century* (St. Louis: Center for Reformation Research, 1982).
2. See Lewis Spitz, *The Protestant Reformation, 1517-1559* (New York: Harper & Row, 1985), p. 149. For a discussion of printers in Basel, see Peter G. Bietenholz, *Basle and France in the Sixteenth Century* (Genève: Librairie Droz, 1971).
3. Guggisberg, *Basel*, pp. 12-17.
4. For Oecolampadius, see ibid., pp. 22-24.
5. The resulting *Reformationsordnung* was issued on April 1 of that year (ibid., pp. 24-32).
6. Ibid., p. 38.
7. Ibid., p. 74.
8. Ibid., p. 39.
9. The court records are found in P. Génard (ed.), "Personen te Antwerpen in de XVIe eeuw voor het 'feit van religie' gerechtelijk vervolgd," *Antwerpsch Archievenblad*, Eerst Reeks, Vols. VII and VIII. See also Mellink "Antwerpen als Anabaptisttencentrum," pp. 155-68.
10. As cited in Bainton, *David Joris*, pp. 57-58; translation from Bainton's original English typescript manuscript (available in the Radical Reformation Microfiche Project, #392-A/1), p. 64.
11. See Ketel's testimony, de Hullu, *Bescheiden*, p. 307. Their decision to move may also have been influenced by the plundering of noble estates in and around Antwerp (including Lier) by the troops of Maarten van Rossem, Duke Karel van Gelder's captain, in July of 1542. Interestingly, Cornelis van Lier was one of the city's 24 district supervisors (*wijkmeesters*) entrusted with overseeing the defence of the city walls during the unsuccessful siege (Floris Prims, *Geschiedenis van Antwerpen* [Brussels: Uitgeverij Kultuur en Beschaving, 1981], Vol. V, p. 79).
12. Since 1541 van Schor, a native of Limburg, had been a tutor in the van Berchem household. See Paul Burckhardt, "David Joris und seine Gemeinde in Basel," *Basler Zeitschrift für Geschichte und Altertumskunde*, Vol. XLVIII, 1949, p. 8.
13. From the confession of Ketel, in de Hullu, *Bescheiden*, pp. 307-308.
14. When Jan van Lier died, the manor was to return to Cornelis' heirs. Jan purchased the right to high justice from Antwerp in August of 1547 and took up residence in the Berchem castle, which he had also repurchased, in 1551 (Prims, *Berchem*, p. 98).
15. Bainton, *David Joris*, p. 58; Ketel said that Joris portrayed himself as "een koopman genoemd Johan van Brugghe" (de Hullu, *Bescheiden*, p. 308). Joris' meeting with the council is noted in the city's *Offnungsbuch* in an entry under April 11, 1544. See Burckhardt, "David Joris," p. 7.
16. Basel magistrates were also impressed with Joris' physical characteristics. He was square of build, with a reddish beard and sparkling eyes. His speech was grave and

his posture imposing. To complete the image Joris and his companions dressed elegantly. See Bainton, *David Joris*, p. 58.

17. The process against Ketel began some time around May 21, 1544 (de Hullu, *Bescheiden*, p. 296).
18. Burckhardt gives the fullest account of Joris' children. They included George (born 1525), Clara (the wife of Joachim van Berchem), Gideon, Susanna, Solomon, Anna (Tanneke), Abigail, David, Sampson and Elias, who was born the year after the Netherlanders arrived in Basel.
19. According to Burckhardt ("David Joris," p. 20), van Lier was still in Basel as late as April, 1545. Burckhardt also remarks that in Strasbourg van Lier "sogar in den Rat kam" (ibid., pp. 7-8).
20. Guggisberg states that "Between the breakthrough of the Reformation and the end of the sixteenth century the total number of conferments of citizenship was approximately three thousand. Among these new citizens are less than two hundred identifiable religious refugees. Considering the fact that the total population of Basel in the second half of the sixteenth century lay between ten and twelve thousand this is indeed very little" (*Basel*, p. 40). Many of the refugees never attempted to become citizens and others could not meet the requirements.
21. Between 1543 and 1548 Blesdijk worked on behalf of Joris in North Germany and the Netherlands. He received citizenship in Basel on November 28, 1549. He married Tanneke sometime in the early 1550s. See Zijlstra, *Blesdijk*, p. 91.
22. Church records indicate that Joris' grandchildren were baptised in the city's churches, usually St. Leonhard. See Burckhardt, "David Joris," p. 21.
23. As Bainton (*David Joris*, pp. 59-60) points out, Joris frequently chastised his supporters for their unsolicited charity. Binningen was the location of the château used by the colonists as a country manor.
24. *Hydeckel*, fols. 458v-60r, to Jacoba van Hackfort, daughter of Count Barent van Hackfort and wife of Gossen van Raesfelt, the Twenthe bailiff.
25. See above, p. xii. Also in the Basel Kunstmuseum is a portrait of a group identified by Prims (*Geschiedenis van Berchem*, pp. 94-98) as Joris' family. Burckhardt ("David Joris," p. 36) points out that the attribution of these paintings to the Dutch painter Jan van Scorel is incorrect. The theory that the work was a self-portrait is disputed by Boon ("De Glasschilder David Joris," pp. 133-35) who suggests that the portrait is the work of a Frisian artist, probably one of many who visited Joris in Basel.
26. As a glasspainter, Joris would have made a number of these for aristocratic families.
27. The Spieshof is currently a municipal building and the Binningen Schloss a fine restaurant. The convent was St. Margaret's. Bainton (*David Joris*, pp. 60-61) lists the other properties and goods in the estate.
28. Probably so as not to alert the authorities. For Joris' glasspainting activities in Basel, see Boon, "De Glasschilder David Joris," pp. 122-37. There are several glass rounds completed by Joris in the Basel Historical Museum (see pages 6 and 22). In an appendix Boon transcribes a plan for another series of glass rounds which Joris had designed (ibid., pp. 136-37).
29. *Historia vitae*, pp. 175-78; see Bainton, *David Joris*, p. 61.
30. See Bainton, *David Joris*, pp. 95-97; Nippold, "David Joris," pp. 494-99; Burckhardt, "David Joris," pp. 28-30; and Zijlstra, *Blesdijk*, p. 136. While Bainton denied the charge, evidence provided by Burckhardt leaves little doubt as to its veracity.
31. Before his death Joris had arranged the marriage of Anna to Boelsen, one of his followers from East Frisia. This marriage could not have taken place any earlier than 1548. See Burckhardt, "David Joris," p. 29. Burckhardt (ibid., p. 30) cites a letter written by Cornelis van Lier describing the financial remuneration offered to Boelsen.

Van Lier then wrote "dat die somm, wye E.L. mich schreyben, vor die twee kinderen wynich und klein sind, als ick dennck op iren lieben und getreuwen vatter," whom Burckhardt logically identifies with Joris.

32. That Joris later arranged the marriage of Anna also indicates that their relationship had not been officially polygamous. Bainton, however, certainly overstated his case when he argued that Joris condemned polygamy. He himself quotes a letter by Joris from 1553 in which Joris complains that "O if only those who have taken one or two [wives] had done so in true faith. . . . I write this to awaken your heart to the Lord that you may not think you are more godly with two than if you had but one. As far as I am concerned it is all the same whether you have one, two or four so long as you obey God and the truth" (*David Joris*, English manuscript, pp. 75-76). At the most Joris was indifferent, but not hostile, to polygamy. He had allowed the Delft group centred around Kaal to maintain the practice in 1538-39.

33. Hsia, "Münster and the Anabaptists," p. 66.

34. Although the Netherlanders got along with their neighbours, there was the odd complaint. Bainton notes Joris' remarks in response to some complaints: "Some uncivil gossip is abroad to the effect that we damage the town and take the bread from the mouths of the poor. On the contrary in the four years we have spent thousands on building. We do not begrudge this, but have spent it cheerfully" (Bainton, *David Joris*, English manuscript, p. 69).

35. *David Georgen ausz Holand desz Ertzkatzers warhafftige histori, seines lebens, unnd verfurischen leer, etc* (Basel, 1559), fol. A5v-B2r. This tract, produced by scholars of the University of Basel, was the earliest erudite attempt to defend the city against the charge that it had knowingly housed the notorious heretic. It appeared shortly after the trial against the Davidites. These scholars also presented a negative assessment of Joris' doctrine in eleven articles.

36. Bainton, *David Joris* (English manuscript), p. 69.

37. He had escaped from Paris and had moved to Antwerp around the same time as Joris, and the two may have met then. If so, Bauhin may have encouraged the refugees to follow him to Basel. Bietenholz (*Basle and France*, p. 63) mentions that Bauhin probably did not have a medical degree, but by 1580 had become the dean of Basel's medical profession.

38. "David Joris," p. 39.

39. The closeness of the two is demonstrated by the fact that when Castellio died Bauhin became guardian of his children. See Bietenholz, *Basle and France*, p. 125.

40. For Castellio, see Guggisberg, *Basel*, pp. 42-43, 55-72, and Bietenholz, *Basle and France*, pp. 122-36.

41. *Christlijcke Sendbrieven* (n.p., n.d.), part 3, fol. 56v. See Bainton's summary in *David Joris* (English manuscript), pp. 69-70; and Nippold, "David Joris," pp. 589-90. Bainton (*David Joris*, p. 62) mistakenly gives the beginning folio number as 45.

42. *Christlijcke Sendbrieven*, fol. 57r.

43. Ibid., fol. 57v.

44. Ibid., fol. 56v. Joris also made this cryptic comment: "Dan also gevoele ick / dat in my oock die sonde gedoodet wert deur die sonde: want hart teghen hart geset is" (ibid., fol. 57v). Could this be a rationalisation for Joris' practice of concubinage?

45. Ibid., fol. 58v. It appears that Joris had written this letter while outside the city as a result of a conflict, probably one of the innumerable skirmishes fought between the Catholic forces, led by the emperor, and the Protestant cities which were a common feature in the Swiss Cantons between 1541 and 1555. If Joris had been in the city, he and Castellio would have likely corresponded in person and there would be no extant letter.

46. Zijlstra, *Blesdijk*, pp. 98-99. The work translated into French was Joris' *Seer schone*

aenwysingen unde grondige ontdeckingen van die verborghen wysheydt Godes, translated as *De la cognoissance de Dieu et de l'homme.*

47. Normally Blesdijk translated Joris' works into Latin and van Schor translated his writings for French readers (ibid., p. 99). The reference to a penny in the above letter may reveal Joris' awareness of Castellio's financial difficulties. Bietenholz (*Basle and France*, p. 126) suggests that Castellio probably benefited by Joris' generosity.

48. The work in "Ciceronian Latin," was published in 1551. In 1555 Castellio published a version in popular French (Guggisberg, *Basel*, p. 59).

49. Bainton, *David Joris*, p. 73. Burckhardt ("David Joris," p. 43) disagreed with Bainton on this point, suggesting that the letter from Joris to Castellio was little more than a greeting. On the other hand, Bietenholz (*Basle and France*, p. 132) affirms that the "scope of Castellio's rationalism was wide enough to allow a genuine affection for the mystical tendencies of . . . the Anabaptists."

50. *Blesdijk*, pp. 99-100.

51. See ibid., pp. 97-104, and Bietenholz, *Basle and France*, pp. 126-32.

52. Other regions included were Holland, Belgium, Holstein, Lübeck and Friesland. Prominent among his letters were chastising missives to fellow Spiritualists such as Caspar Schwenckfeld (*Christlijcke Sendbrieven*, part 3, fol. 45) and the founder of the House of Love, Heinrich Niclaes (ibid., part 1, fol. 100).

53. The numbers for the Antwerp and Basel periods are approximate, for some of those dated to 1544 and included here for the Antwerp residence, may have instead been composed in Basel during the last four months of that year after Joris had emigrated. The count of Joris' works is based on the standard bibliographies, including van der Linde, *David Joris*; Hillerbrand, *Bibliography*; A.M. Cramer, *Bijvoegselen tot de Levensbeschrijving van David Joris* (Leiden: 1844); Bainton, *David Joris*; and Nijhoff and Kronenberg, *Nederlandsche Bibliographie*. Several uncatalogued works were discovered in the Manuscript Department, Universiteit Amsterdam.

54. The best discussion of Joris' Spiritualist thought is still Bainton, *David Joris*, esp. pp. 71-88.

55. Most true Spiritualists rejected any notions which might lead to further sectarianism.

56. *Twonder-Boeck* (1542-43), part I, fol. 51v: "Dit is den beloofden wtuercoren Dauidt / die gheweldige Vorst"; *Twonder-boeck: waer in dat van der werldt aen versloten gheopenbaert is. Opt nieuw ghecorrigeert vnde vermeerdert by den Autheur selue* (n.p., 1551), part I, fol. 57r: "Dit is den principaelsten Geest der kraft / den beloofden wtverkoren David die geweldige vorst."

57. Ibid. (1551), part I, fol. 58r. This passage is not found in the earlier edition. Bainton (*David Joris*, English manuscript, pp. 80-81) discovered similar divergent passages between the two editions. For example, in the first edition, Joris wrote: "I David have power with my spirit to judge you in the Lord according to the Spirit and to bless and curse according to the truth. To forgive or to retain sins, to bind and to loose by the Lord in Heaven, yes at the right time to slay with the rod of my mouth, which is the eternal word of the power of God." In the second edition, Joris had revised this to read "therefore consider this spirit or time of grace in which you shall be blessed or damned, commended or condemned, your sins forgiven or retained, bound or loosed. Yes, he who is sent of the Lord His God has power with other holy apostles and prophets to punish and slay with the rod of his mouth which is the almighty word of the power of God."

58. Bainton, *David Joris*, p. 72. Bainton also argues that the section on the Trinity "is more academic than anything we have seen thus far" (ibid., p. 73).

59. Edited, translated and discussed by Bainton, in *Concerning Heretics. An anonymous work attributed to Sebastian Castellio* (New York: Columbia University Press, 1935),

pp. 305-309. The letter dates from September, 1553. The original is in *Christlijcke Sendbrieven*, part IV, letter 9.

60. Guggisberg, *Basel*, p. 59.

61. Ibid., p. 60. This is the work translated by Bainton as *Concerning Heretics*.

62. See *Blesdijk*, pp. 110-14. Zijlstra shows that several sections in *De haereticis* were nearly word for word identical with Joris' *Ernstelijcke Klage* of 1544. The main objection to Joris' authorship is the relatively clear writing style of Kleinbergius' piece. Joris, however, could be clear, as we saw with his *Apology to Countess Anna*. It is also possible that the translator of Joris' piece, probably Blesdijk or Castellio, had improved its style. Bainton (*Concerning Heretics*, p. 10) summarises the earlier debate on Joris' participation in *De haereticis* and concludes in the negative.

63. It is possible to speculate that had he lived longer, Joris would have turned his pen against the later burning of witches. Aside from his advocacy of toleration, Joris also depreciated or even denied the power of the Devil. Without a belief in a powerful Devil, there was no basis for witch prosecution. See Geoffrey Scarre, *Witchcraft and Magic in 16th and 17th Century Europe* (London: Macmillan Education Ltd., 1987).

64. Bainton cites the following letter: "My dear Eysken [the wife of Reinier van Berchem], I hear that you have complained of me that we have not done for Reinier what we promised and have not treated him as our own son. . . . I hear that he has said that his mother gave us everything. . . . His mother said she could have no peace if I did not accept the gifts and Reinier himself pressed them upon me. I turned everything over to Joachim with the approval of Van Lier and Annelin. Whether or not Joachim made good use of it I testify before the Lord that I did not spend a penny for my own need. I admit that the mother once turned over to me 2,200 gulden. A thousand went for the chateau and some for the upkeep . . ." (*David Joris*, English manuscript, p. 99). The van Berchems had brought in the greatest proportion of funds into the colony. See also Zijlstra, *Blesdijk*, pp. 131-32.

65. For Blesdijk's disillusionment with and fall from the Davidites, see Zijlstra, *Blesdijk*, pp. 121-46.

66. Stayer, "David Joris," p. 358.

67. Bainton, *David Joris* (English manuscript), p. 100.

68. Zijlstra, *Blesdijk*, pp. 124-31.

69. *David Joris*, pp. 92-93.

70. See Zijlstra, *Blesdijk*, pp. 131-36.

71. The events surrounding the "Joris trial" are covered by Bainton, *David Joris*, pp. 98-107. Many of the documents relating to the post mortem trial are included in Vols. II and III of the *Jorislade* and several have been edited by Bainton (*David Joris*, pp. 122-222).

72. Bainton, *David Joris* (English manuscript), p. 110.

73. Guggisberg, *Basel*, p. 45.

74. Bainton, *David Joris*, pp. 102-103. Bainton relates an interesting incident on the popular level. Rumours circulated among the populace that the Davidites had buried an animal in the place of the prophet's corpse, and worshipped Joris' body in their home. The city dug up and reburied Joris' corpse while one of the citizens cut off a piece of his beard to disprove the rumour. Bainton also cites a letter of a Basel citizen who wrote on May 12: "A countess from Holland, perhaps persuaded by stories of demonic incubi, came to Basel shortly after his death to receive the Holy Spirit by intercourse with his corpse which had been preserved by spices" (ibid., English manuscript, p. 113).

75. Bietenholz remarks that "during the official investigation Castellio was not seriously implicated. He had no qualms in condemning a few incoherent articles allegedly

excerpted from Joris' writings. Not with one syllable did he condemn the Anabaptist himself, and he got away with it'' (*Basle and France*, p. 126).

76. This included not being allowed to entertain visitors from the Netherlands, having to deliver all of Joris' books and papers to the authorities, and having to pay fines totaling 4,600 gulden (Bainton, *David Joris*, p. 106).

77. Nippold, "David Joris," p. 627.

78. For example, see the anonymous *Tegenbericht op een Laster en scheldtboecksken gheentituleert David Gergis wt Hollandt, des Ertzketters Waerachtige Historie* (n.p., 1584). While the *Tegenbericht* was not published until 1584, it was written as a response to the University of Basel's 1559 report. In the last decade of the sixteenth century a Davidite by the name of J. Theophilus took on the prominent author Dirck Volckherts Coornhert in *Eenen Sendtbrief aen Dirk Volckertz Cornhert: Op syn Boeck ghenaempt Kleyn Munster / Utgeghaen teghens die Scriften van D.J.* (n.p., n.d.). Also, Andreas Huygelmumzoon, actually Bernard Kirchen, the second husband of Joris' daughter Clara, took on the prominent rector of the Groningen school (Ubbo Emmius, in *Wederleggenghe / unde grove onbeschaemde vnde tastelicke Logenen van Ubbo Emmen* [n.p., 1600]). Interestingly, Huygelmumzoon noted, "I have heard this testimony about the pious David, from himself and from those who were of his party, who would therefore not keep silent about the truth'' (fols. 13-15).

79. See Zijlstra, *Blesdijk*, pp. 134-36.

80. Eugénie Droz, "Sur Quelques Traductions Françaises D'Écrits de David Joris," in *Het Boek*, derde reeks, Vol. XXXVII, 1965, 154-162.

81. The merchant Henrick Jacobsz financed the printing of Mullem's edition of the *Twonder-Boeck*. See ibid., p. 161. That there was in Emden a market for the *Wonder Book* is confirmed by the chronicler Abel Eppens, who noted in the 1580s that with the lack of interest in the Reformed Church in Emden, it was no wonder that the city swarmed with "libertines, Franckists, Schwenckfeldians, Albadians and especially David Jorists" (from W. Bergsma, "Zestiende-Eeeuwse Godsdienstige Pluriformiteit Overwegingen Naar Aanleiding van Abel Eppens," in Buist, *Historisch Bewogen*, p. 9).

82. Nippold, "David Joris," p. 626. Herberts had been a Cistercian monk in Westphalia until he came over to the Reformation in Bocholt sometime before 1570. See J. Reitsma, *Geschiedenis van de Hervorming en de Hervormde Kerk der Nederlanden* (Utrecht: Kemink & Zoon N.V., 1933), pp. 224-25.

83. Interestingly, there is in the Manuscript department at the Universeit Amsterdam a volume entitled "H. Herberti Diversche Stukken," (#II 1976a) which contains works by Joris and Ketel, as well as Herberts. Herberts' teaching on the devil and antichrist are remarkably parallel to Joris'. While the Reformed preacher denied the allegation that he had sponsored the publication of Joris' works, continuing suspicions about his unorthodoxy led to a second investigation of his views conducted by The Hague Synod in 1583 and finally to his removal from office in 1591 by the Dordrecht Synod, although a more equitable settlement was mediated by the government. See Brandt, *History of the Reformation*, p. 400.

84. Alastair Hamilton (*The Family of Love* [Greenwood, S.C.: The Attic Press, Inc., 1981], p. 63) concurs: "For men who were Catholics at heart but were not allowed to practise their religion, for men thoroughly disgusted both with Catholicism and Reformed Protestantism but who retained some form of piety, for men trying to broaden the appeal of Reformed Protestantism by modifying its severity and its exclusiveness, the spirituality of Sebastian Franck, David Joris, Hendrik Niclaes and [Hendrik Jansen van] Barrefelt had an attraction.''

APPENDICES

Anabaptist Leaders Active
after 1535[1]

Name	Group	Locale	Dates
Adriaen Adriaens	P	Poeldijk	died March 1536
Adriaen Jorysz	P	Poeldijk	died March 1536
Adriaen van Benscop	B>D	Holland	1538-
Alexander Overlander	?(Mel)	?	?
Andries Hermans	Mel	Guelders	died April 1537
Andreis Droochscheerder	M/B>D	Groningen	1534-
Andreis Tuchmeister	M>D	Groningen	1534-
Anthon Smedes	D	Westphalia	1537-
Bauke Molenaer	M/B>D	Hilversum	1534-
Bertold Nyemans	B	Emlichem	-1544
Christoffel van Zutphen	M>D	Westphalia	1537-
Claes bij Steenwijk	B	?	?
Claes Janz van Hazersw.	P	Poeldijk	died March 1536
Cornelis Appelman	B	Holland/Münster	1538-d.1544
Cornelis Barbier	?	Gorkum	fugitive 1539
Cornelis Cloot	?	Antwerp	?
Cornelis de Kuiper	D	Delft	1539-d.1544
Cortoys uit Henegouwen	D	Utrecht	died 1539
David Joris	D	Delft	1534-
Dirk Philips	O	Friesland	1534-
Dirick Schoemecker	B>D	Westphalia	1531-d.1546
Frans Jansz	B	Utrecht	1534-d.1541
Gerdt Eilkeman	B	Westph./Fries.	1534-d.1544
Gilles van Ratheim	Mel>O	Maastricht	1534-d.1536
Goris de lantaarnmaker	?(Mel)	Leiden	escaped 1535-
A man from Gorkum	?	Gorkum	?
Hans Scheerder	M/B>D	Leeuwarden	1533-
Heinrich die Goudsmit	?	Gorkum	fugitive 1539
Henrich Herckemaicker	B>D	Giethoorn	1534-d.1544
Heinrich Kaal	M/B>D	Westph./Delft	1535-d.1539
Heinrich Krechting	M	Westphalia	1533-40
Hendrick van Zutphen	M	Netherlands	1534-
Hendrick van Maastricht	M	Netherlands	died Feb. 1536
Herk Dirks	?(Mel)	Utrecht	1534-d.1541

Note to Appendix I is found on page 196.

196 David Joris

Appendix I (continued)

Name	Group	Locale	Dates
Herman van Kelder	D	Delft	died 1539
Jacob up de Kelder	D	Groningen	1537-
Jan de snyder	D	Delft	-1544-
Jan Glaesmaker	D	Friesland	1537-
Jan Matthijs van Middelburg	Mel	England	1534-d.1538
Jan Eisenburg	Mel	Strassburg	1531-d.1541/43
Janne Specke	M	Gron./Antw.	died Nov.1537
Jan Trajectensis	?(Mel)	Overijsel	-1536-?
Jan van Batenburg	B	Netherlands	died April 1538
Jan van Maastricht	Mel	Maastricht/Antw.	died Nov. 1537
Jan van Schoonhoven	Mel	Holland	-1536-
Joost de Snijder	?	Gorkum	fugitive 1539
Jorien Ketel	D	Deventer	1538-d.1544
Lambert Duppijns	D	Haarlem	died 1539
Laurens Droggscheerder	?(Mel)	?	?
Leonard de Boekbinder	M	Holland	1533-?
Lenaert Munsels	?	Alken	-1540-
Leonard van Ijsenbroeck	?	?	1534-?
Luytgen Benninck	B	Emlichem	-1544-
Matthias Belkensis	M	Friesland	-1536-?
Menno Simons	O	Friesland	1536-
Meynart van Emden	M>D	Groningen	1534-
Nicolaas Blesdijk	D	Netherlands	1539-
Obbe Philips	O	Groningen	1534-
Paulus van Druinen	O?	Brabant	died 1538
Peter Glassmaker	D	Appingedam	-1538-
Peter van den Binchorst	P	Hazerswoude	died Jan.1536
Peter van Coelen	?	?	?
Peter van Luyck	?(Mel)	?	?
Rem van Hoorn	M>D	Alkmaar	1534-
Roleff Morveldinck	B	Emlichem	-d.1542
Seward Klerck	M>D	Groningen	-1536-
Steven van Naarden	?	?	?
Thyaert van Sneek	M	Friesland	-d.1539
Willem Dirks Zeylmaker	M/B	Overijsel	1534-d.1544
Willem van Endhoven	M/B	Utrecht	1534-40

Note

1. From Mellink, *De Wederdopers*, and Vos, "Kleine bijdragen," pp. 111-23.
Legend: M=Münsterite; B=Batenburger; D=Davidite; O=Mennonite;
Mel=Melchiorite; P=Poeldijk or Hazerswoude radical; /=or; >=switched affiliation.

Jorien Ketel's Confession[1]

When I [*sic*],[2] Jorien Ketel (a citizen living in Deventer) through the command of the Duke of Bueren, Stadholder of Frisia and the land of Overijsel,
was placed in prison, they asked him of his faith. Thereupon he gave to
them orally and in writing a good confession, which they sent to the Court at
Brussels for judgement.

When they discovered from this that he heartily supported and
defended D[avid] J[oris]'s doctrine and word, and that he clung to what he
had confessed, both orally and in writing, and was a follower and defender
of Joris, the Court of Brussels strongly instructed [the authorities of]
Deventer to use severe torture on the prisoner, in order to discover who the
others of D[avid] J[oris]' sect were. Then the magistrates of Deventer, to
show their faithful obedience and against all imperial laws and also against
their own policy, interrogated him four or five times under severe torture,[3]
so that (even if he had remained alive) he was made unfit for living in the
world.

When they could find no guilt in him except on account of his faith, the
majority of the council members wanted to release him from the matter. But
the Court of Brussels wrote insisting that they must execute him. While the
Burgomasters disagreed amongst themselves over the matter, there was a
meeting of the knights and the foremost of the city who remonstrated to the
council, and they came to an accord to consent to his death.[4]

After being in prison twelve weeks and a day, he was finally led out
into the Bishop's Court. There was the sheriff, according to the local law
and on account of the Imp[erial] Maj[esty] and two Burgomasters sitting on
the bench to hold judgement. They asked Jorien Ketel if they should read
aloud everything that he had written and confessed in prison. Thereupon he
answered: that it was not necessary, but they should only read the things
which they believed were evil or that were done against the Imperial man-
dates, for which he deserved death. Thereupon the secretary so read: "Here
stands Jorien Ketel and confesses, that he is of D[avid] J[oris'] sect and that
he had eaten and drank with D[avid] J[oris], had journeyed and gone about
with him, had known his deeds and views, had read his books and written
teachings, had published and spread them in different lands, and that he does
only that which [Joris] desired. Further, that he is rebaptised and that on this

---

Notes to Appendix II are found on page 200.

account his first wife was also drowned at Utrecht.''

Thereupon Jorien Ketel answered: "it so happened, that D[avid] J[oris] taught me nothing but good, namely God's Word. All his doctrine was proven and confirmed to me with divine Scriptures, namely that I should kill and tread under the old man with all his evil lusts and put on or become a new man. He counselled and taught all this to me, a dunce. Should I therefore not listen to him, believe him and follow after him? Further, it is also true that I am rebaptised, but it has been eleven years since it happened.''

Then the sheriff requested a judgement by the executioner regarding this matter, what one should do concerning him. The executioner judged that one should cut off his head and his body ought to be buried in unconsecrated ground.

Then Jorien Ketel took off his hat and spoke: "the Lord must be eternally trusted and praised," and turning to the people he said further: "O, would to God I were free to speak.'' Thereupon one of the Burgomasters spoke, "Jorien, you know well what is said, to you is given the grace to say a few more words." Jorien answered: "Yes, to me is given grace, O to me is given grace from my God, for he has forgiven my sins.''

Then the monk spoke: "I desire that these spectators will be able to say that you died as a pious, Christian man." Thereupon Jorien answered again: "wherefore I suffer and die, that I have to say the same to them, and they will still hear out of my mouth, therefore you be silent.'' Then he [the monk] desired to place a crucifix in his hand in order to remember the death and suffering of Christ. To this Jorien replied: "No, I will not take your cross, I bear Jesus Christ and his cross in my heart, that is enough for me. Therefore all of you, who stand around me, are there any among you who desire to bear this Jesus Christ and his cross with me in his heart, who will set his feet fast and firm in the forthcoming tempest and need, for there shall be need, and O so great. Whoever does not desire to share the blame of this day, but indeed has reason to grieve over it?''

Further he spoke with lowly heart: "my heart condemns me not in anything, for I have travelled through cities and lands in order to find and serve my God, and I have also found him, namely upon this way, for he is never to be found in any other way, neither in heaven nor in earth.''

When they then let him have a taste of wine, he said, "O my God, you must eternally be praised and worshipped, for just like the mouth of your eternal Son spoke to his disciples, 'I shall no more drink of this fruit of the vine from this time until the day when I will drink it anew with you in the kingdom of my Father' I shall no longer enjoy this alone but with the others in the same Kingdom of the Father.''[5]

Then when he went out to the Market [i.e., the New Market], he was joyful and rejoiced in his God, and went with joy to the place and said: "further, my beloved and pious citizens, I pray you on account of God's will, that you will not think evil of me because I am joyful, for I cannot contain myself. I must now rejoice in my God, because he is so favourable to me."

When he came out of the Bishop's court, they led him through the *Bisschopstraat* to the *Brinck*. All along the way he spoke, but one could not understand such because of the crowd of people and the whispers of the multitude.

Then he came to the place where he was to be beheaded, so he knelt down and said, "I thank you O God, who has made and created the heavens and the earth, that you, out of grace, have confessed me worthy, though a poor worm, that I may die for your most holy and illustrious name. Yes, O God, if it is possible to happen, that even if I rose immediately from this death, and again must die for the truth of God from heaven, you know, O my God, that my heart desires such and would do it with joy. Your name be thanked eternally, that you have given me such a heart, mind and spirit through your Holy Spirit." Further he said, "O Father, just like your servant has sought you with faithfulness, and truth, let him now also enjoy the same. Let, O my God, your servant go in peace, for my eyes have seen your salvation."[6] Having said this he stood up from the ground and spoke to the people: "my beloved citizens, I suffer not as a rogue, thief, murderer or other evildoer, but I die for the eternal righteousness and truth of God. More so, that I am of one mind with D[avid] J[oris], that I confess it openly. I believe in God the Almighty Father and in his Son Jesus Christ, the true anointed of God, which D[avid] J[oris] also does. And my foundation and ground stands upon the teaching of the Apostles and prophets, where D[avid] J[oris]'s foundation also stands upon. That this same is in this way and shall be found eternally in the truth, that I will testify this day, sealed with my blood." This bothered the sheriff very much (as it seemed) and he spoke: "D[avid] J[oris] is the most evil arch-heretic who has ever come or been upon the earth or in the world."[7] Thereupon Jorien answered, "the Day of the Lord will make this known, if you or I have testified correctly." Then he went again upon his knees and spoke: "O Lord, lead your servant in peace, for my eyes have seen your salvation and my soul longs to be with you." And still before the executioner had prepared all things, he called out five or six times: "O Lord, into your hands I commit my spirit."

In this way did this godfearing man, with a joyful, prepared heart, finish his course there with joy, as a certain son of Abraham, who feared not to die, but willingly gave over his life for the Lord. Looking to nothing other than only upon the high trust of eternal blessedness, the cherished word of faith, upon which he had firmly fixed his feet, he sealed it with his blood and testified that he believed it in the truth with diligence and earnest courage, counselling them through his mouth, speaking and teaching. Therefore wake up, you who sleep, namely you who are lusting and are impure in sins. For the day of the Lord, the terrifying judgement of God, is at the door, when everyone who does not improve his life out of wisdom, or who has despised the counsel of the Holy Spirit, her punishment, love and trust, will perish. The Lord, the Almighty, eternal, gracious, good God will be merciful to him concerning his misunderstandings, if a good will is maintained, so that they will not be incinerated on this day (whom the Holy Spirit through his servants has called out and sealed with their blood) nor be practised in malevolence and be overtaken.

Notes

1. From de Hullu, *Bescheiden*, pp. 311-16.
2. The author may have intended to write the account in the first person, or he may have finished a confession started by Ketel himself.
3. There were legally established limits to the number of times an accused heretic could be tortured. Many inquisitors got around the restriction by "continuing" the same session of torture over several days instead of beginning a new one.
4. Blesdijk blames the Groningen Reformed preacher, Dr. Hieronymus, for causing Ketel's execution. It appears that Hieronymus wrote to the Stadholder and to the Deventer authorities gravely warning them of the danger of David Joris' teaching. In Blesdijk's reply to Hieronymus, he included a copy of *Wholesome Teaching*, to show the Groningen preacher what kind of pious Christian he had brought to the executioner's scaffold (*Billijcke Verantwoordinge*, fol. 3r).
5. Reference is to Matthew 26:29.
6. Reference is to Luke 2:29-30.
7. This viewpoint may have come from Hieronymus' pamphlet to the Deventer Council.

APPENDIX III

Ketel's Letter to His Wife[1]

My worthy, dear wife, I say to you out of the innermost of my heart, a thousand good nights, and beg of you, on account of love, which I have had for you and your children, that you will conduct yourself devoutly and sincerely before all men and that you will bring up my children (as God lets you remain with them) in God's fear and to his honour, and remove all unnecessary things which do not further the salvation of God. And place your trust only upon God, that henceforth he will be your husband, this I command you out of a full heart. Beloved friend, I beg that you also will remember my mother, for she has had sorrow on account of me. Now you know my heart, therefore do not judge nor remember what I may have failed to say to you, but forgive me, I have long ago forgiven you. O Lord, take pity on us according to your great mercy, after I have brought my struggle to an end. My dear Lutger, as you are able, so I desire well that my daughter Elseken, who lives at Hoorn, have a remembrance of me, that she might remember me, do to your courtesy. The Lord shall be with you. Amen. I have died so many deaths before I die, that I cannot write it all to you. Written in my last hour.

Note

1. From de Hullu, *Bescheiden*, pp. 316-17.

Leonard van Dam's Vision of the Heavenly Man[1]

A vision of one (named Leon[ard] van Dam)
who loves the truth and justice of God,
which he has seen in the daytime
during the course of the month of May
or beginning of June 1539.

Sitting up in the attic in a house it happened that the Spirit of God came suddenly upon a man named David and he began to speak of the power and word of his God, just as the Lord placed into his mouth. When I heard these words they were inserted into my innermost being, so that the heart and mind of my soul were opened up like a rose. I then could not contain the life and joy of my innermost spirit. I cannot describe this [joy] in words, but it remains with me as unspeakable. And behold I was compelled to stop my work. But I was troubled about this and continued to work in order to overcome my laziness and weakness, although I was pressured to stop. Finally there was a inspiration given to me by the voice of the Spirit, without my advance knowledge or advice, namely in this fashion: "Truly you have heard today (through the living conversations which have proceeded from David's mouth) [and] you have listened to, seen, tasted and felt Jesus in his living, spiritual,[2] true nature, standing at the right hand of God in heaven. Even more truly than had Stephen, Acts 7[:18]. Or like Isaiah, who said in Isa. 6[:1-3], when he saw the glory of God sitting on his seat and throne: "I am a man of unclean lips." Read and speak freely, without timidity also in this way, that you too are a man of unclean lips, and after this you will see in a living fashion [and] in the innermost parts of your heart the majesty of God. After this it was shown to me from the Spirit, that I should read Isa. 6 and Acts 7. I did not know what I would find written there, but I thought, what can it be? At the same time I was full of a living fire and burning in my innermost being, so that I did not know how or what was happening in me. For I was young and did not know the Spirit and in my weakness I could not express what was happening to me. I saw myself as too small and unworthy to speak like a man of God about the exalted word of the Spirit. The Spirit, however, allowed me no rest, but spoke as loudly to me as if it had occurred through a man's mouth, that I should go downstairs. I could neither sleep nor rest, neither in the evening nor night, until one summer afternoon,

Notes to Appendix IV are found on page 206.

around three or four o'clock, when I answered and said: "Lord, you know what the situation is here and the reason why I cannot go downstairs."[3]

This had happened five or six times when the woman of the house (knowing of it) came up to us in the morning, and said, is anyone up here who wants to come down? You can do so, for the people have departed. About this I was full of amazement and decided to go into the hall or room. When I now had gone in and out of the room five or six more times, I finally stopped and stood there in the middle, and a voice said distinctly to me: "Stand and behold." Then I stood with my face towards the wall and away from the light and I saw a naked man, standing before me, also facing away from the light towards the wall, for I saw him only from behind. He stood with his feet upon the surface of the earth, which was amazing to me. Then the Spirit spoke again to me: "Behold." Trembling, I looked and watched as the man quietly sank down, with his feet gradually descending until his head had also gone under and disappeared. I then saw the earth neither opened nor closed. The voice of the Spirit spoke again: "Behold." I then saw the same naked man under the earth just as clearly as I had seen him above the earth. I therefore became dismayed and frightened, and asked in my heart, what does this man rest on; does he stand on his feet or on his head? I observed that he was suspended between heaven and earth, as I have told you, and he moved as a bird does in the sky. But so that you will understand me, he was in the earth, as I have said to you. Then the Spirit or the voice answered me: "His feet stand upon nothing, and rest upon no outer thing, but he is suspended, for where he is, there is an eternal abyss." Thereupon he called me to look again. Then I saw the same naked man growing or rising out of the earth just like a flower or plant does. But then I saw all of this from behind him. The head came up first, then afterwards the neck, then the shoulders, arms, hips, legs, and gradually the feet, all slowly or little by little.

Take note. The head came up first, then afterwards the neck, so that he once again stood up completely upon the earth as before. I then wanted to touch him, to see if he was living or dead. But such was not permitted to me, for the Spirit answered me: "He is still dead and not yet living." Then I looked at his feet and I became aware that they touched the earth and became impure from it. But from the feet up the body was so pure, beautiful and shining, that one had never heard of nor seen of such a clean and majestic image of a man. Furthermore, my eyes fell once more upon the feet and I saw that they were now also pure and beautiful from the earth, for the earth or impurity had disappeared completely from them. And behold, I saw the life enter him; first his hips were pulled to and fro from behind, just like a man or beast that has first been killed and yet lays and wriggles, so that his veins and sinews[4] were pulled to and fro, as is easy to comprehend. A little later he lifted up his arms and let them down again; then he shifted or moved his whole body, so that he now was thoroughly alive. Finally he lifted a leg up from the earth, or stretched it forward, then the other, and set them down again. See, after this he turned completely around with his face towards mine and against the light, and his face shone like the sun. So bright [was it], in fact, that one cannot describe it. He also had a beautiful red beard and he came walking towards me, as if he would go right through me.[5] Whether he went through or around my body, I do not know. But when he came up to walk to me, I was so amazed and frightened in the appearance of his movement, it was as if I had been outside of my body, standing however upon my feet. I cannot write nor describe this [adequately] with the quill. He was also so large and wonderful, so mighty and frightening, that he feared no one. He furthermore saw perfectly, that all great rulers, lords, princes, dukes, indeed, the kings and emperors of this world were in his eyes as worms upon the earth are commonly regarded by men. As worms, which have only a little movement, not even as the beasts, fish or birds, I say, of which no one fears to tread upon or near them, killing them or letting them live. Yet even more insignificant than these were all men, both small and great, strong or sick, noble or common; all swept away by a wind.

When I now wanted to look at him, he was gone and I saw him no more. Then the Spirit spoke to me: "That is God, the Messiah, the new Creature, the first true man of God from heaven." The name of the person, which was pleasant to me at that time, I will still keep secret, it was very well known to me. He will, according to the word, be even more heard, known and loved at the right time. I did not relate any of this for seven or eight days afterwards, until it finally broke out of my heart. I am also certain that this vision came right from God. Moreover, I desired to reveal or bring it to them, for even as I had seen it outwardly, so I saw it also according to the Spirit.[6] When this happened, the man was so amazed he knew not where to go, for he thought, what is the meaning of this? It was also during this time that he kept it concealed, that he did not reveal it to David. Then it happened that David was also inspired that he should go into the room (where one went to and fro, whence the first came). When he came before the light, he turned around to come towards the other brothers. At that moment a voice said that he should kneel down, but David did not do it right away because of his concern about what the others [might think]. Then a voice spoke strongly and loudly to him that he should be obedient. And see, he did it, regardless of whether or not the others might think it to be as strange as he did. Regardless, it had to be done. As soon as he was down, his heart, sense and mind turned to the Lord and his eyes opened up inwardly. Immediately David found himself staring at a quickly rotating clockwork wheel. It turned quickly, and then after it had rotated for a little time it stopped. The thing [i.e., the key] which one normally used to wind it, turned over and over two or three more times and then stopped.

Then the voice said: "Behold, in this way will I from henceforth awaken the hearts of princes, lords, kings and mighty ones against each other. There will be no end nor rest until they have all perished, and in this way will the blow fall upon their necks." There were many more words spoken by the voice which have since been forgotten. He [i.e., Joris] believed, that it signified that they [i.e., the authorities] will not obtain peace and therefore must humble themselves. He was so convinced of this [meaning] that he placed it in a book. But finally the clearest meaning of the contents came to him, namely, that God wanted to entangle their hearts against each other, or make unrest or trouble for them which would not cease until he had finished and declared his will and word. Be this as it may, it [i.e., the vision] certainly happened in this fashion.[7]

Notes

1. Probably published, but available only in Anonymous, pp. 730-31.
2. Original: *unbetrieglichen*.
3. Van Dam is obviously referring to the danger of detection if he went down from the attic into the main part of the house, where he might be seen by strangers or city officials.
4. Literally *adern* and *sennen*.
5. Although Joris' name is not mentioned, his identity as the man in the vision is indisputable; one of Joris' physical characteristics was a long, red beard.
6. It is difficult to ascertain exactly where the tract ends and the anonymous biography continues, but at this point it appears that Leonard van Dam is no longer the narrator and Anonymous has taken up his story again.
7. According to Anonymous, Joris also had another vision in the same room: "For in the same evening that the wonderful vision of the naked man was revealed to him [i.e., van Dam], David had a divine, glorious incident. God (it seemed to him) pulled him totally away and took David (it appeared) out of his own vision and perception, as if he were no longer the same man; indeed, he no longer recognized himself. In this vision he saw himself in Aaron's priestly nature, as a pure bride, [and] a spiritual head of the church."

Public Confession of Sins

One of the unique doctrines or practices espoused by David Joris was the public confession of sins. In his scheme confession was to be made before the brothers and sisters, not before a priest. In this practice Joris therefore combined anticlericalism with traditional practices. Public confession can be seen also as an attempt by Joris to release the pent-up guilt and frustration associated with the traditional suppression of the sex drive in an ascetic context. It may have acted in this way as a form of psychological group therapy.[1] In Joris' perspective, shame over the body and its functions was a by-product of the fall of Adam. Before that fall, Adam and Eve were naked but unashamed, for the sexual passion had not been introduced. Instead they were created good in the image of God.[2] After the fall, Adam and Eve perceived through the devil ("by the deceitful dark eye") that they ought to be ashamed. This type of shame, inspired by the serpent, led only to death. The goal of the new birth (and ultimately of the restitution) was to restore men and women to pre-Fall innocence, where believers would no longer be ashamed of their bodies because fleshly lusts (i.e., sexual desire) had been cast out.

Joris' concept of Adamic innocence closely paralleled that of St. Augustine, who postulated that in pre-Fall society parenthood was possible without the arousal of sexual passion.[3] Joris explained the relationship of shame with the productive members.

> Woe to those who have impure thoughts about God's handiwork, or to those who remain in such shame. For such shame is from the devil and is deadly to the knowledge of perfection. To us is revealed that we still ought to feel shame because of the commandments, but not the shame of the devil.... For this reason, as long as there is shame in us, there is sin. I mean the [shame] over the members, which were not created by man but by God. Therefore to have shame over them must be from the devil.... Why should they bring more shame than the other members, such as your eyes, nose, mouth, ears, hands and feet? Except only through the roguish eye and the inspiration of the devil.[4]

In other words, if the corrupting influence of the devil, as seen in fleshly lusts, could be cast out, then the shame normally associated with sexual activity would also be removed.

Joris, like his fellow lay reformers and Anabaptists, had not visited a confessional for many years — his last appearance in one was in 1528 when he distributed anticlerical tracts. As one scholar has explained,

> An implicit function of sexual ethics in sacramental confession . . . is the reinforcement of clerical supremacy. . . . The subordination of married laity to celibate clergy is reinforced in many ways by sacramental confession.[5]

Sacramental confession, therefore, came to be employed by the clergy as a form of social control.

> In theory and practice, sacramental confession provided a comprehensive and organised system of social control. Its first principle was the sacramentally ordained priest's dominance, which was expressed in a variety of ways.[6]

Sacramental confession was especially resented by reform-minded laymen. In spite of the fact that Joris began his reform career as an opponent of the sacerdotal system, he soon developed his own replacement for sacramental confession with his practice of "public confession." Joris taught that the sins of his followers were to be confessed publicly before the entire group. While this was a rejection of the dominance of the ordained priesthood, it too operated as a form of social control. In fact, if public confession involved confessing one's sins not only in front of the fellowship, but also in the presence of leaders such as Joris, then it could have asserted the dominance of the "charismatic leader" in the place of the ordained priest.

Ironically, the state of shamelessness envisaged by Joris was achieved by an act in which the old flesh or Satan was openly shamed. By publicly revealing the sins committed secretly by the old man, the shame was removed, much as priestly absolution could remove guilt after confession. Joris exhorted his readers to

> confess . . . your sins, your roguishness, and misdeeds. Let them be known publicly, whatever the old man has wrought in you through the devil . . . in this way you will be released from him and become pure, and completely released. So shame him, take off his clothes, remove his abominations, hate him and his works: murder, thievery, buggery, his adultery, his unchastity, his whoredom. . . . [7]

Joris believed that both he and his wife had cast off Satan and hence removed sexual passion from their relationship. Anonymous recorded that

> It is hard to believe at this point, how the man David Joris became so impelled . . . to tread his shame under his feet and to cast it away. This happened also with his wife, for they threw out Belial, the devil and Satan . . . and he was bound by them according to the Scriptures.[8]

Presumably Joris and his wife could therefore sleep together without provoking lust, and hence without the resultant shame and guilt. The following passage, in Joris' own words, may have provided a formula for the act of casting out Satan:

> Go away from me, Satan, or I shall shame you in all your counsel. You deceitful devil and evil spirit, depart. See, I shall reveal all your lies, roguishness and deceit. I will take off your clothes, I will no longer conceal your bidding, your will and desires no longer be done. Therefore go far from me, for the Lord, the Mighty One, the Holy One in Israel, is my love and bridegroom and husband, whose eyes keep me in his presence, and make me content.[9]

While the evidence is sketchy, it is possible that the practice of "public nakedness" was associated with the practice of confession among Davidites. The act seems to have been performed by the group of Davidites in Delft and is inferred in a list of questions about Joris' teaching sent to him from the Oldenburg Münsterites in 1538.[10] Certainly it would not be inconsistent with Joris' teaching concerning public confession and the casting out of shame. Instead, public nakedness, without sexual arousal, could be construed as a sign that a believer had attained a state of innocence.

Notes

1. See Hennig, "Askese," pp. 36-37; and G. Rathray Taylor, *Sex in History* (London: Thames & Hudson, 1953), pp. 43, 51-52.
2. *Hoert, hoert, hoert*, fols. 33v-34r.
3. See St. Augustine's *The City of God* (Garden City: Image Books, 1958), p. 318. Augustine's works were published in Dutch several times between 1513 and 1520 (Nijhoff and Kronenberg, *Nederlandsche Bibliographie*, nos. 149-55).
4. *Hoert, hoert, hoert*, fols. 42v-43r. Shame over the sexual organs was promoted by traditional medieval theology, for "the blacker the colors in which sexual pleasure is seen, the brighter shines the ideal of the sexually chaste man" (Tentler, *Sin and Confession*, p. 165).
5. Ibid., p. 220.
6. Ibid., p. 345.
7. *Hoert, hoert, hoert*, fols. 11r-12r.
8. P. 724.
9. *Hoert, hoert, hoert*, fol. 21v.
10. Unfortunately the original list of questions is not extant and the only source we have is a summary provided by Blesdijk. This makes certain conclusions regarding "public nakedness" and Joris' followers tentative at best (*Historia vitae*, pp. 75-77).

The Internal Restitution

Joris called the true, internal restitution the "renewal of the five senses."[1] While on the surface it is similar to a German-mystical anthropology, Joris added a unique twist of his own. Man was not only divided into body, soul and spirit,[2] but also into inner and outer. Contrary to traditional mystical thought, Joris regarded the outer, or physical body, as not inherently evil, for it was created by God. The inner man, however, could be either good or evil. In this context, the "flesh" was not the physical body, but the inner man when oriented to selfishness and lust. The condition of the inward man or senses determined the orientation of the external senses. Joris explained,

> Moreover, the five senses of your old man must perish completely inwardly and you must begin and continue to oppose him as your murderer and enemy. Otherwise the new heavenly creature will not appear in glorious power.... There is an external hearing, an external sight, an external smell, taste, touching and feeling, but these do not bring death, but are holy, free and good as they were at creation. When goodness rises first from the inside, then is the outer also good. For the external is ruled or carried by the internal, and not the internal by the external.... Therefore purify your hearts and become renewed in your senses.[3]

The fall of Adam had affected the inner man to the point that his inner senses could no longer perceive God. This corrupt inner state was the "old man" or "old Adam." The spiritual restitution involved a reorientation of the believers' inner senses (imagination) away from inclinations to evil and toward the spiritual eye or senses, which looked to, listened to and felt only the things of God. So restored, one's external body and senses would therefore serve one's internal disposition.[4]

The internal purification of the believer's senses meant that his physical or external senses were now also pure, and he could therefore look on anything without any fear of external corruption. Joris recounted that he experienced this process himself during one of his December 1536 visions in which he found himself surrounded by naked persons. He shouted "O Lord, now I can see all things" and wrote the following song:

Notes to Appendix VI are found on page 212.

Although they hop,
they go a straight way, totally upright.
Pure in the midst of wickedness.
Spotless like children.
Without shame and without hypocrisy.
As Adam and Eve were in the beginning,
they are at the end.[5]

According to Joris, therefore, the true restitution returned the believer to a
state of pre-fall Adamic innocence which insulated him from external corrupting influences. In effect it created a new kind of moral superman. This
had significant ramifications for Joris' sexual ethic, as seen in his views on
marriage and sex.

Notes

1. "Die summa van desen sijn die vijf Sinnen genoemt / die gants vernieut ende veran-
   dert / als't van den opganck der Sonnen inden beghinne wesende / wederghebracht sijn
   moet" (*Van die heerlijcke*, fol. 76v).
2. In *Hoert, hoert, hoert* (fol. 35r), Joris wrote: "hier is die in dreen vullenkoemen / aen
   ziele / gheest / vnde lijff."
3. *Dat eynde coemt*, fols. 147r-v. See Steven E. Ozment, *Homo Spiritualis* (Leiden: E.J.
   Brill, 1969), p. 2, and especially his discussion of Gerson's anthropology, pp. 59-64, 83.
   Joris' concept of restoration to Adamic perfection was in the lineage of Gerson's
   approximation of Adamic manhood, but not of Tauler's pre-created perfection.
4. "Alle (seg ick) dat die mensche gheerne hoort / gheerne op siet / geerne ruyct / gheerne
   smaect / tast vn gheuoelt / inwendich na den verborghen olden bedriechlijcken
   mensche / die daer verleydende ofte verdervende is den wtwendigen mensch ofte Gs.
   gelijckenisse vn vercoren vat ofte plaetse / welcke beyde te niet ghedaen vn te verwor-
   pen is" (*Dat eynde coemt*, fol. 142r).
5. Translated in Stayer, "David Joris," p. 355. See Deppermann, *Hoffman*, p. 315, n. 36.
   From Anonymous, p. 715 and also recounted in Blesdijk, *Historia vitae*, pp. 18-19.

BIBLIOGRAPHY

214   *David Joris*

Bibliographies

Hillerbrand, Hans Joachim (ed.). *A Bibliography of Anabaptism, 1520-1630.* Elkhart: Institute of Mennonite Studies, 1962.
Köhler, Hans-Joachim (ed.). *Flugschriften des frühen 16. Jahrhunderts.* Microfiche Serie, Zug/Schweiz, 1978- .
Nijhoff, Wouter and M. E. Kronenberg (eds.). *Nederlandsche Bibliographie van 1500 tot 1540.* 3 vols. The Hague: Martinus Nijhoff, 1923.
Short-Title Catalogue of Books Printed in the Netherlands and Belgium and of Dutch and Flemish Books Printed in Other Countries From 1470 to 1600 Now in the British Museum. London: Trustees of the British Museum, 1965.
Van der Linde, A. (ed.). *David Joris. Bibliografie.* The Hague: Martinus Nijhoff, 1867.

Primary Sources — Unpublished

Jorislade, Universität Basel, in 15 folio volumes, particularly:
I.   *David Joris. Aus eigenen Schriften.*
II. *Akten und Gutachten.*
III. *David Joris. Briefe.*
IV. *Berichte über David Joris und die Niederlander.*
IX. *Hydeckel. Sendbriefe.*
X.   *Niederdeutsche Schriften und Konzepte in Quarto.*
XV. *Druckschriften.*

Primary Sources — Published

Arnold, Gottfried. *Unpartheiische Kirchen- und Ketzer Historie.* Frankfurt, 1729. Reprinted by Hildesheim: Georg Olms, 1967, 2 vols.
Augustine. *City of God.* Garden City: Image Books, 1958.
Bainton, Roland H. (ed.). *Concerning Heretics: An Anonymous Work Attributed to Sebastian Castellio.* New York: Columbia University Press, 1935.
Bergsma, W. and S. Voolstra (eds.). *Uyt Babel ghevolden, in Jerusalem ghetogen. Menno Simon's verlichting, bekering en beroeping.* Amsterdam: Doopsgezinde Historische Kring, 1986.
Bernard of Clairvaux. *Treatises.* Vol. II. *The Steps of Humility and Pride, On Loving God.* Kalamazoo: Cistercian Publications, 1980.
Blesdijk, Nicolaas Meyndertsz van. *Christelijcke Verantwoordinghe ende billijcke nederlegginge des valschen onghegrondeden oordeels, lasterens ende scheldens, by Menno Symonsz in eenen Sendt-brief . . . niet bevonden werden als hy.* N.p., 1607.
————. *Billijcke Verantwoordinge ende eenvoldighe wederlegginghe Nicolaes Meynertsz. van Blesdijck op eenen scheltlasterighen brief door doctorem Hieronimum Wilhelmi . . . int jaer 1544.* N.p., 1610.
————. *Historia vitae, doctrinae ac rerum gestarum Davidis Georgii haeresiarchae.* Deventer, 1642.
Braght, Thielman van. *The Bloody Theatre or Martyr's Mirror.* Scottdale: Herald Press, 1951.
Bullinger, Heinrich. *Der Widertöufferen Ursprung/ fürgang/ Secten/ wasen/*

fürneme und gemeine jier leer artickel. Zurich: Christoffel Froschower, 1561 (photo-duplication, n.p., 1975).

Civilius. *Eine freidige vermanung, zu klarem vnd offentlichem bekentnis Jesu Christi.* Magdeburg: M. Lothar, 1550.

Colledge, Edmund and Bernard McGinn (eds.). *Master Eckhart. The Essential Sermons, Commentaries, Treatises of Defense.* New York: Paulist Press, 1981.

Coornhert, Dirck Volckherts. *Kleyn-Munster. Des Groot roemighen David jorisens roemryke ende wonderbare schriften eleckerlijk tot een proeve voor ghestelt to Dirck Volckharts Coornhert.* N.p., 1590.

Cornelius, C. A. (ed.). *Geschichtsquellen des Bisthums Münster.* II Band. Münster, 1853 (photo-reprinted 1965).

Cousins, Ewert (ed.). *Bonaventure. The Soul's Journey into God. The Tree of Life. The Life of St. Francis.* New York: Paulist Press, 1975.

Cramer, S. and F. Pijper (eds.). *Bibliotheca Reformatoria Neerlandica.* 10 vols. The Hague: Martinus Nijhoff, 1903.

David Georgen ausz Holand desz Ertzkätzers warhafftige histori, seines lebens, vnnd verfürischen leer etc. Basel: H. Curio, 1559.

Delius, Hans-Ulrich (ed.). *Martin Luther Studienausgabe.* Berlin: Evangelische Verlagsanstalt, 1979.

Dillen, J.G. van (ed.). *Bronnen tot de Geschiedenis van het Bedrijfsleven en het Gildewezen van Amsterdam.* Vol. I: *1512-1611.* The Hague: Martinus Nijhoff, 1929.

Dis, Leenert Meeuwis van (ed.). *Reformatorische Rederijkersspelen uit de Eerste Helft van de Zestiende Eeuw.* Haarlem: Drukkerij Vijlbrief, 1937.

Dolan, John P. (ed.). *The Essential Erasmus.* New York: New American Library, 1964.

Emmius, Ubbo. *Den David Jorischen Gheest in Leven ende Leere/ vreeder ende wijdt-loopegher ontdect/ ende grondlicken verklaert/ tegens aen vermom-den schaemtloosen D. Andreas Huygelmumzoon.* The Hague, 1603.

Erb, Peter C. (ed.). *Pietists. Selected Writings.* New York: Paulist Press, 1983.

Fast, Heinold (ed.). *Der linke Flügel der Reformation.* Bremen: Carl Schunemann Verlag, 1962.

Fredericq, Paul (ed.). *Corpus documentorum Inquisitionis Haereticae Pravitatis Neerlandicae.* 5 vols. Ghent and The Hague: Martinus Nijhoff, 1889-1900.

Génard, P. (ed.). "Personen te Antwerpen in de XVIe eeuw voor het 'feit van reli-gie' gerechtelijk vervolgd." *Antwerpsch Archievenblad,* Eerst Reeks, Vols. VII and VIII.

Grosheide, Grete (ed.). "Verhooren en Vonnissen der Wederdoopers, Betrokken bij de Aanslagen op Amsterdam in 1534 en 1535," in *Bijdragen en Mededeel-ingen van het Historisch Genootschap,* 41 Deel, 1920, pp. 1-198.

Hätzer, Ludwig. *Am Urtayl Gottes unsers eegeahels/ wie man sich mit allen gotzen end Beldnissen halten soll.* Zurich (?), 1523.

Historia von des beruffenen Ertzkätzers David Joris oder Georgii, Lehr- und Leben/ welche von vielen Partheyen verworffen/ Auch mit unerhörten greulichen Schmeh- und Lasterungen Beschuldiget worden. N.p., 1713.

Hoffman, Bengt R. (ed.). *The Theologia Germanica of Martin Luther.* New York: Paulist Press, 1980.

Hoffman, Melchior. *Die eedele hoghe ende troostlike sendebrief/ den die heylige Apostel Paulus to den Romeren gescreuen heeft.* N.p., 1533.

Horst, Irvin B. and Dirk Visser (eds.). "Een tractaat van Melchior Hoffman uit 1531." *Doopsgezinde Bijdragen.* Vol. 4 (New Series), 1978, pp. 66-81.

Hullu, J.G. de (ed.). *Bescheiden Betreffende de Hervorming in Overijsel.* Deventer, 1897.

Hulshof, A. (ed.). "Extracten uit de Rekeningen van het Schoutambacht van Haarlem Betreffende Wederdoopers (1535-39)," *Bijdragen en Mededeelingen van het Historisch Genootschap,* 41 Deel, 1920, pp. 199-231.

Huygelmumzoon, Andreas. *Wederleggenghe/ unde grove onbeschaemde vnde tastelicke Logenen van Ubbo Emmen/ Rector der scholen tot Groeningen/ by hem in druck uytghegeven tegen het leven vnde leere van David Jorissoon.* N.p., 1600.

Jessenius, F. *Auffgedeckte larve Davidis Georgii oder Ausführlicher und augenscheinlichen Beweiss Dass der David Georgius kein reiner Evangelisch- und Christlicher Lehrer gewesen.* [Kiel, 1670].

_____. *Historia Davidis Georgii, welche aus der Baselschen Historia/ Ubbone Emmen/ Blesdickio und andern/ kurtzlich zusammen getragen.* [Kiel, 1670].

Joris, David. *Christlijcke Sendbrieven.* N.p., n.d.

_____. *Clare Berichtinge, Hoe die Mensch van Godt ghevallen ende jn wat manieren hy weder tot Godt gebrocht wert een claere ende leuendige opsluytinge.* N.p., 1543.

_____. *Cort Bericht vn schriftlyck Antwoort D.J. op den Brief des Eerwaardighen Heeren J.A.L.* N.p., 1544.

_____. *Dat eynde coemt/ dat eynde coemt over die vier hoecken der aerden.* N.p., n.d.

_____. *Eene onderwysinge ofte raet/ omme die gedachten in den toem tho brengen.* N.p., 1537.

_____. *Een Geestelijck Liedt-Boecxken.* Mennonite Songbooks, Dutch Series, I. Amsterdam: Frits Knof, n.d.

_____. *Een salighe Leeringe voor die hongherighe bekommerde Zielen.* N.p., n.d.

_____. *Een seer schone tractaet off onderwijs van mennigerley aert der menschen vianden.* Deventer: Albert Pafraet, 1539.

_____. *Een zeer zuuerlyck traectaet van de lyeffde, schoenheyt.* Deventer: Albert Pafraet, 1539.

_____. *Het derde boecxk der christelycker sendtbrieven.* N.p., 1611.

_____. *Het tweede boecxk der christlijcker sendt-brieven.* N.p., n.d.

_____. *Hoert/ hoert/ hoert/ Groot wunder/ groot wunder/ groot wunder.* N.p., n.d.

_____. *Hoe sich die gelouighe, die een suster ofte vrouwe tot hem neempt/ draghen of sy beyde haer tegen den ander hebben sullen.* N.p., n.d.

_____. *Onschult Davids Jorisz. Gedaen unde gepresenteert an die Wolgeborene Vrouw/ Vrouw Anna.* N.p., 1540.

_____. *Seer goet onderwysinge der wijsheit . . . Beyde vor ouden ende Jongen.* Deventer: Albert Pafraet, 1539.

_____. *Troost/ Raet/ Leere ende onderwysinghe.* Deventer: Albert Pafraet, 1542.

_____. *Twonder Boeck.* Deventer: Dirk von Borne, 1542.

_____. *Twonder-boeck: waer in dat van der werldt aen versloten gheopenbaert is. Opt nieuw ghecorrigeert vnde vermeerdert by den Autheur selue.* N.p., 1551.

_____. *Van die heerlijcke ende godlijcke Ordeninge der Wonderlijcker werckinghen Godes.* N.p., 1535. Reprinted 1614.

_____. *Van die Vreemde Tonghen of Talen der Menschen.* N.p., 1545.

Karlstadt, Andreas Bodenstein von. *Van Abtuhung der Bylder/ Und das keyn Betdler unther den Christen seyn soll.* Wittenberg, 1522.

Kempis, Thomas à. *The Imitation of Christ.* Middlesex: Penguin Books, 1952.

Ketel, Jorien. *Heelsame Leere en nutte onderwysinge.* N.p., 1544.

Klaassen, Walter (ed.). *Anabaptism in Outline.* Kitchener: Herald Press, 1981.

_____ (ed.). *Sixteenth Century Anabaptism. Defences, Confessions, Refutations.* Translated by Frank Friesen. Waterloo: Conrad Grebel College, 1982.

Kurtzer Auszug von des beruffenen Ketzers David Georgii oder Joris. Lehr und Leben. N.p., 1704.

Lehmann, Helmut T. (ed.). *Luther's Works.* Philadelphia: Fortress Press, 1955- .

Lienhard, Marc, Stephen F. Nelson, and Hans Georg Rott (eds.). *Quellen zur Geschichte der Täufer.* Vol. XV: *Elsass III, Stadt Strassburg 1536-1542.* Gerd Mohn: Gutersloher Verlagshaus, 1986.

McGinn, Bernard (ed.). *Apocalyptic Spirituality.* New York: Paulist Press, 1979.

Mellink, A.F. (ed.). *Documenta Anabaptistica Neerlandica (D.A.N).* Vol. 1: *Friesland en Groningen (1530-1550).* Leiden: E.J. Brill, 1975.

_____. *D.A.N.* Vol. 2: *Amsterdam, 1536-1578.* Leiden: E.J. Brill, 1980.

_____. *D.A.N.* Vol. 5: *Amsterdam, 1531-1536.* Leiden: E.J. Brill, 1985.

Oosterbaan-Lugt, R.C. (ed.). *Melchior Hoffman. De ordonnantie Gods.* Amsterdam: Doopsgezinde Historische Kring, 1980.

Stolterfoht, M. Jacobum. *Historia von David Georgen einem heillosen Mann/ und Gotteslasterlicher Ertzketzer.* Lübeck, 1635.

Straelen, J.B. van der (ed.). *Geschiedenis der Antwerpsche Rederykkamers.* Antwerpen, 1863.

Stupperich, Robert (ed.). *Die Schriften Bernhard Rothmanns.* Münster: Aschendorffsche Verlagsbuchhandlung, 1970.

Teghenbericht, op een Laster ende Scheltboecxken gheentituleert David Gergis wt Hollandt, des Ertzketters Waerachtige Historie. N.p., [1584].

Theophilus, J. *Eenen Sendtbrief aen Dierck Volckertz Cornhert: Op sijn Boeck ghenaempt Kleyn Munster/ Utgeghaen teghens die Scriften van D.J.* N.p., n.d.

Thomas, Christian. *Historie Der Weiszheit und Thorheit.* Halle, 1693.

Thompson, Craig R. (ed.). *Erasmus, Ten Colloquies.* Indianapolis: The Bobbs-Merrill Company, Inc., 1957.

Verheyden, A.L.E. (ed.). *Het Brugsch Martyrologium.* Brussels: "Wilco," 1944.

Vos, Karel. "Brief van David Joris, 1539." *Doopsgezinde Bijdragen,* Vol. LIV, 1917, pp. 163-65.

Waite, Gary K. " 'A Recent Consultation of Lucifer': A Previously Unknown

Work by Sebastian Franck?'' *Mennonite Quarterly Review,* Vol. LVIII, 1984, pp. 477-502.

_____. "David Joris' Apology to Countess Anna of Oldenburg.'' *Mennonite Quarterly Review,* Vol. LXII, 1988, pp. 140-58.

Wenger, J.C. (ed.). *The Complete Writings of Menno Simons.* Scottdale: Herald Press, 1966.

Williams, G.H. and Angel M. Mergal (eds.). *Spiritual and Anabaptist Writers.* Philadelphia: The Westminster Press, 1957.

Yoder, John H. (ed.). *The Legacy of Michael Sattler.* Scottdale: Herald Press, 1973.

Zeidtler, C. G. and J. G. Martius. *Historia Davidis Georgi ejusque asseclarum.* Lips, 1701.

Secondary Sources

Aldridge, John William. *The Hermeneutic of Erasmus.* Richmond: John Knox Press, 1966.

Armour, Rollin Stely. *Anabaptist Baptism.* Scottdale: Herald Press, 1966.

Augustijn, Cornelis. "Anabaptism in the Netherlands: Another Look.'' *Mennonite Quarterly Review,* Vol. LXII, 1988, pp. 197-210.

Autenboer, E. van. *Volksfeesten en Rederijkers te Mechelen (1400-1600).* Gent: Secretariaat van de Koninklijke Vlaamse Academy voor Taal-en Letterkunde, 1962.

_____. "Organisaties en stedelijke cultuurvormen 15de en 16de eeuw," *Varia Historica Brabantica,* Vol. 6-7, 1978, pp. 147-72.

Bainton, Roland. *David Joris. Wiedertäufer und Kämpfer für Toleranz im 16. Jahrhundert.* Leipzig: *Archiv für Reformationsgeschichte,* Texte und Untersuchungen, VI, 1937.

_____. *The Travail of Religious Liberty.* Philadelphia: The Westminster Press, 1951.

Bangs, Jeremy D. "Waarom zou je het Nieuwe jeruzalem zoeken in Hazerswoude, 1535-1536?'' *Doopsgezinde Bijdragen.* Vol. 7 (New Series), pp. 78-86.

Beachy, Alvin J. *The Concept of Grace in the Radical Reformation.* Nieuwkoop: B. De Graaf, 1977.

Bender, Harold S., "Editorial.'' *Mennonite Quarterly Review,* Vol. IX, 1935, pp. 68-69.

Bergsma, Wiebe. *Aggaeus van Albada (c.1525-1587), schwenckfeldiaan, staatsman en strijder voor verdraagzaamheid.* Published doctoral dissertation, University of Groningen, 1983.

Bietenholz, Peter G. *Basle and France in the Sixteenth Century.* Genève: Librairie Droz, 1971.

Bleyswyk, D. van. *Beschrijvinge der Stadt Delft.* 1667.

Blickle, Peter. *The Revolution of 1525.* Baltimore: The Johns Hopkins University Press, 1981.

Blockmans, W. P. and W. Prevenier. "Poverty in Flanders and Brabant from the Fourteenth to Mid-Sixteenth Century: Sources and Problems.'' *Acta Historicae Neerlandicae,* Vol. X, 1978, pp. 20-57.

Blok, P.J. *Geschiedenis Eener Hollandsche Stad.* The Hague: Martinus Nijhoff, 1912.

————. *History of the People of the Netherlands.* Part II. New York: AMS Press, 1970. Reprinted from 1898-1912.

Boheemen, F.C. van and Th. C.J. van der Heijden. *De Delftse rederijkers 'Wy rapen gheneucht.'* Amsterdam: Huis aan de drie Grachten, 1982.

Boon, A. van der. *Monumentale glasschilderkunst in Nederland.* The Hague: Martinus Nijhoff, 1940.

Boon, K.G. "De Glasschilder David Joris, een Exponent van het Doperse Geloof. Zijn Kunst en Zijn Invloed op Dirck Crabeth." *Mededelingen van de Koninklijke Academie voor Wetenschappen, Letteren en Schone Kunsten van België,* Vol. XLIX, 1988, pp. 117-37.

Bornhauser, Christopher. *Leben und Lehre Menno Simons.* Neukirchner Verlag, 1973.

Bowen, James. *A History of Western Education.* Vol. 2. London: Methuen & Co. Ltd., 1975.

Brandt, Gerard. *The History of the Reformation.* London: T. Wood, 1720-23. Translated from Dutch original of 1674. Reprinted AMS Press, Inc., 1979.

Brecht, Martin. "Die Theologie Bernhard Rothmanns." *Jahrbuch für Westfälische Kirchengeschichte,* Vol. LXXVIII, 1985, pp. 49-82.

————. "The Songs of the Anabaptists in Münster and Their Hymnbook." *Mennonite Quarterly Review,* Vol. LIX, 1985, pp. 362-68.

Brinkmann, Hennig. *Miltelalterliche Hermeneutik.* Tübingen: Max Niemeyer Verlag, 1980.

Brucker, Gene. *Giovanni and Lusanna. Love and Marriage in Renaissance Florence.* Berkeley: University of California Press, 1986.

Buist, M.G. et al. (eds.). *Historisch Bewogen.* Groningen: Wolters-Noordhoff, 1984.

Burckhardt, Paul. "David Joris." *Basler Biographien,* I. Basel, 1900, pp. 91-157.

————. "David Joris und seine Gemeinde in Basel," *Basler Zeitschrift für Geschichte und Altertumskunde,* Vol. XLVIII, 1949, pp. 5-106.

Cairncross, John. *After Polygamy was Made a Sin.* London: Routledge & Kegan Paul, 1974.

Clasen, Claus-Peter. "The Anabaptist Leaders: Their Numbers and Background." *Mennonite Quarterly Review,* Vol. XLIX, 1975, pp. 122-27.

————. *Anabaptism: A Social History, 1525-1618.* Ithaca: Cornell University Press, 1976.

Cohn, Henry J. "Anticlericalism in the German Peasants' War, 1525." *Past and Present,* Vol. 83, 1979, pp. 3-31.

Cohn, Norman. "Medieval Millenarism: Its Bearing on the Comparative Study of Millenarian Movements," in Sylvia L. Thrupp (ed.), *Millennial Dreams in Action.* New York: Schocken Books, 1970, pp. 31-43.

————. *The Pursuit of the Millennium.* London: Granada Publishing, 1970.

Cramer, A.M. *Bijvoegselen tot de Levensbeschrijving van David Joris.* Leiden, 1844.

Crew, Phyllis Mack. *Calvinist Preaching and Iconoclasm in The Netherlands 1544-1569.* London: Cambridge University Press, 1978.

Davies, C.S.L. *Peace, Print and Protestantism, 1450-1558.* London: Hart-Davis MacGibbon, 1976.

Davis, Kenneth Ronald. *Anabaptism and Asceticism.* Scottdale: Herald Press, 1974.

________. "Anabaptism as a Charismatic Movement." *Mennonite Quarterly Review,* Vol. LIII, 1979, pp. 219-34.

Davis, Natalie Z. *Society and Culture in Early Modern France.* Stanford: Stanford University Press, 1975.

De Bakker, W.J. "De Vroege Theologie van Bernhard Rothmann. De Gereformeerde achtergrond van het Munsterese Doperijk." *Doopsgezinde Bijdragen,* n.r., no. 3, 1977, pp. 9-20.

De Groot, Renze Otto. "The Faith of the Dutch Anabaptists." D.Th. dissertation, Northern Baptist Theological Seminary, 1947.

De Hoop Scheffer, J.G. *Geschiedenis der Kerkhervorming in Nederland van haar onstaan tot 1531.* Amsterdam: G.L. Funke, 1873.

Deppermann, Klaus. *Melchior Hoffman.* Gottingen: Vandenhoeck and Ruprecht, 1979.

De Vries, Jan. *The Dutch Rural Economy in the Golden Age, 1500-1700.* New Haven and London: Yale University Press, 1974.

De Vries, O.H. *Leer en praxis van de vroege dopers.* Leeuwarden: Uitgeverij Gerben Dykstra, 1982.

Droz, Eugénie. "Sur Quelques Traductions Françaises d'Écrits de David Joris." *Het Boek,* derde reeks, Vol. XXXVII, 1965, pp. 154-62.

Duerksen, Rosella R. "Anabaptist Hymnody of the Sixteenth Century." Doctorate of Sacred Music thesis, Union Theological Seminary, New York, 1956.

Duke, Alastair. "Popular Religious Dissent in the Low Countries, 1520-1530." *Journal of Ecclesiastical History,* Vol. 26, 1975, pp. 42-66.

________. "Building Heaven in Hell's Despite: The Early History of the Reformation in the Towns of the Low Countries," in A. C. Duke and C. A. Tamse (eds.), *Britain and the Netherlands.* The Hague: Martinus Nijhoff, 1981, pp. 45-75.

Dyck, Cornelius J. "Hermeneutics and Discipleship," in Willard M. Swartley (ed.), *Essays on Biblical Interpretation. Anabaptist-Mennonite Perspectives.* Elkhart: Institute of Mennonite Studies, 1984, pp. 29-44.

Eire, Carlos M.N. *War Against the Idols. The Reformation of Worship from Erasmus to Calvin.* Cambridge: Cambridge University Press, 1986.

Elslander, A. van. "Lijst van Nederlandse rederijkerskamers uit de XVe en XVIe eeuw." *Koninklijke Soevereine Hoofdkamer van Retorica De Fonteine Jaarboeck,* Vol. XVIII, 1968, pp. 29-60.

Emmerson, Richard Kenneth. *Antichrist in the Middle Ages.* Seattle: University of Washington Press, 1981.

Emmius, Ubbo. *Friesische Geschichte.* Vol. VI. Translated by Erich von Reeken. Frankfurt am Main: Verlag Jochen Wörner, 1982 (from 1615 edition).

Faber, J.A. "Dearth and Famine in Pre-Industrial Netherlands." *Acta Historicae Neerlandicae,* Vol. XIII, 1980, pp. 51-64.

Fränger, Wilhelm. *The Millennium of Hieronymus Bosch.* New York: Hacker Art Books, 1976.

Friedländer, Max J. *Early Netherlandisch Painting.* Vols. 8-10. Leiden: A.W. Sijthoff, 1962-73.

_____. *From van Eyck to Bruegel.* Ithaca, New York: Cornell University Press, 1981.

Friedman, Jerome. "Servetus and the Psalms: The Exegesis of Heresy," in Olivier Fatio and Pierre Fraenkel (eds.), *Histoire de l'exegese au XVIe siècle.* Geneve: Librairie Droz, 1978, pp. 161-78.

Friedmann, Robert. *The Theology of Anabaptism.* Scottdale: Herald Press, 1973.

George, Timothy. "Early Anabaptist Spirituality in the Low Countries." *Mennonite Quartery Review,* Vol. LXII, 1988, pp. 256-75.

Geyl, Pieter. *History of the Low Countries.* London: Macmillan and Company Ltd., 1964.

Gibson, Walter S. "Artists and Rederijkers in the Age of Bruegel." *The Art Bulletin,* Sept. 1981, Vol. LXIII, pp. 426-46.

Goertz, Hans-Jürgen. *Die Täufer. Geschichte und Deutung.* München: C.H. Beck, 1980.

_____ (ed.). *Profiles of Radical Reformers.* Kitchener: Herald Press, 1982.

Grattan, Thomas Colley. *Holland: The History of the Netherlands.* New York: 1899.

Grosheide, Grete. *Bijdrage tot de Geschiedenis der Anabaptisten in Amsterdam.* Hilversum: J. Schipper, Jr., 1938.

Grotefind, Herman. *Taschenbuch der Zeitreichnung des deutschen Mittelalters und der Neuzeit.* Berlin: Transpress Reprint, 1984.

Guggisberg, Hans R. *Basel in the Sixteenth Century.* St. Louis: Center for Reformation Research, 1982.

Gutmann, Myron P. *War and Rural Life in the Early Modern Low Countries.* Princeton: Princeton University Press, 1980.

Hale, J.R. *Renaissance Europe 1480-1520.* London: Fontana, 1971.

Hamilton, Alastair. *The Family of Love.* Greenwood, S.C.: The Attic Press, Inc., 1981.

Hansen, R. *Der David Jorisen-Prozess in Tönning, 1642.* Kiel, 1900.

Harderwijk, Isak van. *Bijdrage tot de Kennis der Schriften van David Joris.* Leiden, 1845.

Heel, Dudok van. "Katholiek Amsterdams regentenpatriciaat ten tijde van de Hervorming; werd de Familie Huynen door het wederdopersoproer van 1535 gedeclasseerd?" Unpublished Ph.D. dissertation, University of Amsterdam, 1978.

Hein, Gerhard. "David Joris." *Mennonitisches Lexikon.* Vol. II. Frankfurt am Main: D. Christian Neff, 1937, pp. 433-35.

Hennig, Matthias. "Askese und Ausschweifung: Zum Verständnis der Vielweiberei im Täuferreich zu Münster 1534/35." *Mennonitische Geschichtsblätter,* Vol. XL, 1983, pp. 25-45.

Hillerbrand, Hans J. "Anabaptism and History." *Mennonite Quarterly Review,* Vol. XLV, 1971, pp. 107-22.

_____ (ed.). *Radical Tendencies in the Reformation: Divergent Perspectives.* Sixteenth Century Essays and Studies, Vol. IX. Kirksville, MO: Sixteenth Century Journal Publishers, 1988.

Horsch, John. *Is Dr. Kuehler's Conception of Early Dutch Anabaptism Historically Sound?* Scottdale: Mennonite Press, n.d.

————. "The Rise and Fall of the Anabaptists of Münster." *Mennonite Quarterly Review*, Vol. IX, 1935, pp. 92-103, 129-43.

Horst, Irvin B. (ed.). *The Radical Brethren. Anabaptism and the English Reformation to 1558*. Nieuwkoop: B. de Graaf, 1972.

————. *Dutch Dissenters*. Leiden: E.J. Brill, 1986.

Houtte, J.A. van. *An Economic History of the Low Countries, 800-1800*. London: Weidenfeld and Nicolson, 1977.

Hsia, R. Po-chia (ed.). *Society and Religion in Münster, 1535-1618*. New Haven: Yale University Press, 1984.

————. *The German People and the Reformation*. Ithaca: Cornell University Press, 1988.

Huizinga, J. *The Waning of the Middle Ages*. Middlesex: Penguin Books, 1985.

Hulshof, A. *Geschiedenis van de Doopsgezinden te Straatsburg van 1525-1557*. Amsterdam: J. Clausen, 1905.

Hyma, Albert. *The Christian Renaissance*. New York: The Century Co., 1924.

IJsewijn, Josef. "The Coming of Humanism to the Low Countries," in Thomas Brady and Heiko A. Oberman (eds.), *Itinerarium Italicum*. Leiden: E.J. Brill, 1975, pp. 193-301.

Jacobowitz, Ellen S. *The Prints of Lucas van Leyden and His Contemporaries*. Washington: Princeton University Press, 1983.

Jansma, L. G. "Crime in the Netherlands in the Sixteenth Century: The Batenburg Bands after 1540." *Mennonite Quarterly Review*, Vol. LXII, 1988, pp. 221-35.

Jedin, Hubert and John Dolan (eds.), *History of the Church*. Vol. III. New York: The Seabury Press, 1980.

Kautsky, Karl. *Communism in Central Europe in the Time of the Reformation*. New York: Russell and Russell, 1959.

Keeney, William Echard. *The Development of Dutch Anabaptist Thought and Practice from 1539-1968*. Nieuwkoop: B. De Graaf, 1968.

Keller, Ludwig. *Geschichte der Wiedertäufer und ihres Reichs zu Münster*. Münster, 1880.

Kerk, Lucuelle van de. *De Haarlemse Drukkers en Boek-verkopers van 1540 tot 1600*. The Hague: Martinus Nijhoff, 1951.

Keup, Wolfram (ed.). *Origin and Mechanisms of Hallucinations*. New York: Plenum Press, 1970.

Kirchhoff, Karl-Heinz. "Die Täufer im Münsterland. Verbreitung und Verfolgung des Täufertums im Stift Münster, 1533-1550." *Westfälische Zeitschrift*, Vol. CXIII, 1963, pp. 1-109.

————. "Was There a Peaceful Anabaptist Congregation in Münster in 1534?" *Mennonite Quarterly Review*, Vol. XLIV, 1970, pp. 357-70.

————. *Die Täufer in Münster 1534/35*. Münster in Westfalen: Aschendorfsche Verlagsbuchhandlung, 1973.

Klaassen, Walter. "Spiritualization in the Reformation," *Mennonite Quarterly Review*, Vol. XXXVII, 1963, pp. 67-77.

————. *Anabaptism: Neither Catholic nor Protestant*. Waterloo: Conrad Press, 1973.

————. "Anabaptist Hermeneutics: Presuppositions, Principles and Practice," in Willard M. Swartley, *Essays on Biblical Interpretation. Anabaptist-*

Mennonite Perspectives. Elkhart: Institute of Mennonite Studies, 1984, pp. 5-10.

Klassen, William. *Covenant and Community.* Grand Rapids: Wm. Eerdmans Publishing, 1968.

Koegler, Hans. "Einiges über David Joris als Künstler." *Öffentliche Kunstsammlung Basel,* Jahresberichte 1928-30, pp. 157-201.

Krahn, Cornelius. *Dutch Anabaptism.* Scottdale: Herald Press, 1981.

————. *Menno Simons.* Newton: Faith and Life Press, 1982.

Kuehler, W.J. *Geschiedenis der Nederlandsche Doopsgezinden in de Zestiende Eeuw.* 2nd ed. Haarlem: H.D. Teenk Wellink en Zoon, 1961.

Kuratsuka, Taira. "Gesamtgilde und Täufer: Der Radikalisierungsprozess in der Reformation Münsters. Von der reformatorischen Bewegung zum Täuferreich 1533/34." *Archiv für Reformationsgeschichte,* Vol. LXXVI, 1985, pp. 233-61.

Lambert, Audrey M. *The Making of the Dutch Landscape.* London: Seminar Press, 1971.

Lauer, Robert H. and Jeanette C. Lauer. *The Spirit and the Flesh: Sex in Utopian Communities.* Metuchen, N.J.: The Scarecrow Press, 1983.

Leeuw, R.A. (ed.). *De Stad Delft. Cultuur en maatschappij tot 1572.* Delft: Stedelijk Museum, Het Prinsenhof, 1981.

Lerner, Robert E. *The Heresy of the Free Spirit in the Later Middle Ages.* Berkeley: University of California Press, 1972.

Lienhard, Marc (ed.). *The Origins and Characteristics of Anabaptism.* The Hague: Martinus Nijhoff, 1977.

Lifton, Robert J. *Death in Life. Survivors of Hiroshima.* New York: Random House, 1967.

List, Günther. *Chiliastische Utopie.* München: Fink, 1973.

Littell, Franklin Hamlin. *The Origins of Sectarian Protestantism.* New York: The Macmillan Company, 1964.

Lockyer, Roger. *Tudor and Stuart Britain 1471-1714.* New York: St. Martin's Press, 1964.

Martin, Lynnewood F. "The Family of Love in England: Conforming Millenarians." *Sixteenth Century Journal,* Vol. III, 1972, pp. 99-108.

McLaughlin, R. Emmet. *Caspar Schwenckfeld, Reluctant Radical: His Life to 1540.* New Haven: Yale University Press, 1986.

Meeschke, R., et al. (eds.). *Delftse Studiën.* Assen: Van Gorcum & Company, 1967.

Meihuizen, H.W. *Het Begrip Restitutie in het Noordwestelijke Doperdom.* Haarlem: H.D. Tjeenk Willink en Zoon, 1966.

————. "The Concept of Restitution in the Anabaptism of Northwestern Europe." *Mennonite Quarterly Review,* Vol. XLIV, 1970, pp. 141-58.

Meijer, Reinder P. *Literature of the Low Countries* Assen: Van Gorcum & Company, 1971.

Mellink, Albert F. "Antwerpen als Anabaptisttencentrum tot ± 1550." *Nederlands Archief voor Kerkgeschiedenis,* Vol. XLVI, 1963-64, pp. 155-68.

————. *Amsterdam en de Wederdopers.* Nijmegen: Socialistiese Uitgeverij Nijmegen, 1978.

————. "The Beginnings of Dutch Anabaptism in the Light of Recent Research." *Mennonite Quarterly Review,* Vol. LXII, 1988, pp. 211-20.

————. " 'The Radical Underground' in the Dutch Radical Reformation." *Commissie tot de Uitgave van Documenta Anabaptistica Neerlandica,* Bulletin 12 & 13, 1980-81, pp. 43-58.

————. *De Wederdopers in de Noordelijke Nederlanden.* 2nd ed. Leeuwarden: Uitgeverij Gerben Dykstra, 1981.

Mennonite Encyclopedia. 4 vols. Scottdale: Herald Press, 1955-59.

Miskimin, Harry A. *The Economy of Later Renaissance Europe, 1460-1600.* London: Cambridge University Press, 1977.

Moss, Jean Dietz. *"Godded with God." Hendrik Niclaes and His Family of Love.* Philadelphia: The American Philosophical Society, 1981.

Moxey, Keith P.F. "Image Criticism in the Netherlands Before the Iconoclasm of 1566." *Nederlands Archief voor Kerkgeschiedenis,* Vol. LVII, 1977, pp. 148-62.

Nierop, H.F.K. van. *Van ridders tot regenten: De Hollandse adel in de zestiende en de eerste helft van de zeventiende eeuw.* Amsterdam: Stichting Hollandse Historische Reeks, 1984.

Nigg, Walter. *Das Leben des seligen Heinrich Seuse.* Dusseldorf: Patmos-Verlag, 1966.

Nippold, Friedrich. "David Joris von Delft. Sein Leben, seine Lehre und seine Secte." *Zeitschrift für historische Theologie.* Gotha, 1863.

Ozment, Steven E. (ed.). *Homo Spiritualis.* Leiden: E.J. Brill, 1969.

———— *The Reformation in Medieval Perspective.* Chicago: Quadrangle Books, 1971.

————. *Mysticism and Dissent.* New Haven: Yale University Press, 1973.

————. *The Age of Reform, 1250-1550.* New Haven: Yale University Press, 1980.

———— (ed.). *Reformation Europe: A Guide to Research.* St. Louis: Center for Reformation Research, 1982.

————. *When Fathers Ruled.* Cambridge: Harvard University Press, 1983.

Packull, Werner O. *Mysticism and the Early South German-Austrian Anabaptist Movement.* Scottdale: Herald Press, 1977.

————. "Some Reflections on the State of Anabaptist history: The Demise of a Normative Vision." *Studies in Religion,* Vol. VIII, 1979, pp. 313-23.

————. "Melchior Hoffman — A Recanted Anabaptist in Schwäbisch-Hall." *Mennonite Quarterly Review,* Vol. LVII, 1983, pp. 83-111.

————. "Melchior Hoffman's Experience in the Livonian Reformation: The Dynamics of Sect Formation." *Mennonite Quarterly Review,* Vol. LIX, 1985, pp. 130-46.

————. "The Image of the 'Common Man' in the Early Pamphlets of the Reformation (1520-1525)." *Historical Reflections,* Vol. XII, 1985, pp. 253-77.

————. "In Search of the 'Common Man' in Early German Anabaptist Ideology." *Sixteenth Century Journal,* Vol. XVII, 1986, pp. 52-67.

————. "Anna Jansz of Rotterdam, a Historical Investigation of an Early Anabaptist Heroine." *Archiv für Reformationsgeschichte,* Vol. LXXVIII, 1987, pp. 147-73.

————. "The Sign of Thau: The Changing Conception of the Seal of God's

Elect in Early Anabaptist Thought." *Mennonite Quarterly Review,* Vol. LXI, 1987, pp. 363-74.

_____. "Peter Tasch: From Melchiorite to Bankrupt Wine Merchant." *Mennonite Quarterly Review,* Vol. LXII, 1988, pp. 276-95.

Parker, Geoffrey. *The Dutch Revolt.* London: Allen Lane, 1977.

Pater, Calvin A. *Karlstadt as the Father of the Baptist Movements.* Toronto: University of Toronto Press, 1984.

Pollard, A.F. *Henry VIII.* New York: Harper Torchbooks, 1966.

Poole, Reginald L. *The Beginning of the Year in the Middle Ages.* N.p., 1921.

Porter, Jack Wallace. "Bernhard Rothmann 1495-1535. Royal Orator of the Münster Anabaptist Kingdom." Ph.D. dissertation, University of Wisconsin, 1964.

Post, R.R. *Kerkelijke Verhoudingen in Nederland voor de Reformatie van 1500 tot 1580.* Utrecht: Uitgeverij het Spectrum, 1954.

_____. *Scholen en Onderwijs in Nederland Gedurende de Middeleeuwen.* Utrecht: Uitgeverij het Spectrum, 1954.

_____. *The Modern Devotion.* Leiden: E.J. Brill, 1968.

Posthumus, N.W. *Inquiry into the History of Prices in Holland.* Vol. II. Leiden: E.J. Brill, 1964.

Prevenier, W. "Officials in Town and Countryside in the Low Countries. Social and Professional Developments from the Fourteenth to the Sixteenth-Century." *Acta Historicae Neerlandicae,* Vol. VII, 1974, pp. 1-17.

Prims, Floris. *Geschiedenis van Berchem.* Berchem: Gemeentebestuur van Berchem, 1949.

_____. *Geschiedenis van Antwerpen.* Vol. 5. Brussels: Uitgeverij Kultuur en Beschaving, 1981.

Puts, Freddy. "Geschiedenis van de Antwerpse rederijkerskamer De Goudbloem." *Koninklijke Soevereine Hoofdkamer van Retorica De Fonteine Jaarboeck,* Vols. XXIII-XXIV, 1973-74, pp. 5-15.

Rammstedt, Otthein. *Sekte und soziale Bewegung.* Koln: Westdeutscher Verlag, 1966.

Raue, J.J. *Vorming en ruimtelijke ontwikkeling in de late middeleeuwen de Stad Delft.* Delft: Delfste Universitaire Pers, 1983.

Reitsma, J. *Geschiedenis van de Hervorming en de Hervormde Kerk der Nederlanden.* Utrecht: Kemink & Zoon N.V., 1933.

Rembert, Karl. *Die Wiedertäufer im Herzogtum Jülich.* Berlin, 1899.

Rich, E.E. and C. H. Wilson (eds.). *The Cambridge Economic History of Europe.* Vol. IV. Cambridge: Cambridge University Press, 1967.

Roever, Margriet de and Boudewign Bakker (eds.). *Woelige tijden: Amsterdam in de eeuw van de beeldenstorm.* Amsterdam: Gemeentearchief Amsterdam, 1986.

Rothkrug, Lionel. "Holy Shrines, Religious Dissonance and Satan in the Origins of the German Reformation." *Historical Reflections,* Vol. 14, 1987, pp. 143-286.

Rublack, Hans-Christoff. "Martin Luther and the Urban Social Experience." *Sixteenth Century Journal,* Vol. XVI, 1985, pp. 15-32.

Russell, Jeffrey Burton. *Witchcraft in the Middle Ages.* Ithaca: Cornell University Press, 1972.

Scarre, Geoffrey. *Witchcraft and Magic in 16th and 17th Century Europe*. London: Macmillan Education Ltd., 1987.

Schroër, Alois. *Die Reformation in Westfalen*. Münster: Aschendorff, 1979.

Simpler, Steven. *Roland Bainton. An Examination of his Reformation Historiography*. Lewiston: The Edwin Mellen Press, 1985.

Smalley, Beryl. *The Study of the Bible in the Middle Ages*. Oxford: Basil Blackwell, 1983.

Snyder, C. Arnold. *The Life and Thought of Michael Sattler*. Scottdale: Herald Press, 1984.

Spitz, Lewis. *The Protestant Reformation, 1517-1559*. New York: Harper & Row, 1985.

Stayer, James M. "The Münsterite Rationalization of Bernhard Rothmann." *Journal of the History of Ideas*, Vol. XXVIII, 1967, pp. 179-92.

_____. *Anabaptists and the Sword*. Lawrence, Kansas: Coronado Press, 1976.

_____. "Oldeklooster and Menno." *Sixteenth Century Journal*, Vol. IX, 1978, pp. 50-67.

_____. "Vielweiberei als 'innerweltliche Askese.' " *Mennonitische Geschichtsblätter*, Vol. XXXVII, 1980, pp. 24-41.

_____. "Davidite vs. Mennonite." *Mennonite Quarterly Review*, Vol. LVIII, 1984, pp. 459-76.

_____. "David Joris: A Prolegomenon to Further Research." *Mennonite Quarterly Review*, Vol. LXI, 1985, pp. 350-66.

_____. "Was Dr. Kuehler's Conception of Early Dutch Anabaptism Historically Sound? The Historical Discussion of Anabaptist Münster 450 Years After." *Mennonite Quarterly Review*, Vol. LX, 1986, pp. 261-88.

_____. "Anabaptists and Future Anabaptists in the Peasants' War." *Mennonite Quarterly Review*, Vol. LXII, 1988, pp. 99-139.

_____, Werner O. Packull, and Klaus Deppermann. "Monogenesis to Polygenesis: The Historical Discussion of Anabaptist Origins." *Mennonite Quarterly Review*, Vol. LXIX, 1975, pp. 83-121.

_____ and Werner O. Packull (eds.). *The Anabaptists and Thomas Müntzer*. Dubuque, Iowa: Kendall/Hunt Publ. Comp., 1980.

Sterck, J.F.M. "Onder Amsterdamsche Humanisten." *Het Boeck*, 2nd Reeks, Vol. 6, 1917, 282-96.

Strauss, Gerald. *Luther's House of Learning*. Baltimore: The Johns Hopkins University Press, 1978.

Stupperich, Robert. *Das Münsterische Täufertum. Ergebnisse und Probleme der neueren Forschung*. Münster: Aschendorffsche Verlagsbuchhandlung, 1958.

Taylor, G. Rattray. *Sex in History*. London: Thames & Hudson, 1953.

Ten Cate, S. Blaupot. *Geschiedenis der Doopsgezinden in Friesland*. Leeuwarden, 1839.

Tentler, Thomas N. *Sin and Confession on the Eve of the Reformation*. Princeton: Princeton University Press, 1977.

Thomas, Roy G. *Stained Glass: Its Origin and Application*. New York, 1922.

Tracy, James D. "Heresy Law and Centralization under Mary of Hungary: Conflict between the Council of Holland and the Central Government over the

Enforcement of Charles V's Placards." *Archiv für Reformationsgeschichte*, Vol. LXXIII, 1982, pp. 284-307.

Troeltsch, Ernst. *The Social Teaching of the Christian Churches*. 2 vols. Chicago: University of Chicago Press, 1981.

Uytven, R. van. "What is New Socially and Economically in the Sixteenth-Century Netherlands." *Acta Historicae Neerlandicae*, Vol. VII, 1974, pp. 18-53.

Vandecasteele, M. "Letterkundig Leven te Gent van 1500 tot 1539." *Koninklijke Soevereine Hoofdkamer van Retorica De Fonteine Jaarboeck*, Vol. XVI, 1966, pp. 3-58.

Verduin, Leonard. "The Chambers of Rhetoric and Anabaptist Origins in the Low Countries." *Mennonite Quarterly Review*, Vol. XXXIV, 1960, pp. 192-96.

Verheyden, A.L.E. *De hervorming in de Zuidelijke Nederlanden in de XVIe Eeuw*. Brussels: Uitgegeven door de Synode van de Protestantse Kerken, 1949.

_____. *Anabaptism in Flanders, 1530-1650*. Scottdale: Herald Press, 1961.

Vervliet, H.D.L. *Sixteenth-Century Printing Types of the Low Countries*. Amsterdam: Menno Hertzberger & Co., 1968.

Veurman, B.W.E., et al. *Het spel en de knikkers*. Vol. I: *Litteratuur-geschiedenis van ca. 800 tot 1880*. Amsterdam: Meulenhoff Educatief, 1972.

Visser, J.C., et al. *Delftse Studiën*. Assen: Van Gorcum & Company, 1967.

Voolstra, Sjouke (ed.). *Voortrekkers en Stilstaanders. Vijftien generaties dopers leven in Zeeland*. Middelburg: Rijksarchief in Zeeland, 1976.

_____. *Het Woorde is Vlees geworden: De Melchioritisch-Menniste Incarnatieleer*. Kampen: J.H. Kok, 1982.

Vos, Karel. "Meyndert van Emden." *Nederlandsch archief voor kerkgeschiedenis*, Vol. XI, 1914, pp. 164-66.

_____. "Kleine bijdragen over de doopersche beweging in Nederland." *Doopsgezinde Bijdragen*, Vol. LIV, 1917, pp. 106-23.

_____. "Anneke Jans." *Rotterdamsch Jaarboekje*, Vol. VI, 1918, pp. 14-28.

Vyne, The. Hampshire: The National Trust, 1976.

Waite, Gary K. "Spiritualizing the Crusade: David Joris in the Context of the Early Reform and Anabaptist Movements in the Netherlands, 1524-1543." Ph.D. diss., University of Waterloo, 1986.

_____. "The Anabaptist Movement in Amsterdam and the Netherlands, 1531-1535: An Initial Investigation into its Genesis and Social Dynamics." *The Sixteenth Century Journal*, Vol. XVIII, 1987, pp. 249-64.

_____. "Staying Alive: The Methods of Survival as practiced by an Anabaptist Fugitive, David Joris." *Mennonite Quarterly Review*, Vol. LXI, 1987, pp. 46-57.

_____. "David Joris' Thought in the Context of the Early Anabaptist Movement in the Netherlands, 1534-1536." *Mennonite Quarterly Review*, Vol. LXII, 1988, pp. 296-317.

_____. "From Apocalyptic Crusaders to Anabaptist Terrorists: Anabaptist Radicalism after Münster, 1535-1545." *Archiv für Reformationsgeschichte*, Vol. LXXX, 1989, pp. 173-93.

Wee, H. van der. "Prices and Wages as Developmental Variables: A Comparison between England and the Southern Netherlands, 1400-1700." *Acta Historicae Neerlandicae*, Vol. X, 1978, pp. 58-78.

Weigelt, Horst. *Sebastian Franck und die lutherische Reformation*. Gütersloh: Gerd Mohn, 1972.

Willemse, C.W.A. "De briefwisseling tussen David Joris en Johannes a Lasco." *Doopsgezinde Bijdragen*, Vol. IV (New Series), 1978, pp. 9-22.

Williams, George H. *The Radical Reformation*. Philadelphia: The Westminster Press, 1962.

Woltjer, Jan Juliaan. "Stadt und Reformation in den Niederlanden," in Franz Petri (ed.), *Kirche und Gesellschaftlicher Wandel in Deutschen und Niederlandischen Stadten der Werdenden Neuzeit*. Wien: Bohlau Verlag, 1980, pp. 155-67.

Worp, J.A. *Drama en Tooneel*. Rotterdam: Fa. Langerveld, 1903.

Wray, Frank J. "The 'Vermahnung' of 1542 and Rothmann's 'Bekenntnisse.'" *Archiv für Reformationsgeschichte*, Vol. XLVII, 1956, pp. 243-51.

Zijlstra, S. *Nicolaas Meyndertsz van Blesdijk. Een bijdrage tot de Geschiedenis van het Davidjorisme*. Assen: Van Gorcum & Company, 1983.

————. "Menno Simons and David Joris," *Mennonite Quartery Review*, Vol. LXII, 1988, pp. 249-56.

INDEX

Abelsz, Dominicus, 30
Adam (and Eve), 12, 73, 96, 97, 99, 100, 149, 207, 211-12
Aelbrechtsz, Gijsbrecht, 53
Agnes von Limburg, Abbess of Freckenhorst, 122
Alkmaar, 145, 147, 152
Amerbach, Bonifacius, 185
Amersfoort, Joris van (Joris de Koman), 49f.
Amsterdam, 13, 25, 27-39, 55, 57, 76, 77, 145, 147, 151-52
Anabaptism, South German, 2, 23f.; Swiss, 1, 23f. For Dutch Anabaptism, *see* Batenburgers, Covenanters, Davidites, Melchiorites, Mennonites, Münsterites
Angels, 105, 118, 130, 138, 140, 170; evil, 121-22
Anna, Countess of Oldenburg, 121, 171
Antichrist, 14, 25, 54, 57, 74, 99, 183
Anticlericalism, 8-16, 32, 52-54, 90, 92, 207-208
Antwerp, 7, 33, 51, 81, 116, 145, 147, 155, 163-72, 178-79, 183
Apocalypticism, 24-25, 28-29, 32, 57-59, 69, 90, 101, 138, 167; and authorities, 74; and history, 96
Appeldoorn, 153
Appelman, Cornelis, 116, 153-55
Appingedam, 147, 151
Artisans, 10, 36-37; and reform, 8f., 13, 92; and Anabaptism, 29-30, 145f.; and Joris, 147, 150
Asceticism, 104-106; and Joris, 57, 72, 140, 207
Augsburg Confession, 163
Augustinians, 7, 52

Bacher, Barent, 30
Baeck, Gijsbrecht von, bailiff of Isselstein, 153
Baelhuys, Annetgen and Gelis, 34
Balk, Mathijs van, 117
Baptism, of adults, 23-26, 30, 34, 58, 59, 65-66, 89, 97, 118, 153, 197-98; of infants, 114, 171; and Joris, 65f., 113, 148

Basel, 1f., 81, 157, 164, 166, 168, 172, 177-87
Batenburg, Jan van, 28, 39, 103, 113, 116-20, 133, 145, 150-53, 171
Batenburgers, 68, 72, 78, 105, 114, 116, 122, 149, 151-54
Bauhin, Jean, 181-82, 185
Benscop, 116
Benscop, Adriaen van, 30, 37, 114, 151
Berch, Jan Jansz van den, 75-76
Berchem, van, family, 155, 163, 184; Anna, 163, 180; Joachim, 163, 179-80, 184; Reinier, 163, 179; Willem, 163; Wybrecht, 163
Binchorst, Pieter van den, bailiff of the Gravenzande, 116
Binningen, 179-80
Blenckvliet, Adriaan Jansz van, 53
Blesdijk, Nicolaas Meyndertsz van, 52, 116, 121, 150, 153, 155, 157, 164-65, 179, 180, 182, 184-86
Bocholt Conference, 66, 70, 106, 117-19, 139, 151
Boeckbinder, Bartholomeus, 30
Boelsen, Jan, 182
Borne, Dirk van, 155
Breda, 78, 163
Brenz, Johannes, 184
Breuchel, Aelbrecht van, 74, 75
Briell, Cornelius uit, 30
Brugge, Johann van (David Joris), 1, 50, 179, 185
Brugges, 49
Brussels, 7, 33, 34
Bucer, Martin, 164
Bueren, Duke of, 153, 197; Duchess of, 154

Calvinism, 32. *See also* Reformed Church
Campen, Gerrit van, 29, 30, 35, 38
Campen, Jacob van, 30, 34-35, 38, 65, 151
Canin, Jan, 186
Castellio, Sebastian, 168, 181-86
Chambers of Rhetoric, 12-13, 32, 49, 52-54, 181
Charismatic leadership, 119, 121, 137,

140-41, 150, 165, 172, 208
Charles V, Holy Roman Emperor, 36
Children, of God, 70, 90, 97, 100, 103; of Joris, 67, 75f., 81, 163, 180; Joris' concept of, 93, 131, 139, 140
Church, Anabaptist concept of, 23, 100; Joris' concept of, 138, 165; church discipline, 181
Claeszn, Peter, 30
Cloven Hoof, 90-91, 94, 99, 102-103
Community of goods, 26, 28
Confession, sacramental, 9, 14, 212; public confession of sins, 121, 132, 134, 137-38, 154, 171, 184, 207-209
Conventicles, reform, 7, 9, 31-32; Anabaptist, 23, 33, 145
Cornelis, Geertgen, 73, 149
Court of Holland, 8, 13, 30, 34, 73, 74. *See also* The Hague
Covenanters, 59, 65-66, 69, 77. *See also* Melchiorites

Dam, Leonard van, 77-78, 132, 157, 203-206
David, armour of, 97; Key of, 90, 94; king, 49, 99, 102; third, 71, 129, 149-52, 164, 167-71, 183-84
Davidites, 71, 74-76, 113-14, 138, 145-55, 171, 186, 209
Day of the Lord, 57-58, 69, 130-31, 156, 199. *See also* Apocalypticism, Jesus Christ
Deelen, Wouter, 32
Delft, 1, 7, 28, 31-34, 36, 49-55, 58, 65, 67-69, 72, 75, 77-81, 121-22, 129, 147-49, 152, 154, 209
Den Briell, 68
Denck, Hans, 2, 24
Deventer, 74, 76, 79, 145, 147, 151, 153, 155, 179, 197
Devil (Satan), 73, 99, 131-32, 134, 166, 168, 207-209
Devotio Moderna, 8
Dordrecht, 7, 78-79
Dordrecht, Adriaen Ariaensz van, 75
Droochscheerder, Andreis, 114, 151-52

Dutch language, 49-50, 54, 92, 181
East Frisia, 25, 55, 147
Economic conditions and reform, 14, 27-29, 34-35, 97
Education, 11, 15, 135, 154; and Joris, 49-50, 139, 147, 150
Eilkeman, Gerdt, 148
Eisenburg, Johannes, 129, 131-33, 135-37, 139
Elders of Israel, 129, 136, 141
Elijah, eschatological return of, 96, 133, 140
Emden, 55, 57, 147, 186
Emden, Meynart van, 37, 114
England, 51, 67; Anabaptists in or from, 68f., 73, 113, 117-18, 120, 129, 132
Enkhuizen, 51
Erasmus of Rotterdam, 177, 181, 184
Etten, Anna van, Lady of Schilde, 163-64, 179
Eucharist, 8, 27, 118

Fear of God, 90, 132, 135-36
Franck, Sebastian, 28, 168, 183-84
Frederycxz, Frans, 32
Friesland, 29, 114, 117, 145, 147, 151

Gael, Peter, 38
Gansfort, Wesel, 8
Geelen, Jan van, 27, 38
Gelassenheit (resignation), 93f., 104, 136, 169, 181
Gelder, Karel van, 155
Ghent, 7
Giethoorn, 147
Glassmaker, Peter, 132, 153
Glasspainting, 31, 51, 67, 71, 180
Gnapheus, Willem, 8, 11
Goldt, Gerrit, 155
Goor, 145, 147
Goor, Jorien van (Henrickson), 154
Gorkum on the Waert, 67
Gortersdochter, Maritje Jans de (Joris' mother), 49-51, 73, 75, 147
Gouda, 35
"Great Trek," 37, 39, 65, 89
Grebel, Conrad, 23

Greek language, 54, 92
Groningen, city, 36, 145, 147, 150; meeting, 119, 152; province, 114, 148, 151
Groote, Gerard, 8

Haarlem, 32-33, 35-36, 73-75, 147-49, 154
Haestrecht, Jan van, 53
The Hague, 8, 25, 29, 36, 57-58, 77, 117, 147
Hart, Henry, 117
Hazerswoude revolt, 72, 113-17
Hazerswoude, Adriaen Adriaens van, 116-17
Heavenly Flesh of Christ, 25, 69, 104
Heavenly man, 139-40, 203-206
Hebrew language, 54, 92
Herberts, Herman, 186
Herckemaicker, Henrich, 152
Hermeneutics, 90-94
Herroult, Christopher, 155
Heuter, Jan de, sheriff of Delft, 34, 53-54, 72-73, 75
Hilversum, 147, 152
Hoen, Cornelis, 8
Hoffman, Melchior, 24-25, 28, 30, 38, 55, 57-59, 67, 89-106, 113, 118, 129, 132-33, 135, 140
Holland, 13, 28-29, 33-37, 52, 55, 114, 122, 145, 152, 163
Holy days, 9, 13-15
Holy Spirit, 10, 24, 54, 90, 92-93, 96, 132, 139-40, 156, 165, 167-68, 170, 180, 183-84, 199f.; inspiration of, 71, 94, 120, 129f., 133-37, 152, 181, 203
Hoorn, 13, 33
Hoorn, Damas van, 66, 93, 101
Hoorn, Rem van, 114, 152
Houtsager, Peter, 30
Huggen, Katryn, 147
Humanism, 2, 8, 13, 177, 181-82, 184
Hut, Hans, 24
Hymns, *see* Songs

Iconoclasm, 8-9, 11, 33, 52-54, 72, 178
Inner word, 24, 165. *See also* Hermeneutics, Holy Spirit

Inquisition, 33-34, 54-55, 59, 73, 186
Isselstein, 147, 153

Jacobsz, Dammas, 148
Jans, Anneken, 68-70, 73
Jansz, Frans, 77
Jerusalem, heavenly or new, 27-28, 34-35, 67, 179
Jesus Christ, 71, 96, 99f., 135, 157, 168, 170, 199; incarnation of, 56, 91, 118, 183; as mediator, 10, 56; nature, 55; return of, 26, 56, 69, 90, 97, 121, 166f. *See also* Heavenly Flesh of Christ
Jews, 135
Joestez, Jan, 53
Jost, Leonard, 24f., 132-33, 135-37
Jost, Ursula, 24f., 135
Jülich, Hans van, 118

Kaal, Heinrich, 72, 114, 148, 151-52
Karel, Duke, van Gelder (of Guelders), 36
Karel van Gelder, former stadholder of Groningen, 155
Karlstadt, Andreas Bodenstein van, 8, 53
Kelder, Jacob up de, 152
Ketel, Jorien, 77, 132, 147, 150, 153-57, 163-65, 177-79, 199-201
Kleinbergius, Georgius (as Joris), 184
Klerck, Seward, 117, 150
Krechting, Heinrich, 28, 39, 113, 118, 119, 120

Lasco, Johannes à, 165
Latin, culture, 13; language, 50, 54, 92, 121, 150, 153, 181-82; schools, *see* Education
Leeuwarden, 147
Leeuwarden, Hans van, 30
Leiden, 9, 33, 35-36, 74, 76-77, 147-48, 155
Leiden, Jan van, 26, 30, 38, 100, 104, 116, 119, 150, 152, 171
Letter-spirit, 129f., 136, 140. *See also* Inner word, Hermeneutics
Lier, Anna van, 163-64
Lier, Cornelis van, Lord of Berchem, 163-64, 179

Lippe, Peter von der, 152
Loisten sect, 155, 179
Lord's Supper, *see* Eucharist
Lübeck, 36, 165
Luther, Martin, 7f., 52-53, 56, 177, 184
Lutherans, 13, 24; theology, 26

Maestricht, Jan, 117
Mantz, Felix, 23
Marriage, 104, 121, 129, 131-32, 134, 212; and concubinage, 180; and divorce, 131; of Joris, 68. *See also* Polygamy
Martyrdom, 13, 25, 33, 57, 66, 79f., 101, 155-56
Mary, veneration of, 9, 11, 25, 52, 55
Mass, 9, 11ff., 55-56, 133. *See also* Eucharist, Sacraments
Matthijs, Jan, 26, 30-31, 34, 38, 65, 67, 89, 94
Mechelen, Peter van, 178, 185
Melchiorites, in the Netherlands, 25, 27-30, 35-39, 58f., 65, 72, 89-90, 97, 100, 103, 113-14, 117f., 121; in Strasbourg, 129-41, 165, 171; radical, 150. *See also* Covenanters, England
Mennonites, 2, 32, 113f., 151, 156, 165, 171
Merchants and reform, 13, 49; and Joris, 147, 150, 154, 179
Middelburg, Jan Matthijs van, 30, 32, 35, 117-18, 132
Migration, 28-29, 34-36
Molenaer, Bauke, 152
Monnikendam, 32-33, 36
Mortification, 12, 68, 92, 97, 149, 169
Morveldinck, Johan, 153
Mullem, Dirk, 186
Münster, kingdom of, 2, 25-27, 34-35, 38f., 65, 89-93, 96-102, 104-106, 113, 116, 120, 150-52; fall of, 67, 69, 114, 130; plans to recapture, 119; territory of, 148
Münsterites, after Münster, 68, 116; in Oldenburg, 28, 39, 72, 113-14, 118, 120-22, 140, 165, 171, 209. *See also* Oldenburg

Müntzer, Thomas, 2, 23-24

Naarden, 152
Nicodemism, 27, 32, 37, 39, 57, 75, 163, 165, 179, 186f.
Nobility, 147, 154; and Joris, 163-64, 184
Nudity, public, 73, 121, 140, 184, 209

Oecolampadius, Johannes, 177-78
Oldeklooster, attack on, 27, 151
Oldenburg, 129; meeting in, 66, 72, 78. *See also* Münsterites
Original sin, 105
Overijsel, 114, 118, 153; stadholder of, 154-55

Pacifism, 27, 100f., 116
Paeuw, Jan, 30, 35, 38
Pafraet, Albert, 155
Pamphlets, 9, 52-54, 57
Pastor, Adam, 2, 165, 171
Peasants' War of 1525, 23, 178
Perfection, 93, 102, 118, 121, 132, 138-40, 169, 207
Persecution, 14-15, 25, 27, 33-34, 58, 69, 74, 96, 148, 178; and Joris, 1, 130, 163
Philip, Landgrave of Hesse, 155, 163
Philips, Dirk, 27, 30, 39
Philips, Obbe, 1, 25, 27-28, 30, 38-39, 66, 117, 151
Philipsz, Fransz, 149
Pistorius, Jan, 8, 10f.
Poeldijk, attack on, 68, 72, 113-17
Polygamy, 26, 28, 104-106, 118, 148-49, 171, 180
Poor relief, 11, 15, 35-36, 181
Pouwels, Jan, 30-31, 38
Printers and printing, 9, 155, 177-78, 186
Processions, 9, 31, 52-53
Purgatory, 13, 15

Radical Reformation, 1f., 28
Raesfelt, 148, 152
Rebirth, 12, 69, 168-69, 183
Rebstock, Barbara, 24, 129, 131, 132, 135-37
Reenen, Jan van, 35

Reekers, Henrick, 152
Reformed church, 27-28, 141, 186f.
Regensburg, 155, 164
Restitution, 94-103, 118, 137, 167, 207, 211-12
Revolution and Anabaptism, 27, 39, 96, 101, 116-17, 122, 148
Reyersdochter, Dieuwer, 9
Rol, Heinrich, 26, 153
Rothmann, Bernhard, 26, 89-106, 148, 169

Sacramentarians, 8, 26, 66, 147
Sacraments, 8-9, 12-14, 52-53, 120, 153, 165, 168. *See also* Baptism, Confession, Mass, Purgatory
Saints, veneration of, 9, 11, 13-14, 55; Anabaptists as, 101-103, 140, 166
Sandys, William, treasurer of Henry VIII, 51
Sartorius, Johannes, 7
Schaliedecker, Loy de, 179. *See also* Loisten sect
Scheerder, Hans (van Leeuwarden), 114, 151-52, 155
Schellen, Ael, 148
Schleitheim Confession, 1, 23
Schoemaker, Heinric, 133
Schoemecker, Dirick, 149
Schoenmaker, Harmen, 66, 89, 151
Schoonhoven, Jan van, 53, 117
Schor, Heinrich van, 179, 185
Schwenckfeld, Caspar, 2, 28, 168
Scilde, 147, 163, 179
Scriptures, vernacular, 9, 11-12, 54; Vulgate, 9; as proof-texts, 134, 138; interpretation of, *see* Hermeneutics
Separatism, 23-24, 27, 58, 138, 147
Servetus, Michael, 184
Sexual ethic, 104-105, 131, 134, 140, 154, 180, 207-209
Shame, 105, 121, 138, 207-209
Simons, Menno, 1f., 27, 39, 114, 129, 147, 150f., 153, 164-65, 171-72
Sloten, 147, 152
Smedes, Anthon, 120, 122, 152
Sneek, Tjaard van, 117

Songs, of Joris, 50, 52, 56-58, 65-67, 69, 97f., 101, 212
Sostardt, Elsa von, 153
Spiritualism, 2, 28, 39, 165-68, 170-71, 181, 183, 187
Steinmetzer, Merieke, 148
Stillstand (suspension of baptism), 26, 37-38, 58, 66, 89, 97, 113
Strasbourg, 24-25, 34, 38, 67, 79, 98, 121, 179; conference in, 66, 72, 129-41, 154, 157, 169, 171; and Dutch Anabaptists, 2, 24, 26, 28, 104, 113, 117-19, 122
Sword, 58, 91, 94, 97, 102, 116, 120, 180; Anabaptists and, 23, 25, 38, 101, 149; of the Spirit, 56, 103
Symons, Jacob, 30, 65

Tasch, Peter, 132-33, 135-37
Theologia Deutsch, 52
Toleration, religious, 168, 178, 184, 186
Torture, 9, 54, 73-76, 156, 186, 197
Trajectensis, Jan, 117f.
Trijpmaker, Jan Volkerts, 25, 55, 57, 66, 101, 113
Tuchmeister, Andreis, 150, 152
"Twistreden," 132 f.
Tyetteye van Goegna, Jacob, 30
Tyrnes, Peter Simonszoen van, 30

Urbanism, and Anabaptism, 24-25, 28f., 34-37; and Joris, 114, 145-48, 168
Utrecht, 74, 76, 81, 114, 116, 147-49, 153-55, 198

Vengeance, 28, 58, 70, 73, 96-97, 101-103, 105, 116-18, 149
Vilvoorde, 120
Visions, 24, 135, 157, 203; and Joris, 66, 68, 70, 72, 74, 80, 92, 119, 129, 131, 133, 211
Vlissingen, 67

Wael, Hans de, 150, 153
Waldeck, Franz von, Bishop of Münster, 26, 34, 120
Wassenberg preachers, 26

Waterland conference, 66, 77, 89, 93, 100
Westphalia, 114, 120, 129, 145, 147-48, 152
Willem, Dirkgen, wife of Joris, 52, 57, 67, 72, 74, 76-77, 81, 185, 208
Willemszoon, Dirck, 55
Wolfartsz, Cornelis, 148
Women, and Anabaptism, 29; and Joris, 105, 129-31, 136, 145, 148
Wou, Gherrijt van, 30
Wouter of Utrecht ("Lutheran monk"), 7, 31-32, 52

't Zandt, 66, 89, 151
Zealand, 13, 54, 67
Zierikzee, 13
Zutphen, Christoffel, 118, 120, 122, 152-53
Zutphen, Hendrik, 118
Zwingli, Ulrich, 8, 23
Zwolle, Gerdt van, 148